*Necessary Truth*

# STUDIES IN PHILOSOPHY

*Consulting Editor:*

V. C. CHAPPELL, *The University of Chicago*

A RANDOM HOUSE STUDY
IN THE HISTORY OF PHILOSOPHY

# Necessary Truth:

## A Book of Readings

EDITED BY

**L. W. SUMNER**
*University of Toronto*

**JOHN WOODS**
*University of Toronto*

RANDOM HOUSE
*New York*

# PREFACE

Philosophy courses that stress problems, as opposed, say, to historical surveys, are well served by short collections of the important readings in the problems scheduled for study. When the department of philosophy at the University of Toronto asked us to recommend texts for various undergraduate courses offered here, we were surprised to discover that the problem of necessary truth was not represented by any such anthology. Thinking this a lack serious enough to remedy, we set ourselves the task of assembling a useful set of, for the most part, contemporary readings. This volume is the result.

To be quite clear about its nature and limitations, it was designed to be used, if desired, over a relatively short period of instruction. We have therefore concentrated on providing discussions both readable and of high philosophic quality and have attempted to avoid, as much as possible, overlap of content and preoccupation with peripheral rather than central matters. In consequence many outstanding papers could not be included. While an anthology on necessary truth not containing the classic contributions of Carnap, Waismann, and Goodman cannot be definitive, we have made no such claim for this volume and have pursued no such policy. The definitive anthology on necessary truth remains to be produced; when it appears it will be both impressively thick and punishingly priced.

Of the papers in this collection several have been used at the University of Toronto, with considerable success, in courses having few or no philosophy prerequisites. Of course, not all of these selections can be managed by freshmen (Hintikka's contribution, for example), but the entire offering, and more besides, has worked well both in upper-level undergraduate and graduate courses. It is our opinion that necessary truth is a topic which rewards study at all levels, elementary through advanced; we hope that these readings will be as useful in facilitating such study elsewhere as they have been here.

In order both to control the overall length of this volume and to achieve greater continuity, all footnotes have been excised from reprinted material. The chief drawback of this policy is the loss of those bibliographical references supplied by the authors, but we have tried to compensate in two complementary ways. Appended to most of the selections will be found a list of Further Reading, comprising works germane to the topic and of sufficient reputation to be considered standard. In addition, we have compiled a full bibliography, which we have reason to think the most complete and comprehensive available for the problem of necessary truth. The reader who wishes to pursue the problem beyond the confines of this volume is invited to make full use of it.

Our thanks are due the authors, or their estates, editors, and publishers who have given us permission to reprint. Not the least part of our gratitude goes to our many students whose response to a mountain of material on necessary truth has constituted, for us, a virtual editorial guideline.

*Toronto*                                                        L. W. S.
                                                                   J. W.

# CONTENTS

*Necessary Truth*

# INTRODUCTION

It is a belief common to most philosophers that all truths partition into those which are necessary and those which are merely contingent. A distinction so palpably tempting cannot be entirely new. This one seems to have been marked by Aristotle and the Stoics, and it, or something like it, was a philosophic staple of virtually every major figure in the period bounded by Descartes and Hume. The qualifier "or something like it" is essential. If one resolutely resists reading contemporary distinctions into the writings of his predecessors and sets out to find therein an explicit division of truths into necessary and contingent he is unlikely to be often satisfied. There is, indeed, abundant reference to "truths of reason", "relations of ideas", "necessary connection (co-existence, dependence) of ideas", "innate ideas", "indubitable truths", "self-evident truths", "certain knowledge", "intuitive knowledge", "instructive real knowledge", "demonstrable propositions", "trifling propositions", "propositions whose falsehood is inconceivable", "propositions whose falsehood is unimaginable", and so on and on. But it is a nice question which of these expressions, if any, is properly treated as a forerunner of our concept of necessity.

If it were important to answer this question, one would begin by making clear just what our concept of necessity is. The simple, and unilluminating, explication is this: a statement, $p$, is necessary if and only if its denial, not-$p$, is impossible. The rather more decorative account holds $p$ to be necessary if and only if it is true "in all possible worlds", where possible worlds now emerge as something like Carnap's state descriptions or Hintikka's model sets. By these lights it is unarguable that the contemporary concept of necessity is to be found at least in Leibniz. Given enough determination it is possible, perhaps likely, that one could mine from the works of most of the other figures in the aforementioned period a concept of necessity acceptably close to this one; the whole enterprise, however, remains haunted by the specter of anachronism.

One moves onto more familiar ground with Kant, who is generally regarded as the father of the present-day vocabulary of "necessary", "a priori", and "analytic"; even here, however, there is uncertainty. Analytic statements may indeed be true in all possible worlds, but what of those truths which are a priori and synthetic? Are they true as well in all possible worlds, or merely in all worlds which we are capable of experiencing? It is a moot point whether Kant possesses a concept of necessity univocal as between "necessary analytic" and "necessary synthetic".

Whatever the outcome of all these conceptual speculations, whether or not our predecessors had just the concept of necessity we have, it seems clear that they did not have the *problem* of necessity we have. Even the most empiricistic among them did not feel much impelled to ask such questions as: Are there any necessary truths? If so, what makes them necessary? It is with Mill, who answered the first question in the negative, thus avoiding the second, that one comes hard upon "the problem of necessary truth". It is not far from the mark to say that the cluster of perplexities corporately displayed under this description is in its own right a philosophic problem only since his time. If this is so, it is a fact worth explaining. One goes some way toward such an explanation by showing why necessary truth is a problem especially troubling to an empiricist.

The empiricist's problems with necessary truth are dominated, if not defined, by Kant and Mill. Whatever the empiricist of old may have thought about necessary truth, his positivistic successor can be characterized as one who, in reaction to Kant, denies knowledge a priori of synthetic truths, and, in reaction to Mill, reaffirms the existence of necessary truths. He proclaims the fundamental dogma—all necessary, all analytic truths and only these are known a priori; and therewith a problem. If Frege had dispelled Mill's skepticism by his brilliant and painstaking display of the necessity (analyticity) of the truths of logic, what was one to make of those Kantian paradigms of the synthetic a priori, the truths of mathematics, which although necessary appear for all the world not to be truths of logic? Frege's solution was to defeat the appearance and reduce mathematics to logic.

Even so there is room for the question whether an empiricist account of necessity really is compatible with the epistemological doctrine that all knowledge *arises from, makes reference to,* and *can be justified only by appeal to* the sundry sensory assaults to which we all are prey. If the formal reconstruction of logic and the reduction thereto of mathematics does not evacuate both of content, leaving precious little to be known a priori, is it not dangerously likely that the empiricist pays for the shock of newly discovered, far distant theorems and for the considerable utility of the nine times table either by appealing to the Deliverances of the Intellect or by finding for mathematics and logic an appropriate sensory base, in either case departing his empiricism?

If one's belief in the necessity of logic and mathematics arises from the certainty which attends the theorems with which we make our way through life, if such necessity is ascribed on the basis of a community of universally shared intuitions and upon universally satisfactory projections therefrom, it needs to be asked whether the positivist is *entitled* to insist upon the necessity of logic and mathematics. One of the ironies of the magnificent recent developments is that our "community of shared intuitions" has been savagely decimated. How, it might be asked, especially since Russell's paradox—known to the set theorist simply as The Catastrophe—and the advances in infinitistic set theory, can logic and mathematics be regarded as necessary, much less as accommodable by the deliverances of sense-experience, while all the while pole-axing the not sensorily more distant nor less universally agreed upon proclamations of metaphysics? What, one wonders, is to befall those brilliant attempts to defeat the Kantian syntheticity of mathematics? To be sure, Frege may have reduced arithmetic to logic, but what of logic since Gödel; and since most of logic is set theory, what, again, of logic since The Catastrophe? Even if, *per impossibile,* an informative mathematics were to be reproduced by nothing more than that safe haven of analyticity, the logic of truth-functions, whence the necessity of the logic of truth-functions? How, again, does an empiricist know that "$p$ or not-$p$" is necessarily true? How, indeed, does he know that it is true?

To the harassed empiricist the only solution for many of these perplexities has seemed to be conventionalism. Doubtless the theory has its attractions. For it would appear that logic at least is utterly certain given the way we use language; that metaphysics is nonsense given the way metaphysicians misuse language; and that the residue is neither because underdetermined by merely linguistic facts. But, of equal importance, language is a sensory phenomenon—stretches of sound punctuated by silence, laryngially producible, neurologically recoverable, and nicely rooted, it would seem, in the very topsoil of what is empirically accessible.

Yet it is difficult to avoid the thought that the conventionalist wants it, or at least must have it, both ways. On the one hand he must be assured that language generates and guarantees the necessity of what is necessary, while on the other he must be satisfied that this source of necessity is as empirically scrutinizable as anything within the domains of physics and neurology. One soon comes to suspect this stance of gravely jeopardizing the view that all knowledge of analytic truths is a priori. Facts about language are, it seems, facts about the world; statements reporting such facts will be synthetic and contingent —how then can they guarantee the necessity of anything?

Furthermore, just what is being claimed when it is said that language generates and guarantees the necessity *of what is necessary?* Of what is necessary in independence of the way language works? in which case conventionalism proclaims its own falsity. Of whatever we decide to make necessary? in which case why the pretence that necessities are true in all possible worlds and why the Humean inconvenience, to our own world, of natural connections forever deprived of necessity? And if by "generate and guarantee the necessity of" one means "necessitate", conventionalism skates perilously close to circularity; yet if linguistic conventions do not necessitate the necessity of necessary truths conventionalism is a false theory. Or perhaps the message is that there just are no necessary truths, that those which appear necessary are in reality contingent statements about language, in which case what is conventionalism a theory about?

These difficulties are reflected in the literature perhaps most vividly by the difficulty of finding a prolonged and complete statement of the conventionalist position which preserves the distinction between necessary and contingent truths. It is not surprising that the more thorough and sensitive treatments of the theory are to be found in the writings of those not disposed to accept it. Conventionalism may, then, be false, and mathematics and a substantial part of logic may fail to be necessary. Nonetheless, it would repay one to be quite clear about just what conventionalism fails to account for, and just what property logic and mathematics may legitimately be doubted to have, for in that case we should be in a better position to get the right theory, or at least to decide what it is a theory about. Let us pause, then, to examine the traditional apparatus; it takes only a little effort to uncover conceptual entanglements of distressing proportions.

The most graphic method of demonstration will be to catalogue a representative assortment of the timeworn modal and epistemological pairs, and to see what results. Consider the following list:

### Group A

| | | | |
|---|---|---|---|
| $Analytic_1$ | (predicate contained in subject) | $\times$ | $Synthetic_1$ |
| $Analytic_2$ | (cannot be denied without contradiction) | $\times$ | $Synthetic_2$ |
| $Analytic_3$ | (logical truth or reducible to such by putting synonyms for synonyms) | $\times$ | $Synthetic_3$ |

### Group B

| | | | |
|---|---|---|---|
| $Necessary_1$ | (contradictory is impossible) | $\times$ | $Contingent_1$ |
| $Necessary_2$ | (immune from overthrow) | $\times$ | $Contingent_2$ |
| $Necessary_3$ | (true in all possible worlds) | $\times$ | $Contingent_3$ |

### Group C

| | | | |
|---|---|---|---|
| $A\ priori_1$ | (does not admit of empirical test) | $\times$ | $A\ posteriori_1$ |
| $A\ priori_2$ | (does not require empirical test) | $\times$ | $A\ posteriori_2$ |
| $A\ priori_3$ | (true by virtue of meanings alone) | $\times$ | $A\ posteriori_3$ |

### Group D

| | | | |
|---|---|---|---|
| $Logical_1$ | (not about the world) | $\times$ | $Factual_1$ |
| $Logical_2$ | (empty, vacuous, conveying no information) | $\times$ | $Factual_2$ |

It should be observed that:

(a) within each group "columnar coextensiveness" fails. Thus "$p$ or not-$p$" is analytic$_3$ but not analytic$_1$; "I exist" may be a priori$_2$ but not a priori$_3$.

(b) it is doubtful whether intergroup coextensionalities exist. This may be illustrated as follows:

(1) "All bachelors are unmarried" can be said to be analytic$_{123}$, necessary$_1$, a priori$_3$, a posteriori$_{12}$, factual$_{12}$.

(2) "Everything red is colored" can be said to be analytic$_1$, synthetic$_{23}$, necessary$_{123}$, a priori$_{23}$, a posteriori$_1$, factual$_{12}$.

(3) "I am in pain" can be said to be synthetic$_{123}$, contingent$_{13}$, necessary$_2$, a priori$_{12}$, a posteriori$_3$, factual$_{12}$.

(4) "$7 + 5 = 12$" can be said to be synthetic$_1$, analytic$_2$, necessary$_1$, a posteriori$_1$, a priori$_2$, logical$_1$, factual$_2$, and perhaps analytic$_3$.

(5) "John is either ten years old or not" can be said to be synthetic$_1$, analytic$_{23}$, necessary$_{123}$, a posteriori$_1$, a priori$_{23}$, factual$_1$, logical$_2$.

Further examples could be multiplied at will. It is of some importance to bear in mind that few, if any, of these attributions are so knockdown as to rule out heated debate. That is just the point—any such debate as is likely to ensue is bound to be heated, and where there is that much heat there is correspondingly little light.

This strongly suggests that the modal and epistemological terms presupposed in discussions of such claims as "All knowledge a priori is of analytic statements" are so vague and ambiguous as to virtually force protagonists into premature and ill-advised dogmatism. And this in turn is tantamount to saying that many of the aforementioned problems with conventionalism and the status of logical and mathematical statements may well spring from the much more deep-seated problem of massive terminological unclarity.

This is not yet to fall back to what C. I. Lewis and, more recently, W. V. Quine have said with such forcefulness—that in the classical sense, so characteristic of the positivist tradition, there just aren't any necessary truths. Quine's position in particular represents a repudiation of the very views which serve to 'define' positivistic empiricism in this century. This has not always been fully appreciated. How often have we heard the complaint that Quine in "Two Dogmas of Empiricism" has done nothing more than lay bare the enormous difficulties of achieving an acceptably clear definition of analyticity, that Quine has erred grievously in inferring from these difficulties that analyticity cannot be defined, and that there is, therefore, no distinction between the analytic and the synthetic? So to infer would indeed be an error, but Quine does not commit it. The main force of his arguments is located in the last two sections of his article. There he says explicitly that no statement is immune to revision. If so, then there is no true statement whose falsity is impossible; but this is to say that no true statement is necessary, that there are no necessary truths.

If Quine is right it is small wonder that conventionalism fails as an account of necessary truth: there is nothing to account for. Small wonder, too, that one should be troubled in showing the necessity of set theory and mathematics: there is no such necessity. The empiricist's problems with necessary truth are thus neatly laid to rest. It is, however, of some importance to note that Quine himself has not been content to leave the matter there. Indeed, in Chapter Two of his later book, *Word and Object,* Quine seems to hold immune from revision both truth-functional tautologies and what he calls "observation-sentences" —a rather startling departure from the attractive solution of "Two Dogmas".

We began with the intuition that there are two kinds of truths: necessary and contingent. Upon reaching a certain level of sophistication we were inclined to reexamine both the accuracy and fruitfulness of this intuition. Now, one step beyond, do we find ourselves at the point at which we began?

# ∾ THE DISTINCTION BETWEEN PURE AND EMPIRICAL KNOWLEDGE

*Immanuel Kant*

There can be no doubt that all our knowledge begins with experience. For how should our faculty of knowledge be awakened into action did not objects affecting our senses partly of themselves produce representations, partly arouse the activity of our understanding to compare these representations, and, by combining or separating them, work up the raw material of the sensible impressions into that knowledge of objects which is entitled experience? In the order of time, therefore, we have no knowledge antecedent to experience, and with experience all our knowledge begins.

But though all our knowledge begins with experience, it does not follow that it all arises out of experience. For it may well be that even our empirical knowledge is made up of what we receive through impressions and of what our own faculty of knowledge (sensible impressions serving merely as the occasion) supplies from itself. If our faculty of knowledge makes any such addition, it may be that we are not in a position to distinguish it from the raw material, until with long practice of attention we have become skilled in separating it.

This, then, is a question which at least calls for closer

From Immanuel Kant, *Critique of Pure Reason,* translated by Norman Kemp Smith (London: Macmillan, 1929), pp. 41–45, 48–51, 189–191. Reprinted by permission of The Macmillan Company of Canada, Ltd., St. Martin's Press, Inc., and Macmillan & Co. Ltd., London.

examination, and does not allow of any off-hand answer:—
whether there is any knowledge that is thus independent of
experience and even of all impressions of the senses. Such
knowledge is entitled *a priori,* and distinguished from the *empirical,* which has its sources *a posteriori,* that is, in experience.

The expression '*a priori*' does not, however, indicate with
sufficient precision the full meaning of our question. For it
has been customary to say, even of much knowledge that is
derived from empirical sources, that we have it or are capable
of having it *a priori,* meaning thereby that we do not derive
it immediately from experience, but from a universal rule—a
rule which is itself, however, borrowed by us from experience.
Thus we would say of a man who undermined the foundations
of his house, that he might have known *a priori* that it would
fall, that is, that he need not have waited for the experience of
its actual falling. But still he could not know this completely
*a priori.* For he had first to learn through experience that
bodies are heavy, and therefore fall when their supports are
withdrawn.

In what follows, therefore, we shall understand by *a priori*
knowledge, not knowledge independent of this or that experience, but knowledge absolutely independent of all experience.
Opposed to it is empirical knowledge, which is knowledge
possible only *a posteriori,* that is, through experience. *A priori*
modes of knowledge are entitled pure when there is no admixture
of anything empirical. Thus, for instance, the proposition, 'every
alteration has its cause', while an *a priori* proposition, is not a
pure proposition, because alteration is a concept which can
be derived only from experience.

## We Are in Possession of Certain Modes of A Priori Knowledge, and Even the Common Understanding Is Never Without Them

What we here require is a criterion by which to distinguish
with certainty between pure and empirical knowledge. Experience teaches us that a thing is so and so, but not that it cannot
be otherwise. First, then, if we have a proposition which in
being thought is thought as *necessary,* it is an *a priori* judgment;
and if, besides, it is not derived from any proposition except

one which also has the validity of a necessary judgment, it is an absolutely *a priori* judgment. Secondly, experience never confers on its judgments true or strict, but only assumed and comparative *universality,* through induction. We can properly only say, therefore, that, so far as we have hitherto observed, there is no exception to this or that rule. If, then, a judgment is thought with strict universality, that is, in such manner that no exception is allowed as possible, it is not derived from experience, but is valid absolutely *a priori*. Empirical universality is only an arbitrary extension of a validity holding in most cases to one which holds in all, for instance, in the proposition, 'all bodies are heavy'. When, on the other hand, strict universality is essential to a judgment, this indicates a special source of knowledge, namely, a faculty of *a priori* knowledge. Necessity and strict universality are thus sure criteria of *a priori* knowledge, and are inseparable from one another. But since in the employment of these criteria the contingency of judgments is sometimes more easily shown than their empirical limitation, or, as sometimes also happens, their unlimited universality can be more convincingly proved than their necessity, it is advisable to use the two criteria separately, each by itself being infallible.

Now it is easy to show that there actually are in human knowledge judgments which are necessary and in the strictest sense universal, and which are therefore pure *a priori* judgments. If an example from the sciences be desired, we have only to look to any of the propositions of mathematics; if we seek an example from the understanding in its quite ordinary employment, the proposition, 'every alteration must have a cause', will serve our purpose. In the latter case, indeed, the very concept of a cause so manifestly contains the concept of a necessity of connection with an effect and of the strict universality of the rule, that the concept would be altogether lost if we attempted to derive it, as Hume has done, from a repeated association of that which happens with that which precedes, and from a custom of connecting representations, a custom originating in this repeated association, and constituting therefore a merely subjective necessity. Even without appealing to such examples, it is possible to show that pure *a priori* principles are indispensable for the possibility of experience, and so to prove their existence *a priori*. For whence could experience derive its certainty, if all the rules, according to which it proceeds, were always themselves empirical, and therefore contingent? Such rules could hardly be regarded as first principles. At present, however, we may be content to have established the fact that our faculty of knowledge does have a pure employment, and to have shown what are the criteria of such an employment.

Such *a priori* origin is manifest in certain concepts, no less than in judgments. If we remove from our empirical concept of a body, one by one, every feature in it which is [merely] empirical, the colour, the hardness or softness, the weight, even the impenetrability, there still remains the space which the body (now entirely vanished) occupied, and this cannot be removed. Again, if we remove from our empirical concept of any object, corporeal or incorporeal, all properties which experience has taught us, we yet cannot take away that property through which the object is thought as substance or as inhering in a substance (although this concept of substance is more determinate than that of an object in general). Owing, therefore, to the necessity with which this concept of substance forces itself upon us, we have no option save to admit that it has its seat in our faculty of *a priori* knowledge.

·   ·   ·

## The Distinction Between Analytic and Synthetic Judgments

In all judgments in which the relation of a subject to the predicate is thought (I take into consideration affirmative judgments only, the subsequent application to negative judgments being easily made), this relation is possible in two different ways. Either the predicate B belongs to the subject A, as something which is (covertly) contained in this concept A; or B lies outside the concept A, although it does indeed stand in connection with it. In the one case I entitle the judgment analytic, in the other synthetic. Analytic judgments (affirmative) are therefore those in which the connection of the predicate with the subject is thought through identity; those in which this connection is thought without identity should be entitled synthetic. The former, as adding nothing through the predicate to the concept of the subject, but merely breaking it up into those constituent concepts that have all along been thought in it, although confusedly, can also be entitled explicative. The latter, on the other hand, add to the concept of the subject a predicate which has not been in any wise thought in it, and which no analysis could possibly extract from it; and they may therefore be entitled ampliative. If I say, for instance, 'All bodies are extended', this is an analytic judgment. For I do not require to go beyond the concept which I connect with 'body' in order to find extension as bound up with it. To meet with this predicate, I have merely to analyse the concept, that is, to become conscious to myself of the manifold which I always think in that concept. The judgment is therefore analytic. But when I say, 'All bodies are heavy', the predicate is something quite different from anything that I think in the mere concept of body in general; and the addition of such a predicate therefore yields a synthetic judgment.

Judgments of experience, as such, are one and all synthetic. For it would be absurd to found an analytic judgment on experience. Since, in framing the judgment, I must not go outside my concept, there is no need to appeal to the testimony of experience in its support. That a body is extended is a proposition that holds *a priori* and is not empirical. For, before appealing to experience, I have already in the concept of body all the conditions required for my judgment. I have only to extract from it, in accordance with the principle of contradiction, the required predicate, and in so doing can at the same time become conscious of the necessity of the judgment—and that is what experience could never have taught me. On the other hand, though I do not include in the concept of a body in general the predicate 'weight', none the less this concept indicates an object of experience through one of its parts, and I can add to that part other parts of this same experience, as in this way belonging together with the concept. From the start I can apprehend the concept of body analytically through the characters of extension, impenetrability, figure, etc., all of which are thought in the concept. Now, however, looking back on the experience from which I have derived this concept of body, and finding weight to be invariably connected with the above characters, I attach it as a predicate to the concept; and in doing so I attach it synthetically, and am therefore extending my knowledge. The possibility of the synthesis of the predicate 'weight' with the concept of 'body' thus rests upon experience. While the one concept is not contained in the other, they yet belong to one another, though only contingently, as parts of a whole, namely, of an experience which is itself a synthetic combination of intuitions.

But in *a priori* synthetic judgments this help is entirely lacking: [I do not here have the advantage of looking around in the field of experience.] Upon what, then, am I to rely, when I seek to go beyond the concept A, and to know that another concept B is connected with it? Through what is the synthesis made possible? Let us take the proposition, 'Everything which happens has its cause'. In the concept of 'something which happens', I do indeed think an existence which is preceded by a time, etc., and from this concept analytic judgments may be obtained. But the concept of a 'cause' lies entirely outside the other concept, and signifies something different from 'that which happens', and is not therefore in any way contained in this latter representation. How come I then to predicate of that which happens something quite different, and to apprehend that the concept of cause, though not contained in it, yet belongs, and indeed necessarily belongs, to it? What is here the unknown = X which gives support to the understanding when it believes that it can discover outside the concept A a predicate B foreign to this concept, which it yet at the same time considers to be connected with it? It cannot be experience, because the suggested principle has connected the second representation with the first, not only with greater universality, but also with the character of necessity, and therefore completely *a priori* and on the basis of mere concepts. Upon such synthetic, that is, ampliative principles, all our *a priori* speculative knowledge must ultimately rest; analytic judgments are very important, and indeed necessary, but only for obtaining that clearness in the concepts which is requisite for such a sure and wide synthesis as will lead to a genuinely new addition to all previous knowledge.

.   .   .

## The Highest Principle
## of All Analytic Judgments

The universal, though merely negative, condition of all our judgments in general, whatever be the content of our knowledge, and however it may relate to the object, is that they be not self-contradictory; for if self-contradictory, these judgments are in themselves, even without reference to the object, null and void. But even if our judgment contains no contradiction, it may connect concepts in a manner not borne out by the object, or else in a manner for which no ground is given, either *a priori* or *a posteriori,* sufficient to justify such judgment, and so may still, in spite of being free from all inner contradiction, be either false or groundless.

The proposition that no predicate contradictory of a thing can belong to it, is entitled the principle of contradiction, and is a universal, though merely negative, criterion of all truth. For this reason it belongs only to logic. It holds of knowledge, merely as knowledge in general, irrespective of content; and asserts that the contradiction completely cancels and invalidates it.

But it also allows of a positive employment, not merely, that is, to dispel falsehood and error (so far as they rest on contradiction), but also for the knowing of truth. For, *if the judgment is analytic,* whether negative or affirmative, its truth can always be adequately known in accordance with the principle of contradiction. The reverse of that which as concept is contained and is thought in the knowledge of the object, is always rightly denied. But since the opposite of the concept would contradict the object, the concept itself must necessarily be affirmed of it.

*The principle of contradiction* must therefore be recognised as being the universal and completely sufficient *principle of all analytic knowledge;* but beyond the sphere of analytic knowledge it has, as a *sufficient* criterion of truth, no authority and no field of application. The fact that no knowledge can be contrary to it without self-nullification, makes this principle a *conditio sine qua non,* but not a determining ground, of the truth of our [non-analytic] knowledge. Now in our critical enquiry it is only with the synthetic portion of our knowledge that we are concerned; and in regard to the truth of this kind of knowledge we can never look to the above principle for any positive information, though, of course, since it is inviolable, we must always be careful to conform to it.

Although this famous principle is thus without content and merely formal, it has sometimes been carelessly formulated in a manner which involves the quite unnecessary admixture of a synthetic element. The formula runs: It is impossible that something should *at one and the same time* both be and not be. Apart from the fact that the apodeictic certainty, expressed through the word 'impossible', is superfluously added—since it is evident of itself from the [very nature of the] proposition —the proposition is modified by the condition of time. It then, as it were, asserts: A thing = $A$, which is something = $B$, cannot at the same time be not-B, but may very well in succession be both $B$ and not-$B$. For instance, a man who is young cannot at the same time be old, but may very well at one time be young and at another time not-young, that is, old. The principle of contradiction, however, as a merely logical principle, must not in any way limit its assertions to time-relations. The above formula is therefore completely contrary to the intention of the principle. The misunderstanding results from our first of all separating a predicate of a thing from the concept of that thing, and afterwards connecting this predicate with its opposite—a procedure which never occasions a contradiction with the subject but only with the predicate which has been synthetically connected with that subject, and even then only when both predicates are affirmed at one and the same time. If I say that a man who is unlearned is not learned, the condition, *at one and the same time,* must be added; for he who is at one time unlearned can very well at another be learned. But if I say, no unlearned man is learned, the proposition is analytic, since the property, unlearnedness, now goes to make up the concept of the subject, and the truth of the negative judgment then becomes evident as an immediate consequence of the principle of contradiction, without requiring the supplementary condition, *at one and the same time.* This, then, is the reason why I have altered its formulation, namely, in order that the nature of an analytic proposition be clearly expressed through it.

# ∾ OF DEMONSTRATION AND NECESSARY TRUTHS

*John Stuart Mill*

---

If . . . the foundation of all sciences, even deductive or demonstrative sciences, is Induction; if every step in the ratiocinations even of geometry is an act of induction; and if a train of reasoning is but bringing many inductions to bear upon the same subject of inquiry, and drawing a case within one induction by means of another; wherein lies the peculiar certainty always ascribed to the sciences which are entirely, or almost entirely, deductive? Why are they called the Exact Sciences? Why are mathematical certainty, and the evidence of demonstration, common phrases to express the very highest degree of assurance attainable by reason? Why are mathematics by almost all philosophers, and (by some) even those branches of natural philosophy which, through the medium of mathematics, have been converted into deductive sciences, considered to be independent of the evidence of experience and observation and characterized as systems of Necessary Truth?

The answer I conceive to be, that this character of necessity ascribed to the truths of mathematics, and even (with some reservations to be hereafter made) the peculiar certainty attributed to them, is an illusion; in order to sustain which, it is necessary to suppose that those truths relate to, and express the

---

From John Stuart Mill, *System of Logic,* Tenth Edition (London: Longmans, Green, 1879), pp. 147–148, 149, 151–153, 166–169, 183–184.

properties of, purely imaginary objects. It is acknowledged that the conclusions of geometry are deduced, partly at least, from the so-called Definitions, and that those definitions are assumed to be correct representations, as far as they go, of the objects with which geometry is conversant. Now we have pointed out that, from a definition as such, no proposition, unless it be one concerning the meaning of a word, can ever follow; and that what apparently follows from a definition, follows in reality from an implied assumption that there exists a real thing conformable thereto. This assumption, in the case of the definitions of geometry, is not strictly true: there exist no real things exactly conformable to the definitions. There exist no points without magnitude; no lines without breadth, nor perfectly straight; no circles with all their radii exactly equal, nor squares with all their angles perfectly right. It will perhaps be said that the assumption does not extend to the actual, but only to the possible existence of such things. I answer that, according to any test we have of possibility, they are not even possible. Their existence, so far as we can form any judgment, would seem to be inconsistent with the physical constitution of our planet at least, if not of the universe. To get rid of this difficulty, and at the same time to save the credit of the supposed system of necessary truth, it is customary to say that the points, lines, circles, and squares which are the subject of geometry, exist in our conceptions merely, and are part of our minds; which minds, by working on their own materials, construct an *a priori* science, the evidence of which is purely mental, and has nothing whatever to do with outward experience. By howsoever high authorities this doctrine may have been sanctioned, it appears to me psychologically incorrect. The points, lines, circles, and squares which any one has in his mind are (I apprehend) simply copies of the points, lines, circles, and squares which he has known in his experience. Our idea of a point I apprehend to be simply our idea of the *minimum visibile,* the smallest portion of surface which we can see. A line as defined by geometers is wholly inconceivable. We can reason about a line as if it had no breadth; because we have a power, which is the foundation of all the control we can exercise over the operations of our minds; the power, when a perception is present to our senses or a conception to our intellects, of *attending* to a part only of that perception or conception, instead of the whole. But we cannot *conceive* a line without breadth; we can form no mental picture of such a line; all the lines which we have in our minds are lines possessing breadth. If any one doubts this, we may refer him to his own experience. I much question if any one who fancies that he can conceive what is called a mathematical line, thinks so from the evidence of his consciousness: I suspect it is rather because he supposes that unless such a conception were possible, mathematics could not exist as a science: a supposition which there will be no difficulty in showing to be entirely groundless.

. . .

When, therefore, it is affirmed that the conclusions of geometry are necessary truths, the necessity consists in reality only in this, that they correctly follow from the suppositions from which they are deduced. Those suppositions are so far from being necessary, that they are not even true; they purposely depart, more or less widely, from the truth. The only sense in which necessity can be ascribed to the conclusions of any scientific investigation, is that of legitimately following from some assumption, which, by the conditions of the inquiry, is not to be questioned. In this relation, of course, the derivative truths of every deductive science must stand to the inductions, or assumptions, on which the science is founded, and which, whether true or untrue, certain or doubtful in themselves, are always supposed certain for the purposes of the particular science.

. . .

It remains to inquire, what is the ground of our belief in axioms—what is the evidence on which they rest? I answer, they are experimental truths; generalizations from observation. The proposition, Two straight lines cannot enclose a space—or, in other words, two straight lines which have once met do not meet again, but continue to diverge—is an induction from the evidence of our senses.

. . .

It is not necessary to show that the truths which we call axioms are originally *suggested* by observation, and that we should never have known that two straight lines cannot enclose a space if we had never seen a straight line: thus much being admitted by Dr. Whewell and by all, in recent times, who have taken his view of the subject. But they contend that it is not experience which *proves* the axiom; but that its truth is perceived *a priori,* by the constitution of the mind itself, from the first moment when the meaning of the proposition is apprehended, and without any necessity for verifying it by repeated trials, as is requisite in the case of truths really ascertained by observation.

They cannot, however, but allow that the truth of the axiom, Two straight lines cannot enclose a space, even if evident independently of experience, is also evident from experience. Whether the axiom needs confirmation or not, it receives confirmation in almost every instant of our lives, since we cannot look at any two straight lines which intersect one another without seeing that from that point they continue to diverge more and more. Experimental proof crowds in upon us in such endless profusion, and without one instance in which there can be even a suspicion of an exception to the rule, that we should soon have stronger ground for believing the axiom, even as an experimental truth, than we have for almost any of the general truths which we confessedly learn from the evidence of our senses. Independently of *a priori* evidence we should certainly believe it with an intensity of conviction far greater than we accord to any ordinary physical truth: and this too at a time of life much earlier than that from which we date almost any part of our acquired knowledge, and much too early to admit of our retaining any recollection of the history of our intellectual operations at that period. Where then is the necessity for assuming that our recognition of these truths has a different origin from the rest of our knowledge, when its existence is perfectly accounted for by supposing its origin to be the same? when the causes which produce belief in all other instances exist in this instance, and in a degree of strength as much superior to what exists in other cases as the intensity of the belief itself is superior? The burden of proof lies on the advocates of the contrary opinion: it is for them to point out some fact inconsistent with the supposition that this part of our knowledge of nature is derived from the same sources as every other part.

This, for instance, they would be able to do, if they could prove chronologically that we had the conviction (at least practically) so early in infancy as to be anterior to those impressions on the senses upon which, on the other theory, the conviction is founded. This, however, cannot be proved: the point being too far back to be within the reach of memory and too obscure for external observation.

.　.　.

What we have now asserted, however, cannot be received as universally true of Deductive or Demonstrative Sciences, until verified by being applied to the most remarkable of all those sciences, that of Numbers; the theory of the Calculus; Arithmetic and Algebra. It is harder to believe of the doctrines of this science than of any other, either that they are not truths *a priori,* but experimental truths, or that their peculiar certainty is owing to their being not absolute, but only conditional truths. This, therefore, is a case which merits examination apart; and the more so because on this subject we have a double set of doctrines to contend with; that of the *a priori* philosophers on one side; and on the other, a theory most opposite to theirs, which was at one time very generally received, and is still far from being altogether exploded among metaphysicians.

This theory attempts to solve the difficulty apparently inherent in the case, by representing the propositions of the science of numbers as merely verbal, and its processes as simple transformations of language, substitutions of one expression for another. The proposition, Two and one is equal to three, according to these writers, is not a truth, is not the assertion of a really existing fact, but a definition of the word three; a statement that mankind have agreed to use the name three as a sign exactly equivalent to two and one; to call by the former name whatever is called by the other more clumsy phrase. According to this doctrine the longest process in algebra is but a succession of changes in terminology, by which equivalent expressions are substituted one for another; a series of translations of the same fact, from one into another language; though how, after such a series of translations, the fact itself comes out changed, (as when we demonstrate a new geometrical theorem by algebra) they have not explained; and it is a difficulty which is fatal to their theory.

It must be acknowledged that there are peculiarities in the processes of arithmetic and algebra which render the theory in question very plausible, and have not unnaturally made those sciences the stronghold of Nominalism. The doctrine that we can discover facts, detect the hidden processes of nature, by an artful manipulation of language, is so contrary to common sense, that a person must have made some advances in philosophy to believe it; men fly to so paradoxical a belief to avoid, as they think, some even greater difficulty, which the vulgar do not see. What has led many to believe that reasoning is a mere verbal process is, that no other theory seemed reconcilable with the nature of the Science of Numbers. For we do not carry any ideas along with us when we use the symbols of arithmetic or of algebra. In a geometrical demonstration we have a mental diagram, if not one on paper; AB, AC, are present to our imagination as lines, intersecting other lines, forming an angle with one another, and the like; but not so *a* and *b*. These may represent lines or any other magnitudes, but those magnitudes are never thought of; nothing is realized in our imagination but *a* and *b*. The ideas which, on the particular occasion, they happen to represent, are banished from the mind during every intermediate part of the process, between the beginning, when the premises are translated from things into signs, and the end, when the conclusion is translated back from signs into things. Nothing, then, being in the reasoner's mind but the symbols, what can seem more inadmissible than to contend that the reasoning process has to do with anything more? We seem to have come to one of Bacon's Prerogative Instances; an *experimentum crucis* on the nature of reasoning itself.

Nevertheless, it will appear on consideration, that this apparently so decisive instance is no instance at all; that there is in every step of an arithmetical or algebraical calculation a real induction, a real inference of facts from facts; and that what disguises the induction is simply its comprehensive nature and the consequent extreme generality of the language. All numbers must be numbers of something; there are no such things as numbers in the abstract. *Ten* must mean ten bodies, or ten sounds, or ten beatings of the pulse. But though numbers must be numbers of something, they may be numbers of anything. Propositions, therefore, concerning numbers have the remarkable peculiarity that they are propositions concerning all things whatever; all objects, all existences of every kind, known to our experience. All things possess quantity; consist of parts which can be numbered; and in that character possess all the properties which are called properties of numbers. That half of four is two, must be true whatever the word four represents, whether four hours, four miles, or four pounds weight. We need only conceive a thing divided into four equal parts (and all things may be conceived as so divided) to be able to predicate of it every property of the number four, that is, every arithmetical proposition in which the number four stands on one side of the equation. Algebra extends the generalization still farther: every number represents that particular number of all things without distinction, but every algebraical symbol does more, it represents all numbers without distinction. . . .

There is another circumstance, which, still more than that which we have now mentioned, gives plausibility to the notion that the propositions of arithmetic and algebra are merely verbal. That is, that when considered as propositions respecting Things, they all have the appearance of being identical propositions. The assertion, Two and one is equal to three, considered as an assertion respecting objects, as for instance, "Two pebbles and one pebble are equal to three pebbles", does not affirm equality between two collections of pebbles, but absolute identity. It affirms that if we put one pebble to two pebbles, those very pebbles are three. The objects, therefore, being the very same, and the mere assertion that "objects are themselves" being insignificant, it seems but natural to consider the proposition, Two and one is equal to three, as asserting mere identity of signification between the two names.

This, however, though it looks so plausible, will not bear examination. The expression "two pebbles and one pebble", and the expression "three pebbles", stand indeed for the same aggregation of objects, but they by no means stand for the same physical fact. They are names of the same objects, but of those objects in two different states: though they *de*note the same things, their *con*notation is different. Three pebbles in two separate parcels, and three pebbles in one parcel, do not make the same impression on our senses; and the assertion that the very same pebbles may by an alteration of place and arrangement be made to produce either the one set of sensations or the other, though a very familiar proposition, is not an identical one. It is a truth known to us by early and constant experience—an inductive truth; and such truths are the foundation of the science of Numbers. The fundamental truths of that science all rest on the evidence of sense; they are proved by showing to our eyes and our fingers that any given number of objects, ten balls, for example, may by separation and rearrangement exhibit to our senses all the different sets of numbers the sum of which is equal to ten. All the improved methods of teaching arithmetic to children proceed on a knowledge of this fact. All who wish to carry the child's *mind* along with them in learning arithmetic; all who wish to teach numbers, and not mere ciphers—now teach it through the evidence of the senses, in the manner we have described.

We may, if we please, call the proposition, "Three is two and one", a definition of the number three, and assert that arithmetic, as it has been asserted that geometry, is a science founded on definitions. But they are definitions in the geometrical sense, not the logical; asserting not the meaning of a term only, but along with it an observed matter of fact. The proposition, "A circle is a figure bounded by a line which has all its points equally distant from a point within it", is called the definition of a circle; but the proposition from which so many consequences follow, and which is really a first principle in geometry, is, that figures answering to this description exist. And thus we may call "Three is two and one" a definition of three; but the calculations which depend on that proposition do not follow from the definition itself, but from an arithmetical theorem presupposed in it, namely, that collections of objects exist, which while they impress the senses thus, °₀° , may be separated into two parts, thus, O O O . This proposition being granted, we term all such parcels Threes, after which the enunciation of the above-mentioned physical fact will serve also for a definition of the word Three.

The Science of Numbers is thus no exception to the conclusion we previously arrived at, that the processes even of deductive sciences are altogether inductive, and that their first principles are generalizations from experience.

.   .   .

I consider [the Principle of Contradiction] to be, like other axioms, one of our first and most familiar generalizations from experience. The original foundation of it I take to be, that Belief and Disbelief are two different mental states, excluding one another. This we know by the simplest observation of our own minds. And if we carry our observation outwards, we also find that light and darkness, sound and silence, motion and quiescence, equality and inequality, preceding and following, succession and simultaneousness, any positive phenomenon whatever and its negative, are distinct phenomena, pointedly contrasted, and the one always absent where the other is present. I consider the maxim in question to be a generalization from all these facts.

In like manner as the Principle of Contradiction (that one of two contradictories must be false) means that an assertion cannot be *both* true and false, so the Principle of Excluded Middle, or that one of two contradictories must be true, means that an assertion must be *either* true or false: either the affirmative is true, or otherwise the negative is true, which means that the affirmative is false. I cannot help thinking this principle a surprising specimen of a so-called necessity of Thought, since it is not even true, unless with a large qualification. A proposition must be either true or false, *provided* that the predicate be one which can in any intelligible sense be attributed to the subject (and as this is always assumed to be the case in treatises on logic, the axiom is always laid down there as of absolute truth). "Abracadabra is a second intention" is neither true nor false. Between the true and the false there is a third possibility, the Unmeaning; and this alternative is fatal to Sir William Hamilton's extension of the maxim to Noumena. That Matter must either have a minimum of divisibility or be infinitely divisible, is more than we can ever know. For in the first place, Matter, in any other than the phenomenal sense of the term, may not exist; and it will scarcely be said that a non-entity must be either infinitely or finitely divisible. In the second place, though matter, considered as the occult cause of our sensations, do really exist, yet what we call divisibility may be an attribute only of our sensations of sight and touch, and not of their uncognizable cause. Divisibility may not be predicable at all, in any intelligible sense, of Things in Themselves, nor therefore of Matter in itself; and the assumed necessity of being either infinitely or finitely divisible may be an inapplicable alternative.

# ∾ THE A PRIORI

*A. J. Ayer*

The view of philosophy which we have adopted may, I think, fairly be described as a form of empiricism. For it is character-istic of an empiricist to eschew metaphysics, on the ground that every factual proposition must refer to sense-experience. And even if the conception of philosophizing as an activity of analysis is not to be discovered in the traditional theories of empiricists, we have seen that it is implicit in their practice. At the same time, it must be made clear that, in calling ourselves empiricists, we are not avowing a belief in any of the psychological doctrines which are commonly associated with empiricism. For, even if these doctrines were valid, their validity would be independent of the validity of any philosophical thesis. It could be established only by observation, and not by the purely logical considerations upon which our empiricism rests.

Having admitted that we are empiricists, we must now deal with the objection that is commonly brought against all forms of empiricism; the objection, namely, that it is impossible on em-piricist principles to account for our knowledge of necessary truths. For, as Hume conclusively showed, no general proposi-tion whose validity is subject to the test of actual experience can

From A. J. Ayer, *Language, Truth and Logic,* Second Edition (London: Victor Gollancz, 1946, and New York: Dover Publications, n.d.), ch. 4. Reprinted by permission of the publishers.

ever be logically certain. No matter how often it is verified in practice, there still remains the possibility that it will be confuted on some future occasion. The fact that a law has been substantiated in $n-1$ cases affords no logical guarantee that it will be substantiated in the $n$th case also, no matter how large we take $n$ to be. And this means that no general proposition referring to a matter of fact can ever be shown to be necessarily and universally true. It can at best be a probable hypothesis. And this, we shall find, applies not only to general propositions, but to all propositions which have a factual content. They can none of them ever become logically certain. This conclusion, which we shall elaborate later on, is one which must be accepted by every consistent empiricist. It is often thought to involve him in complete scepticism; but this is not the case. For the fact that the validity of a proposition cannot be logically guaranteed in no way entails that it is irrational for us to believe it. On the contrary, what is irrational is to look for a guarantee where none can be forthcoming; to demand certainty where probability is all that is obtainable. We have already remarked upon this, in referring to the work of Hume. And we shall make the point clearer when we come to treat of probability, in explaining the use which we make of empirical propositions. We shall discover that there is nothing perverse or paradoxical about the view that all the "truths" of science and common sense are hypotheses; and consequently that the fact that it involves this view constitutes no objection to the empiricist thesis.

Where the empiricist does encounter difficulty is in connection with the truths of formal logic and mathematics. For whereas a scientific generalization is readily admitted to be fallible, the truths of mathematics and logic appear to everyone to be necessary and certain. But if empiricism is correct no proposition which has a factual content can be necessary or certain. Accordingly the empiricist must deal with the truths of logic and mathematics in one of the two following ways: he must say either that they are not necessary truths, in which case he must account for the universal conviction that they are; or he must say that they have no factual content, and then he must explain how a proposition which is empty of all factual content can be true and useful and surprising.

If neither of these courses proves satisfactory, we shall be obliged to give way to rationalism. We shall be obliged to admit that there are some truths about the world which we can know independently of experience; that there are some properties which we can ascribe to all objects, even though we cannot conceivably observe that all objects have them. And we shall have to accept it as a mysterious inexplicable fact that our thought has this power to reveal to us authoritatively the nature of objects which we have never observed. Or else we must accept the Kantian explanation which, apart from the epistemological difficulties which we have already touched on, only pushes the mystery a stage further back.

It is clear that any such concession to rationalism would upset the main argument of this book. For the admission that there were some facts about the world which could be known independently of experience would be incompatible with our fundamental contention that a sentence says nothing unless it is empirically verifiable. And thus the whole force of our attack on metaphysics would be destroyed. It is vital, therefore, for us to be able to show that one or other of the empiricist accounts of the propositions of logic and mathematics is correct. If we are successful in this, we shall have destroyed the foundations of rationalism. For the fundamental tenet of rationalism is that thought is an independent source of knowledge, and is moreover a more trustworthy source of knowledge than experience; indeed some rationalists have gone so far as to say that thought is the only source of knowledge. And the ground for this view is simply that the only necessary truths about the world which are known to us are known through thought and not through experience. So that if we can show either that the truths in question are not necessary or that they are not "truths about the world," we shall be taking away the support on which rationalism rests. We shall be making good the empiricist contention that there are no "truths of reason" which refer to matters of fact.

The course of maintaining that the truths of logic and mathematics are not necessary or certain was adopted by Mill. He maintained that these propositions were inductive generalizations based on an extremely large number of instances. The fact that the number of supporting instances was so very large accounted, in his view, for our believing these generalizations to be necessarily and universally true. The evidence in their favor was so strong that it seemed incredible to us that a contrary instance should ever arise. Nevertheless it was in principle possible for such generalizations to be confuted. They were highly probable, but, being inductive generalizations, they were not certain. The difference between them and the hypotheses of natural science was a difference in degree and not in kind. Experience gave us very good reason to suppose that a "truth" of mathematics or logic was true universally; but we were not possessed of a guarantee. For these "truths" were only empirical hypotheses which had worked particularly well in the past; and, like all empirical hypotheses, they were theoretically fallible.

I do not think that this solution of the empiricist's difficulty with regard to the propositions of logic and mathematics is acceptable. In discussing it, it is necessary to make a distinction which is perhaps already enshrined in Kant's famous dictum that, although there can be no doubt that all our knowledge begins with experience, it does not follow that it all arises out of experience. When we say that the truths of logic are known independently of experience, we are not of course saying that they are innate, in the sense that we are born knowing them. It is obvious that mathematics and logic have to be learned in the same way as chemistry and history have to be learned. Nor are we denying that the first person to discover a given logical or mathematical truth was led to it by an inductive procedure. It is very probable, for example, that the principle of the syllogism was formulated not before but after the validity of syllogistic reasoning had been observed in a number of particular cases. What we are discussing, however, when we say that logical and mathematical truths are known independently of experience, is not a historical question concerning the way in which these truths were originally discovered, not a psychological question concerning the way in which each of us comes to learn them, but an epistemological question. The contention of Mill's which we reject is that the propositions of logic and mathematics have the same status as empirical hypotheses; that their validity is determined in the same way. We maintain that they are independent of experience in the sense that they do not owe their validity to empirical verification. We may come to discover them through an inductive process; but once we have apprehended them we see that they are necessarily true, that they hold good for every conceivable instance. And this serves to distinguish them from empirical generalizations. For we know that a proposition whose validity depends upon experience cannot be seen to be necessarily and universally true.

In rejecting Mill's theory, we are obliged to be somewhat dogmatic. We can do no more than state the issue clearly and then trust that his contention will be seen to be discrepant with the relevant logical facts. The following considerations may serve to show that of the two ways of dealing with logic and mathematics which are open to the empiricist, the one which Mill adopted is not the one which is correct.

The best way to substantiate our assertion that the truths of formal logic and pure mathematics are necessarily true is to examine cases in which they might seem to be confuted. It might easily happen, for example, that when I came to count what I had taken to be five pairs of objects, I found that they amounted only to nine. And if I wished to mislead people I might say that on this occasion twice five was not ten. But in that case I should not be using the complex sign "$2 \times 5 = 10$" in the way in which it is ordinarily used. I should be taking it not as the expression of a purely mathematical proposition, but as the expression of an empirical generalization, to the effect that whenever I counted what appeared to me to be five pairs of objects I discovered that they were ten in number. This generalization may very well be false. But if it proved false in a given case, one would not say that the mathematical proposition "$2 \times 5 = 10$" had been confuted. One would say that I was wrong in supposing that there were five pairs of objects to start with, or that one of the objects had been taken away while I was counting, or that two of them had coalesced, or that I had counted wrongly. One would adopt as an explanation whatever empirical hypothesis fitted in best with the accredited facts. The one explanation which would in no circumstances be adopted is that ten is not always the product of two and five.

To take another example: if what appears to be a Euclidean triangle is found by measurement not to have angles totalling

180 degrees, we do not say that we have met with an instance which invalidates the mathematical proposition that the sum of the three angles of a Euclidean triangle is 180 degrees. We say that we have measured wrongly, or, more probably, that the triangle we have been measuring is not Euclidean. And this is our procedure in every case in which a mathematical truth might appear to be confuted. We always preserve its validity by adopting some other explanation of the occurrence.

The same thing applies to the principles of formal logic. We may take an example relating to the so-called law of excluded middle, which states that a proposition must be either true or false, or, in other words, that it is impossible that a proposition and its contradictory should neither of them be true. One might suppose that a proposition of the form "*x* has stopped doing *y*" would in certain cases constitute an exception to this law. For instance, if my friend has never yet written to me, it seems fair to say that it is neither true nor false that he has stopped writing to me. But in fact one would refuse to accept such an instance as an invalidation of the law of excluded middle. One would point out that the proposition "My friend has stopped writing to me" is not a simple proposition, but the conjunction of the two propositions "My friend wrote to me in the past" and "My friend does not write to me now": and, furthermore, that the proposition "My friend has not stopped writing to me" is not, as it appears to be, contradictory to "My friend has stopped writing to me," but only contrary to it. For it means "My friend wrote to me in the past, and he still writes to me." When, therefore, we say that such a proposition as "My friend has stopped writing to me" is sometimes neither true nor false, we are speaking inaccurately. For we seem to be saying that neither it nor its contradictory is true. Whereas what we mean, or anyhow should mean, is that neither it nor its apparent contradictory is true. And its apparent contradictory is really only its contrary. Thus we preserve the law of excluded middle by showing that the negating of a sentence does not always yield the contradictory of the proposition originally expressed.

There is no need to give further examples. Whatever instance we care to take, we shall always find that the situations in which a logical or mathematical principle might appear to be confuted are accounted for in such a way as to leave the principle unassailed. And this indicates that Mill was wrong in supposing that a situation could arise which would overthrow a mathematical truth. The principles of logic and mathematics are true universally simply because we never allow them to be anything else. And the reason for this is that we cannot abandon them without contradicting ourselves, without sinning against the rules which govern the use of language, and so making our utterances self-stultifying. In other words, the truths of logic and mathematics are analytic propositions or tautologies. In saying this we are making what will be held to be an extremely controversial statement, and we must now proceed to make its implications clear.

The most familiar definition of an analytic proposition, or judgment, as he called it, is that given by Kant. He said that an analytic judgment was one in which the predicate B belonged to the subject A as something which was covertly contained in the concept of A. He contrasted analytic with synthetic judgments, in which the predicate B lay outside the subject A, although it did stand in connection with it. Analytic judgments, he explains, "add nothing through the predicate to the concept of the subject, but merely break it up into those constituent concepts that have all along been thought in it, although confusedly." Synthetic judgments, on the other hand, "add to the concept of the subject a predicate which has not been in any wise thought in it, and which no analysis could possibly extract from it." Kant gives "all bodies are extended" as an example of an analytic judgment, on the ground that the required predicate can be extracted from the concept of "body," "in accordance with the principle of contradiction"; as an example of a synthetic judgment, he gives "all bodies are heavy." He refers also to "$7 + 5 = 12$" as a synthetic judgment, on the ground that the concept of twelve is by no means already thought in merely thinking the union of seven and five. And he appears to regard this as tantamount to saying that the judgment does not rest on the principle of contradiction alone. He holds, also, that through analytic judgments our knowledge is not extended as it is through synthetic judgments. For in analytic judgments "the concept which I already have is merely set forth and made intelligible to me."

I think that this is a fair summary of Kant's account of the distinction between analytic and synthetic propositions, but I do not think that it succeeds in making the distinction clear. For even if we pass over the difficulties which arise out of the use of the vague term "concept," and the unwarranted assumption that every judgment, as well as every German or English sentence, can be said to have a subject and a predicate, there remains still this crucial defect. Kant does not give one straightforward criterion for distinguishing between analytic and synthetic propositions; he gives two distinct criteria, which are by no means equivalent. Thus his ground for holding that the proposition "$7 + 5 = 12$" is synthetic is, as we have seen, that the subjective intension of "$7 + 5$" does not comprise the subjective intension of "$12$"; whereas his ground for holding that "all bodies are extended" is an analytic proposition is that it rests on the principle of contradiction alone. That is, he employs a psychological criterion in the first of these examples, and a logical criterion in the second, and takes their equivalence for granted. But, in fact, a proposition which is synthetic according to the former criterion may very well be analytic according to the latter. For, as we have already pointed out, it is possible for symbols to be synonymous without having the same intensional meaning for anyone: and accordingly from the fact that one can think of the sum of seven and five without necessarily thinking of twelve, it by no means follows that the proposition "$7 + 5 = 12$" can be denied without self-contradiction. From the rest of his argument, it is clear that it is this logical proposition, and not any psychological proposition, that Kant is really anxious to establish. His use of the psychological criterion leads him to think that he has established it, when he has not.

I think that we can preserve the logical import of Kant's distinction between analytic and synthetic propositions, while avoiding the confusions which mar his actual account of it, if we say that a proposition is analytic when its validity depends solely on the definitions of the symbols it contains, and synthetic when its validity is determined by the facts of experience. Thus, the proposition "There are ants which have established a system of slavery" is a synthetic proposition. For we cannot tell whether it is true or false merely by considering the definitions of the symbols which constitute it. We have to resort to actual observation of the behaviour of ants. On the other hand, the proposition

"Either some ants are parasitic or none are" is an analytic proposition. For one need not resort to observation to discover that, there either are or are not ants which are parasitic. If one knows what is the function of the words "either," "or," and "not," then one can see that any proposition of the form "Either *p* is true or *p* is not true" is valid, independently of experience. Accordingly, all such propositions are analytic.

It is to be noticed that the proposition "Either some ants are parasitic or none are" provides no information whatsoever about the behaviour of ants, or, indeed, about any matter of fact. And this applies to all analytic propositions. They none of them provide any information about any matter of fact. In other words, they are entirely devoid of factual content. And it is for this reason that no experience can confute them.

When we say that analytic propositions are devoid of factual content, and consequently that they say nothing, we are not suggesting that they are senseless in the way that metaphysical utterances are senseless. For, although they give us no information about any empirical situation, they do enlighten us by illustrating the way in which we use certain symbols. Thus if I say, "Nothing can be colored in different ways at the same time with respect to the same part of itself," I am not saying anything about the properties of any actual thing; but I am not talking nonsense. I am expressing an analytic proposition, which records our determination to call a color expanse which differs in quality from a neighboring color expanse a different part of a given thing. In other words, I am simply calling attention to the implications of a certain linguistic usage. Similarly, in saying that if all Bretons are Frenchmen, and all Frenchmen Europeans, then all Bretons are Europeans, I am not describing any matter of fact. But I am showing that in the statement that all Bretons are Frenchmen, and all Frenchmen Europeans, the further statement that all Bretons are Europeans is implicitly contained. And I am thereby indicating the convention which governs our usage of the words "if" and "all."

We see, then, that there is a sense in which analytic propositions do give us new knowledge. They call attention to linguistic usages, of which we might otherwise not be conscious, and they reveal unsuspected implications in our assertions and beliefs.

But we can see also that there is a sense in which they may be said to add nothing to our knowledge. For they tell us only what we may be said to know already. Thus, if I know that the existence of May Queens is a relic of tree-worship, and I discover that May Queens still exist in England, I can employ the tautology "If *p* implies *q*, and *p* is true, *q* is true" to show that there still exists a relic of tree-worship in England. But in saying that there are still May Queens in England, and that the existence of May Queens is a relic of tree-worship, I have already asserted the existence in England of a relic of tree-worship. The use of the tautology does, indeed, enable me to make this concealed assertion explicit. But it does not provide me with any new knowledge, in the sense in which empirical evidence that the election of May Queens had been forbidden by law would provide me with new knowledge. If one had to set forth all the information one possessed, with regard to matters of fact, one would not write down any analytic propositions. But one would make use of analytic propositions in compiling one's encyclopædia, and would thus come to include propositions which one would otherwise have overlooked. And, besides enabling one to make one's list of information complete, the formulation of analytic propositions would enable one to make sure that the synthetic propositions of which the list was composed formed a self-consistent system. By showing which ways of combining propositions resulted in contradictions, they would prevent one from including incompatible propositions and so making the list self-stultifying. But insofar as we had actually used such words as "all" and "or" and "not" without falling into self-contradiction, we might be said already to know what was revealed in the formulation of analytic propositions illustrating the rules which govern our usage of these logical particles. So that here again we are justified in saying that analytic propositions do not increase our knowledge.

The analytic character of the truths of formal logic was obscured in the traditional logic through its being insufficiently formalized. For in speaking always of judgments, instead of propositions, and introducing irrelevant psychological questions, the traditional logic gave the impression of being concerned in some specially intimate way with the workings of thought. What it was actually concerned with was the formal relationship of classes, as is shown by the fact that all its principles of inference are subsumed in the Boolean class-calculus, which is subsumed in its turn in the propositional calculus of Russell and Whitehead. Their system, expounded in *Principia Mathematica,* makes it clear that formal logic is not concerned with the properties of men's minds, much less with the properties of material objects, but simply with the possibility of combining propositions by means of logical particles into analytic propositions, and with studying the formal relationship of these analytic propositions, in virtue of which one is deducible from another. Their procedure is to exhibit the propositions of formal logic as a deductive system, based on five primitive propositions, subsequently reduced in number to one. Hereby the distinction between logical truths and principles of inference, which was maintained in the Aristotelian logic, very properly disappears. Every principle of inference is put forward as a logical truth and every logical truth can serve as a principle of inference. The three Aristotelian "laws of thought," the law of identity, the law of excluded middle, and the law of non-contradiction, are incorporated in the system, but they are not considered more important than the other analytic propositions. They are not reckoned among the premises of the system. And the system of Russell and Whitehead itself is probably only one among many possible logics, each of which is composed of tautologies as interesting to the logician as the arbitrarily selected Aristotelian "laws of thought."

A point which is not sufficiently brought out by Russell, if indeed it is recognized by him at all, is that every logical proposition is valid in its own right. Its validity does not depend on its being incorporated in a system, and deduced from certain propositions which are taken as self-evident. The construction of systems of logic is useful as a means of discovering and certifying analytic propositions, but it is not in principle essential even for this purpose. For it is possible to conceive of a symbolism in which every analytic proposition could be seen to be analytic in virtue of its form alone.

The fact that the validity of an analytic proposition in no way depends on its being deducible from other analytic propositions is our justification for disregarding the question whether the propositions of mathematics are reducible to propositions of formal logic, in the way that Russell supposed. For even if it is the case that the definition of a cardinal number as a class of classes similar to a given class is circular, and it is not possible to reduce mathematical notions to purely logical notions, it will still remain true that the propositions of mathematics are analytic propositions. They will form a special class of analytic propositions, containing special terms, but they will be none the less analytic for that. For the criterion of an analytic proposition is that its validity should follow simply from the definition of the terms contained in it, and this condition is fulfilled by the propositions of pure mathematics.

The mathematical propositions which one might most pardonably suppose to be synthetic are the propositions of geometry. For it is natural for us to think, as Kant thought, that geometry is the study of the properties of physical space, and consequently that its propositions have factual content. And if we believe this, and also recognize that the truths of geometry are necessary and certain, then we may be inclined to accept Kant's hypothesis that space is the form of intuition of our outer sense, a form imposed by us on the matter of sensation, as the only possible explanation of our *a priori* knowledge of these synthetic propositions. But while the view that pure geometry is concerned with physical space was plausible enough in Kant's day, when the geometry of Euclid was the only geometry known, the subsequent invention of non-Euclidean geometries has shown it to be mistaken. We see now that the axioms of a geometry are simply definitions, and that the theorems of a geometry are simply the logical consequences of these definitions. A geometry is not in itself about physical space; in itself it cannot be said to be "about" anything. But we can use a geometry to reason about physical space. That is to say, once we have given the axioms a physical interpretation, we can proceed to apply the theorems to the objects which satisfy the axioms. Whether a geometry can be applied to the actual physical world or not, is an empirical question which falls outside the scope of the geometry itself. There is no sense, therefore, in asking which of the various geometries known to us are false, and which are true. Insofar as they are all free from contradiction, they are all true. What one can ask is which of them is the most useful on any given occasion, which of them can be applied most easily and most fruitfully to an actual empirical situation. But the proposition which states that a certain application of a geometry is possible is not itself a proposition of that geometry. All that the geometry itself tells us is that if anything can be brought under the definitions, it will also satisfy the theorems. It is therefore a purely logical system, and its propositions are purely analytic propositions.

It might be objected that the use made of diagrams in geometrical treatises shows that geometrical reasoning is not purely abstract and logical, but depends on our intuition of the properties of figures. In fact, however, the use of diagrams is not essential to completely rigorous geometry. The diagrams are introduced as an aid to our reason. They provide us with a particular application of the geometry, and so assist us to perceive the more general truth that the axioms of the geometry involve certain consequences. But the fact that most of us need the help of an example to make us aware of those consequences does not show that the relation between them and the axioms is not a purely logical relation. It shows merely that our intellects are unequal to the task of carrying out very abstract processes of reasoning without the assistance of intuition. In other words, it has no bearing on the nature of geometrical propositions, but is simply an empirical fact about ourselves. Moreover, the appeal to intuition, though generally of psychological value, is also a source of danger to the geometer. He is tempted to make assumptions which are accidentally true of the particular figure he is taking as an illustration, but do not follow from his axioms. It has, indeed, been shown that Euclid himself was guilty of this, and consequently that the presence of the figure is essential to some of his proofs. This shows that his system is not, as he presents it, completely rigorous, although of course it can be made so. It does not show that the presence of the figure is essential to a truly rigorous geometrical proof. To suppose that it did would be to take as a necessary feature of all geometries what is really only an incidental defect in one particular geometrical system.

We conclude, then, that the propositions of pure geometry are analytic. And this leads us to reject Kant's hypothesis that geometry deals with the form of intuition of our outer sense. For the ground for this hypothesis was that it alone explained how the propositions of geometry could be both true *a priori* and synthetic: and we have seen that they are not synthetic. Similarly our view that the propositions of arithmetic are not synthetic but analytic leads us to reject the Kantian hypothesis that arithmetic is concerned with our pure intuition of time, the form of our inner sense. And thus we are able to dismiss Kant's transcendental æsthetic without having to bring forward the epistemological difficulties which it is commonly said to involve. For the only argument which can be brought in favour of Kant's theory is that it alone explains certain "facts." And now we have found that the "facts" which it purports to explain are not facts at all. For while it is true that we have *a priori* knowledge of necessary propositions, it is not true, as Kant supposed, that any of these necessary propositions are synthetic. They are without exception analytic propositions, or, in other words, tautologies.

We have already explained how it is that these analytic propositions are necessary and certain. We saw that the reason why they cannot be confuted in experience is that they do not make any assertion about the empirical world. They simply record our determination to use words in a certain fashion. We cannot deny them without infringing the conventions which are presupposed by our very denial, and so falling into self-contradiction. And this is the sole ground of their necessity. As Wittgenstein puts it, our justification for holding that the world could not conceivably disobey the laws of logic is simply that we could not say of an unlogical world how it would look. And just as the validity of an analytic proposition is independent of the nature of the external world; so is it independent of the nature of our minds. It is perfectly conceivable that we should have employed different linguistic conventions from those which we actually do employ. But whatever these conventions might be, the tautologies in which we recorded them would always be necessary. For any denial of them would be self-stultifying.

We see, then, that there is nothing mysterious about the apodeictic certainty of logic and mathematics. Our knowledge that no observation can ever confute the proposition

"7 + 5 = 12" depends simply on the fact that the symbolic expression "7 + 5" is synonymous with "12," just as our knowledge that every oculist is an eye-doctor depends on the fact that the symbol "eye-doctor" is synonymous with "oculist." And the same explanation holds good for every other *a priori* truth.

What is mysterious at first sight is that these tautologies should on occasion be so surprising, that there should be in mathematics and logic the possibility of invention and discovery. As Poincaré says: "If all the assertions which mathematics puts forward can be derived from one another by formal logic, mathematics cannot amount to anything more than an immense tautology. Logical inference can teach us nothing essentially new, and if everything is to proceed from the principle of identity, everything must be reducible to it. But can we really allow that these theorems which fill so many books serve no other purpose than to say in a round-about fashion 'A = A'?" Poincaré finds this incredible. His own theory is that the sense of invention and discovery in mathematics belongs to it in virtue of mathematical induction, the principle that what is true for the number 1, and true for $n + 1$ when it is true for $n$, is true for all numbers. And he claims that this is a synthetic *a priori* principle. It is, in fact, *a priori*, but it is not synthetic. It is a defining principle of the natural numbers, serving to distinguish them from such numbers as the infinite cardinal numbers, to which it cannot be applied. Moreover, we must remember that discoveries can be made, not only in arithmetic, but also in geometry and formal logic, where no use is made of mathematical induction. So that even if Poincaré were right about mathematical induction, he would not have provided a satisfactory explanation of the paradox that a mere body of tautologies can be so interesting and so surprising.

The true explanation is very simple. The power of logic and mathematics to surprise us depends, like their usefulness, on the limitations of our reason. A being whose intellect was infinitely powerful would take no interest in logic and mathematics. For he would be able to see at a glance everything that his definitions implied, and, accordingly, could never learn anything from logical inference which he was not fully conscious of already. But our intellects are not of this order. It is only a minute proportion of the consequences of our definitions that we are able to detect at a glance. Even so simple a tautology as "91 × 79 = 7189" is beyond the scope of our immediate apprehension. To assure ourselves that "7189" is synonymous with "91 × 79" we have to resort to calculation, which is simply a process of tautological transformation—that is, a process by which we change the form of expressions without altering their significance. The multiplication tables are rules for carrying out this process in arithmetic, just as the laws of logic are rules for the tautological transformation of sentences expressed in logical symbolism or in ordinary language. As the process of calculation is carried out more or less mechanically, it is easy for us to make a slip and so unwittingly contradict ourselves. And this accounts for the existence of logical and mathematical "falsehoods," which otherwise might appear paradoxical. Clearly the risk of error in logical reasoning is proportionate to the length and the complexity of the process of calculation. And in the same way, the more complex an analytic proposition is, the more chance it has of interesting and surprising us.

It is easy to see that the danger of error in logical reasoning can be minimized by the introduction of symbolic devices, which enable us to express highly complex tautologies in a conveniently simple form. And this gives us an opportunity for the exercise of invention in the pursuit of logical enquiries. For a well-chosen definition will call our attention to analytic truths, which would otherwise have escaped us. And the framing of definitions which are useful and fruitful may well be regarded as a creative act.

Having thus shown that there is no inexplicable paradox involved in the view that the truths of logic and mathematics are all of them analytic, we may safely adopt it as the only satisfactory explanation of their *a priori* necessity. And in adopting it we vindicate the empiricist claim that there can be no *a priori* knowledge of reality. For we show that the truths of pure reason, the propositions which we know to be valid independently of all experience, are so only in virtue of their lack of factual content. To say that a proposition is true *a priori* is to say that it is a tautology. And tautologies, though they may serve to guide us in our empirical search for knowledge, do not in themselves contain any information about any matter of fact.

## FURTHER READING

Britton (2)*
Carnap (1), (5)
Hahn
Hempel (1), (2)
Malcolm (1)
Schlick (1)

---

* In many cases, we have cited more than one work by an author in the Bibliography on pages 207–223, and for convenience we have numbered such works chronologically. These numbers in parentheses correspond to the bibliography numbers.

# THE LINGUISTIC THEORY OF LOGICAL NECESSITY

*Arthur Pap*

## Are Necessary Propositions Necessarily Necessary?

If all of this is correct, then we come to the conclusion that there is no way of improving on the definition of "a priori truth" which constituted our starting point, viz. a true statement whose truth is ascertainable by reflecting on its meaning alone, or by logical deduction from statements of this sort. In which case, as pointed out, it will be difficult to escape from the conclusion that the thesis "all a priori truth is analytic" is either a tautology or else false. But let us make one more effort to see clearly what, on the above definition, we are saying about a statement in calling it "true a priori." Do we mean that any rational person could be brought to assent to the statement by just carefully explaining to him what the statement means (by definition of "rational," of course, a rational person would be able to follow a formal demonstration)? If so, then "*p* is a priori" would be a prediction of psychological reactions, and we would only be warranted in saying, with regard to any given *p*, "the evidence makes it probable that *p* is a priori." Now, that "*p* is a priori" should itself be an empirical statement would be an innocent consequence

From Arthur Pap, *Semantics and Necessary Truth* (New Haven and London: Yale University Press, 1958), pp. 119–127, 163–173, 182–185. Copyright © 1958 by Yale University Press. Reprinted by permission of the publisher.

if it were meant in the sense of "this sentence is presently used to express an a priori proposition." But this very statement about usage suggests that "a priori" is directly predicable of *propositions,* though derivatively of sentences that express a priori propositions. And would any philosopher be willing to admit that once we know which proposition *p* is expressed by a given sentence, it is still a *question of empirical fact* whether *p* is a priori? Should we not say, rather, that necessity is an *intrinsic* property of a proposition in the sense that it would make no sense to suppose that a necessary proposition *might not have been* necessary?

The question whether "it is necessary that *p*" is, if true, itself a necessary proposition is of fundamental importance for the problem of explicating the concept of necessary truth, since it is likely that any philosopher who answers it affirmatively will adopt the necessity of the necessity of *p* as a *criterion of adequacy* for proposed explications of necessary truth. He will, in other words, reject any explication which entails the contingency of such modal propositions as failing to explicate the explicandum he has in mind. The same holds, of course, for the concept of logical truth: since all logical truths are necessary truths (whether or not the converse of this proposition be true also), any criterion of adequacy for explications of "necessary truth" is at the same time a criterion of adequacy for explications of "logical truth." This question cannot be decided by formal reasoning within an uninterpreted system of modal logic, containing the usual explicit definition of "necessary" in terms of "possible": *p* is necessary = not-*p* is not possible. Indeed, an uninterpreted system of modal logic can be constructed without even raising the question of the necessity of the necessity of *p;* thus there is no postulate or theorem in Lewis' system $S_2$ that bears on the question, nor is the question informally discussed in the metalanguage. In Appendix II to Lewis and Langford's *Symbolic Logic* (New York and London, 1932) it is pointed out that Lewis' system of strict implication "leaves undetermined certain properties of the modal functions, $\Diamond p$, $\sim \Diamond p$, $\Diamond \sim p$, and $\sim \Diamond \sim p$." Accordingly *"Np -3 NNp,"* as well as *"Np ⊃ NNp"* (*N* . . . = it is necessary that . . .), is both independent of and consistent with the axioms of the system, and whether an axiom of modal iteration, e.g. "what is possibly possible, is possible" (which can be shown to be equivalent to "what is necessary, is necessarily necessary") should be adopted must be decided by extrasystematic considerations based on *interpretation* of the modal functions. Now, let us refer to the thesis that necessary propositions are necessarily necessary henceforth as the "*NN* thesis." What appears to be the strongest argument in favor of the *NN* thesis is based on the semantic assumption that "necessary" as predicated of propositions is a *time-independent* predicate, where a "time-independent" predicate is defined as a predicate $P$ such that sentences of the form "$x$ is $P$ at time $t$" are meaningless. The argument runs as follows.

Anybody who maintained that the proposition "it is necessary that every father have at least one child" is itself contingent, could only mean that the *sentence* "every father has at least one child," which is in fact used to express a necessary proposition, might have been used to express a contingent proposition (e.g. "father" might have been used in the sense in which "man" is used). Indeed, a statement of the form "$S$ expresses a necessary proposition" is incomplete, requiring expansion into "$S$ expresses, in present usage, a necessary proposition," and once so expanded shows itself as a contingent, indeed historical, statement about verbal usage. But while the predicate "expresses a necessary proposition" is clearly time-dependent, "necessary" as predicated of propositions is just as clearly time-independent. This can be shown convincingly if we consider statements of the form "$p$ entails $q$," which are reducible to the form "$p$ is necessary" where $p$ is a conditional proposition (thus "that somebody is a father entails that somebody has at least one child" is reducible to "it is necessary that if somebody is a father, then somebody has at least one child"). Suppose a logic teacher—engaged in the demonstration that premises of the forms "all $A$ are $B$" and "some $A$ are not $C$" entail that some $B$ are not $C$, while the entailment does not hold if the universal premise is replaced by its converse "all $B$ are $A$"— were asked by a befuddled yet critical student: "You have shown that the conclusion is entailed by the first pair of premises but not by the second pair *at the present time.* How do you propose to prove that these logical relations will *always* hold?" Surely this student will have to be told that he has not understood what is meant by "entailment," that in terms of the intended meaning of "entailment" his question does not make sense; that he might just as well have asked how we know that the square root of 9 was equal to 3 before the symbols "3" and "9" were invented by mankind. Thus it must be concluded that it is inconceivable that an entailment which in fact holds from $p$ to $q$ should fail to hold between the same propositions at some other time, simply because it does not make sense to say that an entailment holds *at some time*.

But this argument for the *NN* thesis assumes that the only ground on which the *NN* thesis could be rejected is the interpretation of "$p$ is necessary," like "$S$ expresses a necessary proposition," as a *historical* statement; once this assumption is granted, the *NN* thesis is easily established, since it is easy to show that modal statements are not historical statements. If this assumption is challenged, then some other argument is needed. Such an independent argument might be constructed on the following premise: if and only if $S$ expresses a *contingent* proposition $p$, then it is possible that two people who both take $S$ to express $p$ nevertheless disagree about the truth-value of $S$. Let "$p$" be of the form "$p$ entails $q$" (i.e. "it is necessary that if $p$, then $q$"). The question before us then reduces to the question whether two people who are in disagreement as to whether proposition $p$ entails proposition $q$ may nevertheless be interpreting the sentence "$p$ entails $q$" in the same way. And since it is clearly possible that they should agree in their interpretation of "entails" and yet disagree as to whether $p$ entails $q$, this is to ask whether the disputants could put the identical interpretation on the sentences "$p$" and "$q$." Some analysts would deny this possibility and hence conclude that true entailment statements are themselves necessary; thus Schlick said that correct interpretation and verification coincide in the case of analytic statements. But it seems to me obvious that they are wrong. Consider an entailment between fairly complex propositions, e.g. propositions of the forms "if $p$, then (if $q$, then $r$ or not-$s$)" and "if $q$, then (if $s$ and not-$r$, then not-$p$)." They in fact entail one another, but a person not trained in formal logic may have difficulty seeing this and hence might conceivably dispute the entailment. Yet, if he explicitly agrees to the truth-table definitions of the connectives and moreover shows himself familiar with the relevant syntactic rules, it could hardly be denied that the two sentences express for him the same propositions as for the logician who recognizes their logical equivalence.

But then the only possible source of the disagreement is that one of the disputants is either unaware of some relevant rule of deduction or else employs an invalid rule of deduction or else makes a mistake in applying the relevant rules of deduction; for short, let us say that he commits a deductive error. Should we conclude, now, that the *NN* thesis is false, since the criterion of necessary propositions—viz. that if the proposition *p* expressed by *S* is necessary, then anybody who honestly denied *S* would not interpret *S* to mean *p*—does not seem to be satisfied by entailment propositions? Such a conclusion would be most unwise, since the same argument would prove that not even *first-order* propositions (i.e. propositions which are not about propositions) of appreciable complexity are necessary. Deductive mistakes might lead one, for example, to deny an arithmetical equation which expresses a necessary proposition. And if the best reason one can adduce against *NNp* (where *Np* is equivalent to an entailment proposition) is at the same time an argument against *Np,* then the thesis that *if Np, then NNp,* has in fact been supported rather than undermined.

On the other hand, a seductive argument *against* the *NN* thesis is that to establish a proposition as necessary we must, in many cases, perform calculatory or deductive operations which are subject to error just like the processes of interpreting sense data that enter into the verification of empirical propositions about the physical world. Consider, e.g., the truth-table test for determining whether a given formula expresses a tautology. If after performing the test we say confidently that the proposition expressed by the formula is a tautology, it is because we confidently assume that no mistake was made in the calculations of truth-values. Since there is a finite probability of error in the calculation (proportional, roughly, to the complexity of the formula), we ought to say critically "on the evidence of the calculation test, it is highly probable that the proposition expressed by the formula is a tautology"; and since it does not make sense to ascribe probability to a necessary proposition, so the argument might conclude, "*p* is a tautology" is not itself a necessary proposition.

Before exposing the subtle error of this argument, I wish

to reduce it to absurdity by showing that if it were valid it would prove that there are no tautologies at all, not even in the realm of first-order propositions. Let us ask ourselves by what sort of evidence we could establish the *truth* (not necessity) of a proposition of the form "*p* or not-*p*" (to take the simplest case of a tautology), say "$p_1$ or not-$p_1$," where $p_1$ is an empirical proposition. The naive method would consist in verifying either $p_1$, or not-$p_1$, and then inferring, with the help of the principle "*p* entails (*p* or *q*)," the truth of "either $p_1$ or not-$p_1$." Clearly, in using this method we establish the disjunction as an *empirical* truth only. But if we are not naive, i.e. if we recognize that the truth of this compound proposition is independent of the truth-value of its atomic component, then we shall adduce evidence for the truth of "$p_1$ or not-$p_1$" which is at the same time evidence for the *necessary* truth of this proposition: the evidence of the truth-table. That is, we assert the truth of "$p_1$ or not-$p_1$" on the ground that any proposition of the same form is true, i.e. on the ground that it is *necessarily* true. It follows that if the evidence of the truth-table be regarded as empirical evidence which only lends probability to the propositions it is evidence for, then not only " '$p_1$ or not-$p_1$' is a tautology" but likewise "$p_1$ or not-$p_1$" itself is an empirical proposition. (Note that the truth-table verdict is the only evidence on which "$p_1$ or not-$p_1$" can be asserted in case the truth-value of "$p_1$" is unknown.) Analogous considerations apply if the test by which a formula is established as a tautology is the deduction test.

But just in case some nihilist or ultra-empiricist among analytic philosophers should boldly accept the consequence that there are no necessary propositions at all, it is advisable to refute the argument against the *NN* thesis unconditionally. The subtle error of the argument consists in a confusion of *necessity* as a *logical* property of propositions, and *certainty* as a *psychological* state. It is tacitly assumed that "*p* is necessary" is equivalent to, or at least entails, "*p* can be known with absolute certainty." Yet, it is easy to see that on this assumption the proposition of arithmetic "$63 \times 45 = 2835$" would be no more necessary than the empirical proposition that day always follows and is followed by night (in fact, for a man with a poor training in arithmetic, the latter proposition would be necessary to a higher degree). The evidence on which one asserts such an equation is that calculations performed by oneself led to this result each time, and that calculations performed by other people competent at multiplication confirmed the result. Nevertheless, it remains logically possible that such a finite series of repetitions of the same calculation should have been infected with errors, and that future calculations should lead to a different result. We may feel confident that no mistake was involved in any of the steps of the calculation, yet it is logically possible that a mistake was made. Remember that the only certainty which Descartes' demon was powerless to undermine was the certainty of "I am uncertain"; the propositions of arithmetic fell a prey to the demon just like the propositions of physics. Some philosophers hold that it is the distinctive mark of empirical propositions that no matter how much confirming evidence may have been accumulated at a given time, it always remains possible that in the future disconfirming evidence will turn up. But this is surely an unsuccessful way of distinguishing empirical propositions from necessary propositions. The more complex a deduction, the greater the probability of a deductive error, and hence the greater the probability that a future repetition of the deduction should lead to a different result. Yet we know that the proposition which we judge in terms of deductive evidence is either necessarily true or necessarily false.

What marks a proposition as a priori is not that it is capable of being known, either as true or as false, with *absolute certainty*. It is rather that the only kind of cognitive activity which we admit as appropriate to its validation is conceptual analysis and deduction—the "mere operation of thought." In this sense of "a priori," "*p* is a priori" is itself a priori whether or not it be true, for it is by "the mere operation of thought" that we determine whether a proposition is a priori. For example, if by analysis of truth possibilities I establish the truth of the proposition "if New York is overcrowded, and if it is unpleasant to live in New York if New York is overcrowded, then it is unpleasant to live in New York," without investigating empirically whether the atomic components of this compound proposition are true or false, then I have *by the same analysis* established the *necessary truth* of this proposition. For the analysis establishes that *all* propositions expressed by sentences of the form "if (*p* and (if *p*, then q)), then *q*" are *true*. And if the nonempirical evidence in terms of which *p* is established as true coincides with the evidence in terms of which *p* is established as necessarily true, then *"p* is necessary" is necessary in the same sense in which *"p"* is necessary. What is decisive is that if a necessary proposition is not mistakenly believed to be contingent, then its truth is known simply as a corollary of its necessity, by the principle "if *Np,* then *p*" (whatever is necessarily the case, is the case). To add a simple illustration: by reflecting on the meanings of "square" and "equilateral" we come to know that *"x* is square" entails *"x* is equilateral." The entailment, however, can be expressed in the form "it is necessary that there be no square which is not equilateral," and by "if *Np,* then *p*" this entails "there is no square which is not equilateral."

What led us into this discussion, ending in final acceptance, of the *NN* thesis was the doubt whether the definition of "a priori" in terms of the psychological concept "assent" did not entail that in classifying a proposition as a priori we assert a generalization of psychology. But it now appears that the definition "capable of being known by conceptual analysis and deduction alone," whether or not it be considered "psychologistic," is quite consistent with the view that we are making in no sense an *empirical* statement about a proposition when we classify it as a priori. For, to repeat, the same intellectual operations by which we would normally establish such a proposition as true also establish it as *necessarily* true.

.    .    .

## Are Necessary Propositions a Species of Empirical Propositions?

When the linguistic theory was first expressed, by such ardent "positivists" as Ayer, it easily lent itself to the *reductio ad absurdum* that necessary propositions are really a special kind of empirical propositions, viz. generalizations about linguistic usage. But in the meantime it has been formulated more subtly, by Ayer himself in the introduction to the second edition of his positivist manifesto, and by such Wittgensteinians as N. Malcolm. Let us examine a version of it which brings out what I take to be its central idea, viz. that necessary truth is in some sense the product of linguistic conventions: "The existence of certain linguistic habits relevant to the use of a sentence $S$ is a necessary and sufficient condition for the necessity of the proposition meant by $S$." It is not too difficult to show, however, that linguistic habits can be neither sufficient nor necessary conditions for the necessity of a proposition. The persuasiveness of this theory is probably due to some such reasoning as this: If there exists a linguistic habit of applying the word "yard" to distances of three feet and only to such distances, then the proposition expressed by "every yard contains three feet" is identical with the proposition that every yard is a yard; hence, given that linguistic convention and no further facts at all, the truth of the proposition follows. But suppose we ask, "follows *from what?*" Evidently the answer is "from the law of identity." It has been tacitly assumed, then, that the law of identity ("everything is what it is," in informal language), of which the proposition that every yard is a yard is a substitution instance, is a necessary truth. If it were not, then no amount of linguistic conventions would suffice to make any proposition necessary. The verbalist (as we may call an advocate of the linguistic theory) might reply that such a law of logic itself derives its necessity from linguistic habits as to the usage of such logical constants as "if-then": "if $p$, then $p$" is a familiar version of the law of identity. But if all that is the result of linguistic habits is the *synonymy* of the sentences "every yard contains three feet" and "every yard is a yard" (their expressing the same proposition), then likewise linguistic habits will account only for the *synonymy* of such abstract tautologies as "if $p$, then $p$" and "it is not the case that $p$ and not-$p$." We should not, indeed, *deny* that it is linguistic conventions which "give rise" to the necessity of the proposition thus expressible by different sentences; the question is rather what this assertion *means*. But first let us convince ourselves that the existence of a linguistic habit is not a necessary condition, any more than it is a sufficient condition, for the necessary truth of a proposition. If linguistic habits were to change in such a way that, say, a length of two feet came to be called a "yard," then, of course, the proposition *thereafter* expressed by the sentence "every yard contains three feet" would be false, and hence not necessary. But this has no tendency to prove that the proposition which was formerly expressed by this sentence has ceased to be a necessary truth and turned into a necessary falsehood. Indeed, this consequence of the view that necessary truth "depends" on linguistic habits in the sense in which, say, good health depends on the presence of fresh air, does not even have the virtue of being a meaningful statement: as pointed out above . . . "necessary" is (in the relevant sense) a time-independent predicate, which means that a sentence of the form "*p* is necessary at time *t*—and perhaps not necessary at some other time" makes no more sense than, say, "*p* is a true proposition in New York, but possibly not in London."

The linguistic theory, as formulated, lends itself, moreover, to deduction of a neat paradox. Our theory, while admitting that necessary statements of a natural language are not statements *about* contingent linguistic habits, holds that what characterizes them as necessary is that the existence of such a habit is sufficient to guarantee their truth; one who denied such a statement —who said, e.g., "there are married bachelors"—would thereby break an established linguistic habit. Thus in pointing out that the expressions "bachelor" and "unmarried man" are used synonymously in English, one states a sufficient reason for accepting "all bachelors are unmarried" as true, and therefore the latter statement, according to our theory, is necessary (that actually the synonymy of these expressions is only a sufficient reason for accepting the statement as a logical consequence of a logical truth—$(x)$ $(f)$ $(g)$ $(fx.gx \supset fx)$—is an important argument against the linguistic theory, but will be disregarded in this context). But if an empirical statement *p* describes evidence for another statement *q*—in other words, if in stating *p* one gives an empirical reason for accepting *q*—then *q* is itself empirical. This contradicts the assumption that *q* is necessary. The solution of this little paradox is easy enough if . . . we properly distinguish between "*S* expresses a necessary proposition" and "the proposition that *p*—which happens to be expressed by *S*—is necessary": in pointing to a certain language habit, we may indeed give a reason for accepting the former statement, which is clearly empirical. But since the advocate of the linguistic theory is likely to scoff at the suggestion that necessity is an intrinsic property of extralinguistic propositions . . . , he will probably have no use for this solution.

We thus find that even a formulation of the linguistic theory which does not at the surface entail that necessary propositions are empirical—and that therefore there are not any—entails this paradox if closely analyzed. Let us carefully note, however, that it is one thing to accuse the linguistic theory of denying the existence of necessary propositions, and quite another thing to accuse it of denying the necessity of true propositions of the form "*p* is necessary." It is not obvious that it is inconsistent to hold, on the one hand, that *p* is necessary, and on the other hand, that the proposition expressed by "*p* is necessary" is contingent. . . . It was, indeed, argued [above] that such modal propositions are, if true, themselves necessary. And if that argument is valid, then it is a sufficient refutation of the linguistic theory, since even if this theory could be so formulated as to be compatible with the existence of necessary propositions, it clearly entails the contingency of modal propositions. For if in order to determine whether "*p*" is necessary, one has to examine the present usage of the expressions constituting "*p*," then the truth-value of " '*p*' is necessary" is *empirically* ascertained. But this is at any rate a separate question entirely, since the reasons for holding that there are necessary propositions—to be presented shortly—are independent of the reasons for holding that true modal propositions are themselves necessary propositions.

Let us note also that the same sort of criticism of the linguistic theory would be applicable if "linguistic rule (or convention)" were used in the more restricted sense of "explicitly formulated definition," and the thesis accordingly were that the logical necessity of a proposition is the result of conventional definitions. It is inaccurate to say that a logically true proposition is a proposition which *follows from definitions*. Definitions are, from the formal point of view, rules of substitution *by* which truth, as well as necessary truth, is transmitted from one statement to another. Thus through the definition "father = male parent" necessary truth is transmitted from the statement ($p$) "all male parents are male" to the statement ($q$) "all fathers are male." $p$ would be necessary even if the abbreviation "father" had never been introduced into our language. And since $q$ expresses the same proposition as $p$, the same holds for it. $p$ itself is necessary because of derivability by substitution from a principle of logic: $(x) (f) (g) (fx.gx \supset fx)$. To simplify matters, let us consider this principle as a case of "if $p$ and $q$, then $p$."

In which sense is the necessity of this principle *created* by definitions? All we can say is that, by virtue of the truth-table definitions of the connectives involved, this principle must be true *if* every proposition is either true or false and no proposition is both true and false (this assumption being implicit in the "convention" of assigning just one of the truth-values "true" and "false" to each proposition). If you wish you may say that this assumption is itself logically necessary by virtue of the definition of "proposition": we call "proposition" anything which satisfies the laws of contradiction and of excluded middle. But this still does not end the regress: the definition again does not "create" logical necessity, but merely transmits it from the necessary proposition "every proposition is a proposition."

It may be appropriate to comment in this connection on a recent attempt by an able member of the Wittgenstein school of linguistic analysis to formulate a linguistic theory of necessity in such a way that it is not open to the charge of reducing necessary propositions to empirical propositions about language. Morris Lazerowitz writes (*The Structure of Metaphysics,* p. 271):

> What makes a non-verbal sentence "A flea is an insect" express a logically necessary truth is the fact that the corresponding verbal sentence expresses a true proposition. The fact that "A flea is an insect" expresses a logically necessary proposition entails and is entailed by the fact that "As a matter of usage 'insect' applies to whatever 'flea' applies to" expresses a true empirical proposition.

But it is not clear what "As a matter of usage, '*A*' applies to whatever '*B*' applies to" means. If it is so meant that "As a matter of usage, 'black' applies to whatever 'crow' applies to" is true, although "all crows are black" expresses an empirical proposition, then clearly the mutual entailment asserted by Lazerowitz does not hold. Of course, the fact that "crow" and "black" are used the way they are in English is not a sufficient reason for the truth of "all crows are black." The latter statement is true because (a) "crow" means the property *crow,* (b) "black" means the property *black,* and (c) whatever has the first property also has the second. Lazerowitz, then, must mean that in case the extension of "*B*" is part of the extension of "*A*" by virtue of logical necessity, a rule of usage concerning "*B*" and "*A*" is the *sufficient reason* for the truth of "all *B* are *A*." Yet he emphasizes that it is an empirical fact that this rather than that rule of usage exists. That people who speak English do not apply the predicate "flea but not insect" to anything, regardless of any extralinguistic facts, is itself an empirical proposition. But then he is saying either that the truth of an empirical proposition about usage is a sufficient reason for the truth of a necessary proposition (which is a contradiction, since by definition of "necessary proposition" no empirical fact can entail a necessary proposition except in the vacuous sense in which a necessary proposition is entailed by every proposition) or else that the truth of an empirical proposition about usage is a sufficient reason for the truth of an empirical proposition to the effect that a given sentence expresses a necessary proposition. On the latter interpretation he avoids the paradox that the very concept "necessary proposition" is self-contradictory. But then Lazerowitz has given us at best a criterion for "the sentence '*p*' expresses a necessary proposition," not for "it is necessary that *p*," which latter statement does not mention "*p*," the *sentence*. He has failed, that is, to provide a reasonably complete definition in use of "necessary proposition." In order for a definition in use of "necessary proposition" to be reasonably complete it must contain not only a part elucidating the phrase " '*p*' expresses a necessary proposition" but also a part elucidating the phrase "the proposition *that p* is necessary." To present an analogy from the philosophy of mathematics: the logicist thesis of the definability of number concepts by means of logical constants is not sufficiently substantiated by rules for translating sentences of the form "class *A* has *n* members" into the language of *Principia Mathematica*. Both Frege and Russell supplied further rules of translation for what might be called "substantival" uses of numerical expressions, like "Two is the successor of One." A complete definition in use of "logically necessary" in linguistic terms, then, Lazerowitz has not provided.

The view is sometimes expressed that the conventional nature of logical principles is demonstrated by the fact that in proposing alternatives to the usual, two-valued, logic, one really does nothing else than propose different rules for the usage of logical constants. For example, if a three-valued logic is proposed in which the law of the excluded middle is replaced by the trichotomy "every proposition is either true or false or indeterminate," then, whatever "indeterminate" may mean, "true" and "false" must have different meanings from those they have in the two-valued logic; for, in the two-valued logic, "*p* is not true" entails "*p* is false," and as this entailment is constitutive of the meanings of "true" and "false," its not being valid in the three-valued logic indicates that "true" and "false" have changed their meanings. But I confess that this, undoubtedly correct, observation seems to me to prove nothing else than that the principles of two-valued logic are *necessary* propositions. For if from the fact that so-and-so denies *S* *it follows* that so-and-so has changed the usual meaning of *S*, then it follows that the proposition usually expressed by *S* is necessary. What is in an intelligible sense "conventional" is that a given sentence is used to express one rather than another proposition; but what could be meant by saying that a proposition is necessary "by virtue of linguistic conventions" is simply obscure. To be sure, one could specify the meanings of logical constants "implicitly" by ruling that specified sentences containing them are to be true. For example: let "if, then" be so used that "if (if *p*, then *q*), then (if not-*q*, then not-*p*)" is true (presupposing a prior assignment of meaning to "not"). Is it not clear, then, that the logical law thus functioning as implicit definition is "true by convention"? But if the method of specifying the meaning of a term *T* by saying that *T* is meant in such a way that statement *S* containing *T* is true justified the assertion that the truth expressed by *S* is conventional, then any true statement could be made out as a conventional truth. Thus suppose that all the terms in the statement "the city busses running on Broadway are red" except "red" have been assigned meanings, and we now explain the meaning of "red" by saying " 'red' means that color *C* for which 'the city busses running on Broadway are *C*' is true." Is the fact that the city busses running on Broadway are red, then, a result of linguistic convention?

## Necessity and Linguistic Rules

Perhaps, however, the arguments advanced against the linguistic theory so far have missed its real point, which may be that *there are no necessary propositions,* that there are only contingent propositions plus certain kinds of linguistic rules; that sentences ordinarily said to express necessary propositions do not, indeed, express empirical propositions, but rather express no propositions at all. Thus a sentence like "if John is taller than Bill, then Bill is shorter than John" (*S*) might be said to *express a linguistic rule,* not a proposition in the sense in which a proposition is something that may be true or false, believed or disbelieved, verified or refuted. Perhaps the advocates of this theory would say that the illusion of there being necessary propositions has an origin similar to that of the illusion, in the opinion of the emotivists, that there are ethical propositions. We frequently use *declarative* sentences in expressing desires and aversions, instead of using openly expressive (or imperative) forms of speech; we say to the naughty child "stealing apples is wrong," instead of "don't steal apples," and this leads us to suppose that "stealing apples is wrong" expresses a proposition which calls for verification or refutation, belief or disbelief. Similarly, if instead of uttering a declarative conditional sentence we said (to the person whom we wish to instruct in the correct use of the words "taller" and "shorter") "instead of saying 'John is taller than Bill' you may, if you wish, say 'Bill is shorter than John' (it means the same thing), but don't ever say both '*x* is shorter than *y*' and '*y* is shorter than *x*'; that would be contradicting yourself," the directive, noncognitive function of the language used would be obvious. If we "inform" the person of the speech habits in the community, we do so in the same indirect manner in which we inform the naughty child of the moral attitudes of his elders. There is here, indeed, a striking analogy between the reasons for which emotivists deny that ethical sentences are descriptive (as contrasted with expressive) of emotions and the reasons for which advocates of the linguistic theory, like Ayer, deny that sentences commonly held to express necessary propositions are *descriptive* of linguistic habits.

That a sentence like *S* is directive in function even though its grammatical form suggests that its primary function is cognitive (or assertive) is a plausible view. It is sometimes held against the linguistic theory that necessary propositions cannot be characterized as linguistic rules, since, after all, truth is predicable of necessary propositions while it is not of rules; a rule can be good or useful, but it is nonsense to call it "true." If this argument is used against the characterization of such sentences as $S$ as linguistic rules, it is absurd. For the same argument could be used to maintain that "stealing is wrong" expresses a proposition and cannot be regarded as equivalent in function to the imperative "don't steal": it is syntactically correct to say "it is true that stealing is wrong," while it is syntactically incorrect to say "it is true that don't steal." And that in fact philosophers do not in general regard the declarative form of a sentence as sufficient proof that the sentence expresses a proposition, or that its primary function is cognitive, should require no argument (*vide* the view that there are no ethical propositions). The only argument that is commonly given for denying the propriety of labeling such sentences as $S$ "linguistic rules" is that truth is properly predicable of them; yet if the reason for this latter claim is that $S$ expresses a proposition, the question has been begged, and if the reason is that $S$ is a declarative sentence, the conclusion does not follow.

It would be futile to debate the question of whether $S$ expresses a proposition or is just a linguistic rule unless we can agree on a *general* criterion of propositional significance. The confirmability criterion offered by the logical empiricists is not helpful in this context, for the following reason: in order to escape from the consequence that only empirical statements are cognitively meaningful (in other words, that a sentence either expresses no proposition or else expresses an empirical proposition), the more recent advocates of the criterion have benevolently recognized analytic and even self-contradictory propositions, by ruling that a sentence expresses a proposition if and only if it is either confirmable (in which case it expresses an empirical proposition) *or* analytic or self-contradictory. Obviously, then, nobody who accepts this tolerant form of the confirmability criterion could advocate the version of the linguistic theory under discussion. The very debatability of this theory presupposes a criterion of propositional significance other than the confirmability criterion in the above form. What alternatives are there? That a sentence have declarative form is surely no sufficient condition of propositional significance, for not only "the sum of 2 and 3 is an odd number" but even "the sum of 2 and 3 is a communist" satisfies that condition. Shall we say, then, that a sentence expresses a proposition if truth is significantly (though perhaps not truly) predicable of it? This criterion will readily be perceived to be circular: the range of significant predication of "true," as a predicate applicable to linguistic expressions, can be defined only as the class of sentences that express propositions.

.    .    .

## Necessary Propositions and Rules of Inference

Let us examine, now, the more specific claim made by one variety of linguistic theory, that there are no necessary propositions, since what seem to be necessary propositions are really *rules of inference*. In order to dispel at once the suspicion that fire is being opened here on a strawman, a statement of this view may be quoted:

> In arguing for a conventionalist interpretation of necessary truths, it is important for me to say that I am not prepared to equate such propositions with empirical generalizations about the way in which people actually use words and make transitions from one statement to another. I shall argue that a necessary proposition always lays down a rule and that a rule is never to be equated with an empirical proposition [Karl Britton, "Are Necessary Truths True by Convention?" *Proceedings of the Aristotelian Society,* Supplementary Volume *21* (1947)].

It is clear from the context of the quoted passage that "rule" there means "rule of inference." This view is reminiscent of the teachings of the early logical positivists, like Schlick, that the "eternal" truths of logic and mathematics are really "transformation rules" which we apply to the only genuine propositions there are, viz. empirical propositions. Thus Schlick said that "$7 + 5 = 12$," Kant's celebrated example of synthetic a priori truth, expresses no proposition at all but is simply a rule of substitution of synonymous symbols. Had Schlick been allowed to live through the recent years of progress in semantics, he would no doubt have been the first one to repudiate such a statement: if this equation expresses synonymy, then any other equation expressing the number 12 as a function of other numbers (e.g. $12 = \sqrt{144}$) could be interpreted similarly, and the question would arise how one who understands the meanings of arithmetic symbols could fail to know any true equations connecting them, and indeed could have any need for proofs. After Frege, we say nowadays that the symbols "7 + 5" and "12" have no more the same *sense* than "the evening star" and "the morning star," although the identity of the entities denoted by them admits of a priori proof, while the identity of the objects denoted by the latter descriptions admits only of empirical proof. The really fatal defect, however, of the view that the allegedly necessary statements of logic and mathematics are transformation rules is that such sentences exercise different functions in different contexts. Specifically, while it must be admitted that in the context of empirical inquiries (such as counting empirical classes) the equations of arithmetic are used as rules of inference, it is equally clear that in the context of arithmetical inquiry the same equations are used to express propositions to be proved. As a matter of fact, there is no other way of *justifying* the use of such equations as rules of inference except to show that they express propositions which are necessarily true. The same holds for *logical* rules of inference. Any rule of inference which is, in the metalanguage, formulated by means of variable names of propositions, such as the *ponendo ponens* rule "from $S_1$ and $S_1 \supset S_2$, $S_2$ is derivable," is to be justified by proving that the corresponding object-linguistic formula built up by means of propositional variables, such as "$(p . (p \supset q)) \supset q$," is a tautology, and thus expresses a necessary proposition. There is a danger of circularity in such "justification" if the rule of inference refers to formulae of functional logic, since there the only available technique for proving theorems is the deductive technique, which involves the use of rules of deduction. But the justification is not circular if the rule refers to the propositional calculus only, since here the truth-table test is possible. That in everyday deductive reasoning—as well as deductive reasoning occurring in empirical sciences—the laws of logic function as transformation rules has no tendency at all to prove that they are not propositions in the context of systematic logic in which their regulative use is, without circularity, justified.

Indeed, if the fact that a sentence may in some contexts

function as a rule of inference were a good reason for denying that it is used to assert a proposition in any context, it would follow that even most empirical propositions are not really propositions at all. Whenever a statement of an assumed law of nature is used for purposes of prediction, it is used as a rule of inference (what Carnap called, in the *Logical Syntax of Language,* a "*P*-rule"). And if I speak confidently of "*most* empirical propositions," it is because a careful analysis of singular statements usually brings universal quantifiers to daylight. Even a modest singular statement like "this thing is red" can be analyzed into a universal conditional, viz. if any visually normal observer looked at this thing under standard optical conditions, it would appear red to him. Is utterance of this sentence, then, issuance of an "inference ticket," and not assertion of a proposition?

It remains to state what is perhaps the most decisive objection against the theory that the laws of logic are not propositions but *rules of symbolism.* Briefly, the objection is that whatever rules one may have initially stipulated, and however arbitrary such stipulations may be, one will thereafter have to *find out* what these rules entail, and the statement that such and such is entailed by the rules could hardly be characterized as itself a rule. Consider again the *ponendo ponens* principle, formulated as a rule of deduction in a metalanguage, and let us for the sake of the argument agree that there is no sense in predicating validity or necessary truth of such a rule since it simply constitutes, together with other rules of deduction such as a rule of substitution, a definition of what is to be understood by "logical consequence" in the respective system. When we derive, by applying the rule to the axioms of a logical system, a new theorem, we surely make a discovery. Even if the deductions are performed upon uninterpreted formulae, such that truth is not predicable of the theorems any more than of the axioms, it will be perfectly proper to say after a successful deduction "now I *know* that this is a theorem in the system, i.e. that this formula is entailed by the axioms." But that formula $F_1$ entails formula $F_2$, that any interpretation of the free variables in $F_1$ which turns $F_1$ into a true proposition also turns $F_2$ into a true proposition, is itself a logical truth, and it would be simply nonsense to characterize it as a *rule.* The same point may be illustrated in terms of the method of truth-tables, that automatic decision procedure applicable to the ground floor of logic. It is not unplausible to interpret the law of contradiction "no proposition is both true and false" as the *imperative* "don't contradict yourself!"—and the rule to assign to each elementary proposition no more than one of the truth-values "true" and "false" could accordingly be regarded as the formal expression of compliance with that imperative. To object to such an interpretation of the law of contradiction on the ground that it is, after all, significant to predicate truth (and even necessary truth) of this law, while an imperative is neither true nor false, would be just as question-begging as to object to the emotivist interpretation of "it is wrong to kill a child" as an imperative, that it is, after all, significant to say "it is true that killing children is wrong" but not to say "it is true that don't kill a child." Nevertheless, it remains a *cognitive* problem to decide whether this supreme requirement of consistency is satisfied by such-and-such assertions. For example, it is something that may or may not be *known* (in just the same sense of "knowledge" that is intended when we speak of knowledge of empirical propositions) that if one were to deny a proposition of the form "if (if $p$, then $q$) and (if not-$s$ then not-$r$) and ($p$ or $r$), then (if not-$q$, then $s$)" one would contradict oneself and thus violate the requirement of consistency. It is therefore a complete *nonsequitur* to infer from the fact that a given formula can be established as a tautology without presupposing the truth of any propositions, simply by following *rules* of symbolism, that the formula itself is a rule and does not express a proposition. That decision is not cognition, that it does not make sense to predicate truth or falsehood of a decision, is a trivial observation; that it *is* a cognitive question what behavior is consistent with or necessitated by a given decision is perhaps an equally trivial observation, yet one that is worth repeating in view of such superficial statements as that logical truths are merely rules of symbolic transformation (and so not really "truths" at all); as though there were any sense in the characterization of a statement like "inferences drawn in accordance with the *ponendo ponens* rule invariably lead to true conclusions from true premises" as itself a rule of symbolic transformation!

## FURTHER READING

Ewing (1)
Kneale (1), (2)
Pap (11)
Quine (1)

# ∾ THE VERY IDEA OF A SYNTHETIC-APRIORI

*N. R. Hanson*

The class of propositions is often trisected as follows: the analytic, the synthetic, and the synthetic-apriori. The status of this
third entry is in perennial dispute. Is *any* proposition correctly
labeled 'synthetic-apriori'? Or is this very label somehow nonsen-
sical? Perhaps the expression 'P is a synthetic-apriori proposition'
makes sense, but is never true since there is no suitable value
for the variable P.

These questions require re-orientation. The thesis of what
follows is that 'synthetic-apriori' does not label a *type of proposition* at all. Two quite different things are characterized by
this designation. Moreover, the *idea* of a proposition which is at
once synthetic in structure, yet justified apriori is not inconsistent.
It is just that, as a matter of fact, perhaps there are no synthetic-
apriori propositions.

Consider the bisection of the class of all propositions along
the line 'analytic-synthetic'. P is analytic if, and only if, its negation is of the form (or leads to something of the form) Q. ~ Q.
Analytic propositions are thus non-obvious tautologies; their
tautological character can be revealed by definitional transformations. However, a synthetic proposition is such that its negation,

From N. R. Hanson, "The Very Idea of a Synthetic-Apriori", *Mind*, XXI
(1962), pp. 521–524. © Thomas Nelson and Sons Ltd. 1962. Reprinted
by permission of the Editor of *Mind* and Mrs. N. R. Hanson.

~ P, is not of the form (nor does it entail anything of the form) Q. ~ Q.

This division is exclusive and exhaustive. The negation of *any* proposition must be such that it is either of the form Q. ~ Q (or entails something thus formed),—or its negation is not of this form (nor entails anything thus formed).

It apparently follows from this that analytic propositions cannot but be true. Their negations are self-contradictory, i.e. entail any proposition whatever. And synthetic propositions, since they have equally well-formed and otherwise meaningful negations, must be adjudged true only in virtue of contingent matters of fact.

The knife called 'apriori-aposteriori', however, cuts the class of propositions through quite a different stratum. To characterize a proposition as 'apriori' is to say nothing whatever about its formal structure, or the structure of its negation, or consequences derivable therefrom. It is, rather, to remark the mode whereby the truth of the proposition is discovered. A proposition is apriori if its truth is established without recourse to any possible experience (past, present, or future). A proposition is aposteriori if, in order to justify its truth, reflection alone is insufficient. Some appeal to some experience is required.

No detailed defence should be required for wishing to distinguish (1) characterizing the *structure* of propositions (and their consequences), from (2) characterizing the *mode of justification* of propositions (and their consequences). One can discuss the analyticity or non-analyticity of P without considering what appeals must be made to establish P's truth. (The third paragraph of this paper does just this!) The analyticity-non-analyticity question is settled by entertaining ~ P, tracing its implications, and finding (or not finding) something of the form Q. ~ Q. This kind of enquiry is neutral concerning how P is established—or even *whether* P is established.

*Analytic-synthetic,* therefore, divides types of propositional structures. *Apriori-aposteriori,* however, divides types of propositional justifications. These are quite different.

Suppose one identified 'analytic' with 'apriori',—i.e. gave these terms precisely the same meaning. Only then could the designation 'synthetic-apriori' be a contradiction in terms. But, for reasons given above, there are no grounds for this identification. Indeed, it is difficult to see that any judgment concerning the justification of a proposition follows *logically* from a decision as to its analyticity or non-analyticity. The dichotomies are *that* different.

Many levelheaded philosophers have thought peculiar the very idea of synthetic-apriori propositions. In what would this peculiarity consist? The considerations above are calculated to suggest that the peculiarity cannot reside in the fact that this idea is itself inconsistent. How does one *demonstrate* that a proposition whose negation is consistent cannot be justified without recourse to experience? To have learned that a proposition's negation is structured this way rather than that entails nothing about its mode of justification. Not directly. Crudely put, learning that a proposition is justified aposteriori is to learn something *in addition to* the fact that its negation is consistent. The idea of a proposition being synthetic does not, by itself, rule out the possibility of its justification apriori.

Above all, 'synthetic-apriori' does not designate a new category of *proposition*. Synthetic-apriori propositions (if such there are) are synthetic propositions; propositions whose negations are consistent, and entail nothing inconsistent. This much alone does not mean that there *are* synthetic-apriori propositions. It suggests, however, that the claim that there *couldn't be* synthetic-apriori propositions may be ill-founded, unless based on much broader, and hence more arguable, philosophical considerations. Perhaps there is not one unquestionable candidate for the status 'synthetic-apriori proposition'. But this may just be a matter of fact, and not a consequence of logic.

Let us ask how, in fact, analytic propositions are justified. We know that P is analytic if and only if its negation is inconsistent (or entails what is inconsistent). Hence, demonstrating that P is analytic requires doing the same things as to show that P is forever true. Since its negation is self-contradictory, it could not but be true—a fact we learn from logical manipulation, not from experience. Even so, since the consequences of this distinction will bear down heavily in the case of synthetic propositions, I must insist that *demonstrating P's analyticity is not the same as establishing that P could not be false*. The operations of both procedures may be identical—but the ends are different.

To say that a proposition is analytic is *not* to say just that it is forever and always true. That P is forever true follows from (but is not identical with) the fact that P's negation is self-contradictory.

Confusions result from failing to make this distinction. Thus, when analytic propositions are said to be those which are forever true and couldn't be false, the idea of analyticity collapses into that of invulnerability. Thus the class of analytic propositions becomes populated with all sorts of propositions which, although felt to be certainly true, lack self-contradictory negations. Certain physical principles, religious utterances, and even some moral precepts have been characterized as analytic solely on the grounds that they are invulnerable to disconfirmation. But this locates an accidental feature of analyticity as its defining characteristic. *Of course* analytically true propositions are invulnerable to disconfirmation. This is *because* their negations are self-contradictory. So questions about whether P is analytic remain distinct from questions concerning how P is established. I prove the former by revealing inconsistencies in ~ P, or in its consequences. The latter issue involves arguing from the fact that ~ P (or one of its consequences) *is* inconsistent to the conclusion that therefore P must be forever true. The second undertaking is different from, indeed presupposes, the first.

This distinction becomes critical with synthetic propositions, and for the point of this paper. When I have established that a proposition is synthetic I have *only* established that its negation is consistent. This is done by almost purely logical means. Justifying the truth of the proposition is quite different in this case. For, a proposition may be synthetic whether true or false. P is synthetic if ~ P is consistent as well as P, of course. One must add this to block calling a contradiction, whose negation is consistent, 'synthetic'. Establishing P's truth requires something else to be done. What?

It remains to be shown to me that *what* else must be done to establish P's truth can be read off simply and directly from the fact that ~ P is consistent. But what is logically wrong with the *idea* that the class of non-contradictory propositions having consistent negations (i.e. synthetic propositions) divides into those whose truth is justified without recourse to experience (i.e. *apriori*), and those whose truth is justified only by recourse to experience (*i.e. aposteriori*)? To rule out the former possibility is simply to shout (without giving reasons) one of the central dogmas of empiricism, which latter, I need hardly remark, is *not* a set of deductive principles. But since this is just what is at issue (*i.e.* does 'synthetic-apriori proposition' make sense), the matter thus put need not be pursued.

I have no clear notion of what it would be like to justify by reflection alone the truth of P when ～ P is consistent. But this *may* be only a fact about *me*. I cannot see how of two equally consistent alternative propositions (P and ～ P), reflection alone will determine which describes the facts. But to say this does not *prove* that there cannot be synthetic-apriori propositions. I have but softly expressed an article of the empiricist's faith, to wit, that as a working hypothesis, it seems unlikely that any genuine candidates for synthetic-apriority will be forthcoming. This con-jecture is not justifiable by logic alone. And logic alone cannot demolish a non-empiricist's position.

This discussion must not be allowed to involve a host of propositions which are at once synthetic (*i.e.* having consistent negations) and are yet inconceivably false. It is perhaps invul-nerably true that I cannot be in two places at once, that I am now conscious and typing out these words, that there cannot be a perpetual motion machine, etc. But while these are both invul-nerably true and also synthetic in form, such propositions will not serve as candidates for synthetic apriority. Their invulnera-bility results not so much from a direct, non-experimental dem-onstration of their truth, but rather from an implicit, yet far-flung reference to entire *systems* of empirical knowledge whose very pattern depends upon assuming the truth of such state-ments. The invulnerability of a 'genuine synthetic-apriori state-ment' cannot consist simply in pointing out the disastrous sys-tematic consequences of entertaining the negation to such a proposition. The credentials of such a spectacular propositional entity must be set out directly by reflection on the assertions made by P and by ～ P.

Of propositions which are systematically invulnerable-yet-synthetic, there are many examples at the philosopher's tongue-tip. Of propositions whose negations are consistent, but yet whose truth will be apparent to anyone who understands them —*I* cannot think of one single example. But this implies nothing of logical importance about the *idea* of a synthetic-apriori proposition. No mere fact about what I, or anyone, can or cannot do would have such an implication.

The situation, then, is this: that of all known non-contradictory propositions whose negations are consistent, it is factually true that they are established by recourse to experience. In other words, that they are contingent is (in a sense) a factual truth about such propositions. That they are synthetic is a necessary truth. That certain claims are formally structured such that their negations are inconsistent is a claim which, if true at all, could not but be true. But that their *justifications* are contingent upon experience is a claim of a different kind. This is *just* a matter of fact. It may be said to describe only the 'explored regions' of the modes of justification for synthetic propositions. In itself it contains no argument against a proposition with a consistent negation being justified in some different, possibly non-experiential manner. We *do* know what it is like for some propositions to be justified without recourse to experience. With analytic propositions we know why such recourse is needless. We are not in the same position concerning synthetic propositions. We may not in fact know how a proposition with a consistent negation could be justified without recourse to experience. But, short of reiterating the empiricist's manifesto (again without logically binding reasons), I know of no strict argument for ruling out the very idea of a synthetic-apriori.

FURTHER READING

Langford
Pap (6), (7), (13)
Quinton
Sloman (2)

# ∽ REDS, GREENS, AND LOGICAL ANALYSIS

*Hilary Putnam*

The purpose of this paper is to explain why the statement:

(1)   "Nothing is red (all over) and green (all over) at the same time"

is analytic. The method will be to give two lines of argument, one informal and discursive, the other relatively formal and exact. Both will have essentially the same content. First, however, a brief statement of the significance of the problem.

Philosophers have contended that the qualities green and red are simple and unanalyzable. Hence the a priori character of (1) cannot be explained on the ground of its analyticity—it is claimed—since its denial does not violate the principle of contradiction. By way of contrast, consider:

(2)   "All bachelors are unmarried,"

or, if you prefer:
time."

(3)   "Nothing is both a bachelor and married at the same

The concept *bachelor* is analyzable into *unmarried man.* Accordingly, (2) is analyzable into

From Hilary Putnam, "Reds, Greens, and Logical Analysis", *The Philosophical Review,* LXV (1956), pp. 206–217. Reprinted by permission of the Editors of *The Philosophical Review* and the author.

(4)   "All unmarried men are unmarried"

and the denial of (2), (3) or (4) is:

(5)   "Someone is both married and not married,"

which violates the principle of contradiction.

The difficulty may also be stated in another way. An analytic sentence is one that can be reduced to a theorem of formal logic by putting synonyms for synonyms. If red and green are unanalyzable, then no replacement of their names by synonymous expressions in (1) will turn (1) into a theorem of formal logic. Hence (1) is not analytic, but it is a priori (as everyone admits).

Before replying to this charming argument for the synthetic a priori (and its neatness and force are undeniable), I should like to make a few preliminary comments, by way of orientation. In the first place, the notion of "simplicity," unlike the notion of "analyzability," seems to be psychological rather than logical. Empirical studies by no means indicate universal agreement on what characters in experience are "simple." And yet, no criterion has been presented for simplicity (in the relevant sense) other than what people feel. However, the argument given above does not really depend on the simplicity of red and green, but merely on their unanalyzability; that is, on the fact that "red" and "green" do not possess any synonyms in English or in any other language, actual or merely possible, relevant to this problem (i.e., any synonyms whose substitution for "red" and "green" in (1) would transform it into a theorem of formal logic).

This is established, of course, by reflecting on the sense of "red" and "green" and by "seeing" that any definitions that would make "red" and "green" logically dependent (by making "red" and "green" synonymous with some logically dependent expressions $P$ and $Q$) would involve a violation of the *intended meaning* of these terms.

Thus, to refute this argument, it is necessary to find expressions $P$ and $Q$ which are synonymous with "red" and "green" respectively, and whose substitution for "red" and "green" in (1) turns it into a theorem of logic,—but we must be sure that $P$ is really synonymous with "red" *in the intended sense,* and likewise, "green" with $Q$. In short, we must show that the concepts of red and green involved really are analyzable; the question of simplicity we can drop as irrelevant.

A second remark: The assertion that the concepts red and green are "simple and unanalyzable" may sound very plausible when considered in isolation; but it becomes very paradoxical when we extend the field under consideration. Thus, if "red" and "green" are unanalyzable—what about "colored"? In some ways the notion of being colored seems to me simpler than the notion of being red. Thus it would strike me as very implausible if someone should argue that "colored" is merely short for

"red or green or yellow or . . . or . . ."

But it would be very odd (to say the least) if someone should maintain that

(6)   "Everything red is colored"

is also synthetic a priori.

Furthermore, what about the relational term: "indistinguishable (in color) from"? This is clearly related to the terms just mentioned; e.g., we have:

(7)   "If $X$ is indistinguishable in color from $Y$ then $X$ is colored,"

and if we mean by "red" an *exact shade* of that color, we have further

(8)   "If $X$ is red and $Y$ is red, then $X$ is indistinguishable from $Y$ in color."

Yet the thesis that the relational term "indistinguishable in color from" is analyzable by means of (a finite number of) such nonrelational terms as "red" and "colored" is very dubious.

The point I am leading up to by way of all this is very simple: the color properties are not, after all, isolated; they form a system (or better, a continuum). It is not merely that there are reds and greens; there is the underlying property of being colored, of which red and green are specifications; and there are the varying relations of adjacency in this continuum. If any of the dependencies among the color properties and relations are synthetic a priori, then they all may well be: but this seems difficult to believe.

Turning now to the actual reply: I should like to begin by producing for consideration the sentence:

(9) "If *A* is not exactly the same color as *B,* then if something is the same color as *A*, then it is *not* exactly the same color as *B*."

I think there would be general agreement that (9) *feels* analytic; unlike (1). But at this point our "feelings" about these matters begin to conflict. For, suppose (9) is analytic. Then:

(10) "Nothing is the same color as *A* (all over) and the same color as *B* (all over) at the same time,"

which sounds like a genuine generalization, turns out to be equivalent to:

(11) "*A* and *B* are not exactly the same color"

which is merely "singular."

To show this by means of modern logic: symbolizing (9), (10), and (11) we get

for (9):   $(x)(\sim \text{Ex}[A,B] \supset \cdot \text{Ex}[x,A] \supset \sim \text{Ex}[x,B])$
for (10):   $(x) \sim (\text{Ex}[x,A] \cdot \text{Ex}[x,B])$
for (11):   $\sim \text{Ex}(A,B)$
(Interpret "Ex[*x,y*]" as "*x* is exactly the same color as *y*" [all over].)

The third of these expressions is derivable from the first two quite easily, if one assumes that "Ex" is reflexive, and the second from the first and third. Thus the equivalence of (10) and (11) is indeed a consequence of (9)—and if (9) is analytic, then (10) and (11) are simply equivalent, i.e., each is a consequence of the other. Thus the apparently "universally valid" statement (10) is merely a disguised report about *A* and *B*.

Of course there is a question as to the analyticity of (9). But I don't think that anyone will maintain that *being exactly the same color as* is "simple and unanalyzable." In fact it is not even ostensively definable.

If we reflect on the relation "exactly the same color as" we find, in fact, that it is peculiarly difficult to pin down. It appears to have a close connection with the relation of indistinguishability in color from, which is the relation that one would communicate if one tried to give the meaning of "exactly the same color as" by pointing out examples. It is, however, distinct from this relation, since it is clearly transitive (which is all that (9) says) whereas "indistinguishable in color from" is nontransitive, since we could find a chain $a_1, a_2, \ldots, a_{10}$, let us say, such that $a_1$ is indistinguishable in color from $a_2$, $a_2$ is in turn indistinguishable in color from $a_3$, $\ldots$, $a_9$ is indistinguishable in color from $a_{10}$; and yet $a_1$ is distinguishable in color from $a_{10}$.

We will avoid for the moment the problem of defining "exactly the same color as"; let us try instead to put down all of its intuitive properties (which can later serve as criteria of adequacy for any definition). Only two properties appear clear to me:

I. "Ex" is an *equivalence relation,* i.e., it is transitive, reflexive, and symmetrical.
II. "Ex" is stronger than "indistinguishable from," i.e., if Ex $(x,y)$, then $x$ is indistinguishable in color from y.

If we are willing to admit that I and II determine, completely or incompletely, what we mean by "exactly the same color," then we shall have to admit that (9) is analytic, since it is equivalent to:

(12) $(x)(\mathrm{Ex}[x,A] \supset \cdot \mathrm{Ex}[x,B] \supset \mathrm{Ex}[A,B])$

which formally expresses the transitivity of "Ex." But more than this. It will follow now, not merely that (10) is equivalent to "$A$ is not exactly the same color as $B$," but, by virtue of II, that this latter assertion is implied by "$A$ is distinguishable in color from $B$";—and this, of course, is a mere observation report.

In short, the report proposition that $A$ is distinguishable in color from $B$ is *stronger* than the statement that $A$ is not exactly the same color as $B$; and this latter statement is strictly equivalent to the "universal" judgment that nothing is the same color as $A$ and the same color as $B$ (all over) at the same time.

Or again, if I point to $A$ and to $B$ (let us suppose for the moment that $A$ is red, and $B$ green) and say "Nothing is the same color as $A$ and the same color as $B$ at the same time,"—this "apodictic" judgment is not a discovery of an "incompatibility" between the colors exemplified by $A$ and $B$: it is a mere fragment of a report; it says less, logically speaking, than the straightforward report "*A* is distinguishable in color from *B*."

This, I think, is all that there is to the "factual certainty" of (10). The sentence (10) implies the sentence "*A* is not exactly the same color as *B*"; in this sense it "contains" it, as a factual (and even a corrigible) element. But, except for this apparently trivial presupposition, (10) appears to be (a) universal, and (b) certain. The foregoing analysis is designed to show that the certainty and universality of (10) (relative to this assumption) is *analytic*. In a similar way, one could show that "Nothing is the color that *A appears* to be and the color that *B appears* to be (all over) at the same time"—which could have been considered instead of (10)—is equivalent to "*A* does not appear to be the same color as *B*."

The problem is, how to apply our analysis of (10) to sentence (1). Suppose a speaker has in mind by "red" any shade of red whatsoever, and by "green" any shade of green whatsoever. Then he must be able to imagine at least two objects, *A* and *B*, such that (1) he would apply the term "red" (in that sense) to *A* and the term "green" (in that sense) to *B*; and (2) *A* and *B* are distinguishable in color. Please note: I have not said that "he must never apply 'red' and 'green' (in whichever sense) to the same object." What I have said is that he must be able to *imagine* at least one object which is red but not green, and at least one object which is green but not red. Otherwise, he would simply be using the words "red" and "green" as synonyms (and this particular misuse would, of course, be easily detected). What this amounts to, of course, is that by "that shade of red" and "that shade of green" anyone speaking standard English must mean "exactly the same color as *A*" and "exactly the same color as *B*" where *A* and *B* must be so chosen or imagined as to be distinguishable in color. But if "that shade of red" and "that shade of green" are always the colors of objects which are distinguishable in color, then it is not a cause for wonder that "Nothing is *that* shade of red all over and also *that* shade of green all over at the same time" is always true, no matter who asserts it. And if it is true that no matter which shade of red and which shade of green we choose, nothing is both that shade of red and that shade of green, then it is true that "Nothing is both red and green" even if by "red" and "green" we mean not specific shades but broad classes of such shades.

One more remark before closing the informal part of our argument: the rule of usage described above does not, of course, determine what any particular speaker shall mean by "that shade of red" or "that shade of green" in any particular context; or even what he shall mean by the broader terms "red," "green," and "indistinguishable." Speaking *scientifically* rather than epistemologically (e.g., in terms of what physiology might disclose) I think it not impossible that someone's spectrum might be reversed, i.e., he might see blue where I see red and vice versa. Nevertheless, he would use the color terms "correctly" enough by ordinary standards, i.e., in conformity with such rules as that given above. This acknowledges what was sound in structuralism, as the doctrine was called which held that we can communicate the structure of our experience but not its felt quality.

Now for the formal part of the argument. What I propose to do is to re-present the core of the foregoing informal argument as a sketch for the building up of the color concepts within a constructive system or formal language. Since this method of representing and consolidating a philosophic position is currently out of fashion, it seems desirable to begin with a remark explaining my reasons for preferring it.

Briefly, it appears to me that the most important disagreement among "analysts" today is between those who believe that there is *a correct answer* to such a question as the one we have been discussing, whether this is to be obtained by therapeutically dissolving the puzzle through the examination of usages, or through "straightforward analysis" of the problem; and those who feel, as I do, that there is never one final answer, but a variety of different answers based on different explications of the crucial concepts. On this latter view, a philosophic analysis merely presents one out of many possible reconstructions of a group of concepts; the aim of the analysis is to develop the theory of these concepts; and anyone who feels that *his* meaning for the concepts has not been clarified is invited to develop his own explication, and to discover how an alternative interpretation of the concepts would affect the theory.

In particular, what we have done informally in the preceding pages is to sketch a reconstruction of the color concepts, and to show how this reconstruction would affect the interpretation of some philosophically puzzling sentences. This reconstruction is certainly not the only possible one; it does, however, correspond fairly well to certain rules of English usage (that have been pointed out) and to what are *for me* the intuitive meanings of the concepts involved. Still, it seems important to point out that what has been presented is a reconstruction and not an attempted description of ordinary English usage. For this reason, the analysis will now be presented *explicitly* in constructional form.

The underlying theme of the construction is this: when we think of the color concepts, the most striking fact we observe is that they form a continuum. Likewise with the sounds, etc. This fact enables us to classify a new color we may never have encountered before *as a color;* it fits into one continuum but not into the other. But to say that qualities form a continuum is to say that we can pass by imperceptible stages from one to the other; in the case of colors this "passing by imperceptible stages" is done by means of the relation of *indistinguishability with respect to color.* Thus this relation seems to "constitute" the color-continuum; and it is this relation (which will be symbolized as "Ind") which is taken as primitive.

Into our construction we shall wish to introduce names for specific shades, say *F* and *G*. The general method for doing this has already been indicated; we define a specific shade as the color of some object (physical or phenomenal, depending on which form of language we have chosen). Intuitively, it does seem that whenever we speak or think of "that specific shade" we have some "object in mind"—there is no other way to "pin down" the shade. But this is merely an informal comment by way of supporting the following definition patterns:

(13)  "$F(x)$"  *for*  "$Ex(x,A)$"
      "$G(x)$"  *for*  "$Ex(x,B)$"
         etc.

We can also define the general notion of *a color:*

(14)  "$Col(F)$"  *for*  "$(\exists y)(x)[F(x) \equiv Ex(x,y)]$"

but both of these definitions presuppose that we have already succeeded in defining "exactly the same color as" or "Ex." It is also clear from the informal part of the analysis that it is on our ability to frame a definition for this concept that our construction stands or falls. Fortunately, a definition appears to be possible: "*x* is exactly the same color as *y*" *for* "(for every *z*) *z* is indistinguishable in color from *x* if and only if *z* is indistinguishable in color from *y*."

This last proposal requires a little informal buttressing. The idea of the definition is suggested by this consideration: if *A* and *B* are not exactly the same color, then even if they are indistinguishable, something almost on the theoretical "threshold of distinguishability" with respect to *A* should be (in certain cases) indistinguishable from *A* but distinguishable from *B*. On the other hand, if *A* and *B* are exactly the same color, then anything that is indistinguishable from *A* must also be indistinguishable from *B*.

A somewhat more serious argument for the proposal is this: consider the conditions under which we would say that two objects are exactly the same color. These do not always coincide with the conditions under which we would say that they are indistinguishable, e.g., let *A* and *B* be indistinguishable, but suppose that *C* is indistinguishable from *B* but distinguishable from *A*. Then we would say that the color of *B* is *between* that of *A* and that of *C* (not that it is exactly the same color as *A* or *C*). In other words, that everything that is indistinguishable from *A* be indistinguishable from *B* (and vice versa) is a necessary condition for *A* and *B* being exactly the same color. But is it not also a sufficient condition? If *A* and *B* are not merely indistinguishable, but if in addition everything that is indistinguishable from *A* is also indistinguishable from *B* and vice versa,—then what possible further evidence could prove that *A* and *B* are not "really" the same color?

The most important consideration, however, is that the suggested definition satisfies the criteria of adequacy (I and II) that were put down before. These conditions formulate the intuitive properties of "Ex" (and I hasten to assure the suspicious reader that they were honestly laid down in advance of finding a definition, as *bona fide* criteria of adequacy must be); thus any definition which satisfies them must be considered as formulating an admissible concept of "exactly the same color."

If we are using a physicalistic language, then *stronger* concepts could, of course, be formulated. Thus the meaning of the expression "exactly the same color" might be specified in terms of performable laboratory operations, e.g., by means of reduction sentences. Another good method would be to construe this concept as a theoretical concept, to be implicitly defined by means of theoretical postulates (which would ultimately have to be interpreted, at least partially, in terms of "laboratory operations," or other observables). But a concept so introduced would presumably be even stronger than the one we have defined, for laboratory techniques would make possible even finer distinctions than are possible on the basis of unaugmented human ability to distinguish. Thus, such concepts would also satisfy our criteria of adequacy; which is all that is necessary for the present argument.

We pause to record our definition formally:

(15)   "$\text{Ex}(x,y)$"   *for*   "$(z)\,(\text{Ind}[z,x] \equiv \text{Ind}[z,y])$

and also to postulate the fundamental properties of "Ind"— symmetry and reflexivity (but not transitivity!):

(16)   a.   $(x)\,\text{Ind}(x,x)$
       b.   $(x,y)\,(\text{Ind}[x,y] \equiv \text{Ind}[y,x])$

The first of these postulates permits us to speak of Ind as holding or not holding between $x$ and $y$ even when $x$ and $y$ are not distinct (in this case we count it as trivially true); the second expresses the fact that Ind is fundamentally a characteristic of an *unordered* pair.

We are now in full possession of the results of the informal discussion. Thus, we have as a consequence of (15) (proofs will be omitted) the equivalence of (10) and (11); to say "Nothing is the same color as *this* and simultaneously the same color as *that*" is merely to assert that "this is not the same color as that." Also, we have:

(17)   $\sim \text{Ind}(x,y) \supset \, \sim \text{Ex}(x,y)$
       [from (15) and (16a)].

or in words: "if $x$ and $y$ are distinguishable, then $x$ and $y$ are not exactly the same color"; and from this and the equivalence between (10) and (11) we have the main result of the informal discussion, namely:

(18)  $\sim \text{Ind}(x,y) \supset \cdot (z) \sim (\text{Ex}[z,x] \cdot \text{Ex}[z,y])$,

which means, as was remarked, that the "apodictic" assertion that "Nothing is the same color as this and the same color as that at the same time" (we have confined the discussion to uniformly colored objects, for the sake of simplicity) is a weaker statement than the mere "protocol," "this is distinguishable in color from that."

In closing, I should like to sketch the continuation of the construction. The next step would be to define the second-level predicates "$\text{Red}(F)$" (for "$F$ is a shade of red") and "$\text{Grn}(F)$" (for "$F$ is a shade of green"). In defining these predicates we are restricted by two postulates. The first formulates a feature of English usage pointed out in the informal discussion: Nothing can be classified as both a shade of red and a shade of green (i.e., "that shade of red" and "that shade of green" must never be used as synonyms). The second formulates the fact that red and green are intervals; if $F$ and $H$ are shades of red, and $G$ is between $F$ and $H$ then $G$ is a shade of red. The statement of the first postulate follows:

(19)  $(F) \sim (\text{Red}[F] \cdot \text{Grn}[F])$

The statement of the second postulate requires the definition of "$\text{BTW}(F,G,H)$" (for "$G$ is between $F$ and $H$ with respect to color," as yellow, say, is between red and blue) in terms of "Ind." The possibility of formulating a definition of "BTW" should be evident to any student of the classic constructional systems. The basic idea is to define "between" in terms of "directly between," which is defined as follows:

(20)  "$x$ is directly between $y$ and $z$"  *for*
     "$\text{Ind}(x,y) \cdot \text{Ind}(x,z) \cdot \sim \text{Ind}(y,z)$."

Then the statement of the second postulate is:

(21)  $\text{Red}(F) \cdot \text{Red}(H) \cdot \text{BTW}(F,G,H) \supset \text{Red}(G)$.

and similarly for the other colors. Finally we add postulates giving the relative positions of the colors on the spectrum, e.g.:

(22)   Red($F$) · Orange($G$) · Yellow($H$) $\supset$ BTW($F,G,H$),

and further postulates specifying that there are at least two distinct shades of each color (lest someone think that "red" names a specific shade) and that there is no color between red and orange, etc.

It should be observed that these postulates define the logical structure of the color continuum, but not the actual location of the cutting points (or which end is red). Thus, anyone who uses this formal language according to the rules (of course it is not actually a language, but merely a sketch of a language) would mean by "red" a continuous series of shades, and by "orange" and "yellow," other continuous series of shades (and by "orange" all the shades between "red" and "yellow"); but the rules do not determine beyond this *which* shades he would mean. The relation to natural language should be clear: the rules of natural language also determine that all the shades between red and yellow shall be classified as orange; but they do not determine such a thing as the place where orange stops and yellow begins.

Let us now consider the original problem: "Nothing can be both red and green." Sometimes it is said that "the problem depends on red and green being ostensively defined" (so that they will be "simple and unanalyzable"). But, if they are *literally* defined by pointing, then "red" is being used temporarily as "the color of *this*" and "green" as "the color of *that*"—and this case has been already analyzed. Suppose, however, the assertion is meant as "Nothing can be a shade of red (in color) and a shade of green (in color) at the same time." This symbolizes:

(23)   ($x$) $\sim$ ($F[x]$ · $G[x]$ · Red[$F$] · Grn[$G$]).

This does not follow (as one might first think) from postulate (19) above. Postulate (19) merely tells us that if $F$ is a shade of red and $G$ a shade of green, then $F$ is not the same shade as $G$; but the statement we want is that if $F$ is not the same shade as $G$, then no $x$ is both $F$ and $G$ in color; i.e., (23) would follow from (19) *plus:*

(24)   $(F)(G)(x)(\text{Col}[F] \cdot \text{Col}[G] \cdot F \neq G \supset \sim [F(x) \cdot G(x)])$,

or "nothing is two different shades at once."

This assertion constitutes the heart of our problem. If something were both red and green, it would presumably be two different shades at once; so the falsity of (1) entails the falsity of (24). Assertion (24), however, follows from the definition of "Col"; the usual logical rules for identity; and the crucial definition or explication:—that of "Ex." The truth of (23) and (24) has thus been established by reference to the rules of our language; which makes them analytic in what I, for one, consider to be a perfectly clear sense. And the analyticity of (24), which is the heart of the matter, does not depend on any of our postulates (in case someone wonders whether too much might not have been smuggled in), but merely on the definitions plus logic (which is "good, old-fashioned" analyticity).

# ∾ ONCE MORE: COLORS AND THE SYNTHETIC A PRIORI

*Arthur Pap*

As against my earlier contention that such statements as "Nothing is at the same time both blue and red all over" cannot be analytic—though being unquestionably a priori—because of the unanalyzability of color predicates, Hilary Putnam has recently attempted an elegant proof of their analyticity. He succeeds in the proof of the analyticity of the completely general proposition that nothing can have two colors at the same time by proceeding as follows. He selects "indistinguishable with respect to color" as the sole primitive of a constructional system dealing with colors. While it is an empirical fact that this relation is not transitive, we can define "exactly identical in color" on the basis of this primitive in such a way that the relation designated by it is demonstrably not only symmetrical and reflexive but also transitive:

$$Ex, y = (z) (Iz, x \equiv Iz, y) \qquad D_1.$$

Next we define the second level predicate "color" on the basis of "$E$" as follows: $F$ is a color = there is something, $y$, such that a thing is $F$ if and only if it is exactly identical in color with $y$. Formally:

From Arthur Pap, "Once More: Colors and the Synthetic A Priori", *The Philosophical Review*, LXVI (1957), pp. 94–99. Reprinted by permission of the Editors of *The Philosophical Review* and Mrs. Arthur Pap.

$$C(F) = (\exists y)(x)(Fx \equiv Ex, y) \qquad D_2.$$

I borrow the symbol "$\equiv$" from R. Carnap's *Meaning and Necessity* to express logical equivalence. It seems to me impossible to give the intended definition in extensional terms (material equivalence) for this reason: Suppose that $F$ were a quality other than a color, for example, a shape. It might happen that the predicates "blue" and "round," for example, had the same extension. Now, if $a$ is the standard patch with reference to which "blue" is defined, then in our hypothetical universe anything which has $E$ to $a$ is round and conversely. But then $D_2$ would justify the conclusion that roundness is a color if its definiens were extensional.

Next let us formalize the theorem to be proved on the basis of these (intuitively adequate) definitions; namely, that nothing has two colors at once:

$$(F)(G)[C(F) . C(G) . F \neq G \supset (x)(Fx \supset - Gx)] \qquad T.$$

Putnam is right in saying that $T$ is formally provable on the basis of $D_1$ and $D_2$ with the help of functional logic, without presupposing any extralogical postulates (the apparatus of functional logic needs to be supplemented, however, by a modal operator, since the proof presupposes that $F = G$ if and only if $(x)$ $[Fx \equiv Gx]$). And I admit that I was not aware of this possibility when I argued against the analyticity of the special cases of $T$. I shall show, however, that the claim that the special cases of $T$, like "nothing is both blue and red," are analytic involves us in a paradox which no empiricist can afford to accept.

Let us not be overhasty and say: since it has been formally proved that nothing can have two colors at the same time, no special proof is required for the proposition that nothing can be both blue and red at the same time; for surely you will not question the analyticity of "Blue and Red are colors." In the first place, what is at issue is analyticity in the strict sense of "formal provability with or without help of adequate definitions of extralogical terms," not analyticity in the broad sense of "true *ex vi terminorum*," which I believe means nothing else than old-fashioned, self-evident necessity. I never denied that statements of color incompatibility are true *ex vi terminorum*, in the sense that it is impossible to question them if one understands them; nor would I put "Red is a color" into a different category. But secondly, observe that the substitution instance of $T$ with "Red" substituted for "$F$" and "Blue" substituted for "$G$" reads:

$C$ (Red) . $C$ (Blue) . Red $\neq$ Blue $\supset$ $(x)$ [Red $(x)$ $\supset$ $-$ Blue $(x)$]   $t$.

And the analyticity of $t$—which follows from the analyticity of $T$—is a sufficient ground for asserting the analyticity of the consequent of $t$ only if the antecedent of $t$ is likewise analytic. That the three statements forming the antecedent of $t$ are all analytic is readily shown if we construct explicit definitions of "Red" and "Blue" which conform to Putnam's definition of "color"—*but* these definitions will make use of *proper names,* which is the beginning of the paradox I am about to develop. Let

Red $(x) = df E (x, a)$   $(D_3)$,   and Blue $(x) = df E (x, b)$   $(D_4)$,

where $a$ and $b$ are different particulars. And let identity of properties, as usual, be defined in terms of necessary equivalence. Then we may begin by proving the self-contradictoriness of "Red = Blue," and thereby the analyticity of "Red $\neq$ Blue," as follows:

(Red = Blue) $\equiv$ $(x)$ (Red$(x)$ $\equiv$ Blue$(x)$) $\equiv$ $(x)$ $(E(x, a) \equiv E(x, b))$.

But the latter necessary equivalence entails the identity of $a$ and $b$; for it cannot be self-contradictory to suppose that something has exactly the same color as $a$ without having exactly the same color as $b$ unless $a$ and $b$ are identical. Since "$a = b$" is self-contradictory *ex hypothesi,* "Red = Blue" is self-contradictory. Next we tackle "$C$ (Red)"—but omit the analogous proof for "$C$ (Blue)." On the basis of $D_3$, we can assert: $(x)$ (Red$(x)$ $\equiv$ $E(x, a)$). Hence: $(\exists y)$ $(x)$ (Red$(x)$ $\equiv$ $Exy$), which by $D_2$ means that Red is a color.

This is all very exhilarating for the constructionist, until he pauses to draw from $D_3$ and $D_4$ the startling consequence that the atomic statements "$a$ is red" and "$b$ is blue" are analytic and that his formal definitions therefore warrant an "ontological leap" to the existence, not of God, but of red and blue things. But how could "$a$ is red" be analytic? The first alternative is that "$a$" is an ostensive proper name, a symbolic equivalent of "this" or "that," and therefore meaningless outside of a "token-producing" context. The statement "*a* is red" then says that that which a certain speaker is at a given time pointing at is red; but I discover no self-contradiction in the negation of such a statement. The second alternative is that "*a*" is short for a co-ordinate description. But surely the atomic statements of a Carnapian co-ordinate language are supposed to be synthetic; it is a contingent fact that such and such a quality occupies a specified space-time point or region. Finally, "*a*" may be short for a characterizing description in a thing language, something like "the mail box in front of my house." Now, in order for "Red $((\imath x) Px)$" to be analytic, $P$ must analytically entail Red. But I do not see how a simple quality like Red (I mean an absolutely specific shade of Red) can be analytically entailed by $P$ unless $P$ is a conjunction containing Red. If so, the proof of analyticity will rest on a definition of "$P$" in terms of "Red," and since we have supposed "$a$" to be defined in terms of "$P$", $D_3$ then becomes circular.

Since the definitions in question, if noncircular, give rise to the consequence that there are contingent existential statements which are analytic, they must be rejected by an empiricist for whom "analytic" is incompatible with "contingent." Indeed, even intuitively these definitions are not *meaning analyses*. They are formalizations of ostensive definitions—even fictitious ostensive definitions, for one learns the meanings of color predicates before one knows the meaning of "the same in color," and then only by abstracting a common quality from *several* particulars—but ostensive definition is not meaning analysis. "Red" and "Blue" are what C. G. Hempel and P. Oppenheim, as well as Carnap, have called *purely qualitative* predicates, which means that no reference to a specific particular is necessary to explain their meanings—an idea flatly contradicted by the criticized definitions.

Surprisingly, then, my earlier argument that, because of the unanalyzability of "blue" and "red," the necessary statement "nothing is both blue and red" is not analytic has not been refuted by Putnam's clever demonstration of the analyticity of $T$—which demonstration, be it noted, makes use only of definitions that do not contain individual constants. The philosophical moral I wish to draw from this is that the analytic-synthetic distinction—not to be confused with the necessary-contingent distinction!—has no epistemological significance at all; that is, no essential difference of cognitive faculties is correlated with the difference between analytic and synthetic statements. Anybody who knows that nothing can have two different colors at the same time thereby knows that nothing can be both blue and red at the same time, and the way he knows the more special proposition is surely not different from the way he knows the more general proposition; yet the latter can be plausibly argued to be analytic and the former to be synthetic. In a way this "moral" is implicitly recognized by Carnap when he broadens what Putnam calls the notion of "good old" analyticity, namely, formal provability by means of adequate *explicit* definitions alone, as follows: a statement is analytic in $L$ if it is $L$-implied by the meaning postulates of $L$. The meaning postulates (like the consequent of $t$) are trivially analytic by this definition—every meaning postulate $L$-implies itself—but they are not analytic in the "good old" sense; that is why they are needed as postulates. Carnap's broadened conception of analyticity incorporates the synthetic a priori within the analytic. But all that has happened is that synthetic a priori propositions in the narrower sense of "synthetic," namely, not formally provable with the help of adequate explicit definitions alone, have been *renamed* "meaning postulates." Perhaps this terminological maneuver is justified by the reflection that after all "all bachelors are unmarried" and "nothing is both blue and red" have the important feature in common that nobody who understands what they mean could seriously doubt them. But it should be clear, then, that the modern controversy among analytic philosophers as to whether there are synthetic a priori propositions after all is far removed from the historic battlefield on which empiricists and rationalists met each other in deadly combat. If we reject $D_3$ as a meaning analysis, as we surely must, then "Red is a color" is not analytic in the "good old" sense. Yet, is it not unlikely that Kant, had he reflected on this kind of a priori proposition, would have postulated a new kind of "pure intuition" in order to explain how the predicate can be a priori associated with the subject? Again, consider the statement that $I$ is a symmetrical relation, which presumably would occur as a "meaning postulate" in a system based on "$I$" as a primitive.

Clearly, it cannot be analytic in the good old sense, for "*I*" is a primitive, and the statement is not true by virtue of its form (many statements of the form "for any *x* and *y*, if *xRy*, then *yRx*" are false). But what capital could a rationalist make of such synthetic a priori knowledge? For notice that insofar as "if *xIy*, then *yIx*" differs from a mere substitution instance of "if *p*, then *p*," its necessity, though "synthetic," has a linguistic origin: it so happens that the sentences by which we communicate thoughts are *sequences* of signs. This sequential character is irrelevant to some propositions, such as the proposition that an individual *x* has *I* to an individual *y*—though it is relevant to propositions about relations that are not symmetrical. The postulate "if *xIy*, then *yIx*" merely expresses this irrelevance of the sequential character of sentences of the form "*xIy*." If we had a tonal language, with simple tones symbolizing individuals and differences of pitch symbolizing relations between the individuals, the postulate might be redundant: the proposition that *aIb* might be expressed by sounding, say, a major third containing the tones symbolizing *a* and *b*, and this nonsequential "sentence" would be identical with the sentence corresponding to "*bIa*." This example shows that a synthetic a priori proposition, in the only sense in which I ever maintained that there are such, may even be purely *verbal* and not "about the world" at all!

# RED AND GREEN ALL OVER AGAIN: A REJOINDER TO ARTHUR PAP

*Hilary Putnam*

Professor Arthur Pap's paper does not contain anything with which I disagree. It does compel me, however, to restate points which were unclearly or even inadequately stated in the paper to which he refers.

(i) I did not say in that paper that "Nothing is both red and green" is analytic in the *narrower* sense, i.e., true as a consequence of explicit definitions. What I said was that "Nothing is two different colors at once" (*T*) is analytic, even in the narrower sense, and that "Nothing is both red and green" is analytic in a wider sense (true as a consequence of the rules of the language), which I tried to express by showing that it follows from the analytic sentence (*T*) and certain meaning postulates whose status as linguistic stipulations is, I think, pretty clear in this particular case.

(ii) Pap calls into question the device of "Meaning Postulates." As a device for explicating the notion of analyticity in a particular language, I believe that meaning postulates are unexceptionable (provided that the analytic character of the particular postulates is intuitively clear; and provided they are *complete*, i.e., no analytic truth in the particular language has

From Hilary Putnam, "Red and Green All Over Again: A Rejoinder to Arthur Pap", *The Philosophical Review*, LXVI (1957), pp. 100–103. Reprinted by permission of the Editors of *The Philosophical Review*, and the author.

been "overlooked"). I agree, however, that they do not explain the notion of *analyticity in any language;* and it is this that is of philosophic interest. Explicating this notion is an important problem in analytic philosophy, unless one accepts the view (which I find prima facie unacceptable) that there is no difference to be explicated.

As a first stab, let me suggest *truth as a consequence of the rules of the language* (as explicatum for analyticity in the wider sense). There are (at least) three obvious objections: (1) the notion of a "rule of language" is itself in need of explicating; (2) one can in this way beg the philosophic questions (by taking the sentences traditionally alleged to be "synthetic a priori" as rules of language); and (3) there is no need for a concept of "analyticity in the wider sense": we already have the distinction between necessary and contingent truths as well as that between analytic (in the narrower sense) and nonanalytic, and the former distinction suffices for the purpose in question.

To take the last objection first: Pap classifies "If $x$ is indistinguishable in color from $y$ then $y$ is indistinguishable in color from $x$" as "synthetic a priori," although he also says that it is purely *verbal* (and gives a neat argument to show why). But to do this is to admit that the division of necessary truths into those whose necessity is linguistic or verbal and those (if any) whose necessity is not is not explicated by the narrower concept of analyticity. Thus a wider concept is needed. And it seems more natural to say that the statement just mentioned is analytic (though not in the narrower sense) than to say that it is "synthetic a priori" (though verbal). Likewise, it seems to me more natural to say that the difference, among analytic truths, between those whose analyticity is of the narrower kind ("All bachelors are unmarried") and those whose analyticity is not ("Red is a color") is no philosophically interesting difference at all, than to say, as Pap does, that the analytic-synthetic distinction ("not to be confused with the necessary-contingent distinction") is devoid of epistemological significance.

But this last difference is purely terminological! The important point, however one expresses it, is that there are no necessary truths whose "necessity" differs in a fundamental and mysterious way from that of the analytic truths. And on this point Pap and I are in complete agreement. Since $T$ and its special cases have sometimes been cited as truths of the "mysterious" kind, I hope to have contributed to the argument for this point by showing that $T$ is analytic, even in the narrower sense.

With respect to objection (2): I agree that one could fall into this trap and side-step or evade the traditional problem entirely. For example, I could have taken "Nothing is both red and green" as a meaning postulate. But I think it important that I *did not* do this. What I am prepared to take are things whose analytic character (in whichever sense) the traditional philosopher admits. I know of *no* philosopher who has thought that "Red is a color" is an apodictic truth in the sense in which, say, the phenomenologists have thought "Nothing is both red and green" is an apodictic truth.

I am prepared to admit the difficulty in objection (1); but only to the extent that the general notion of a *rule* is in need of clarification. For example, there are no difficulties that affect the notion of a rule of language and that do not equally affect the notion of a rule of a game. Is the notion of a rule of chess or mah-jongg clearer because the rules of chess and mah-jongg are written down? But surely some languages have written rules, and some games have unwritten ones. And surely the rules that are written down are a codification of pre-existing rules in the case of a game as well as a language; they do not define what it is to be a rule of a game. In the case of some languages, as in the case of some games, I am relatively sure of the rules; and in some cases of both kinds I am unsure. And in both cases I would have difficulty in providing a formal definition, of a kind that would satisfy Quine, of the general concept *rule*.

(iii) Pap's paper also raises some technical points which I find fascinating indeed, and to which I do not have space to do justice here. I shall make only one or two remarks:

(a) My paper visualizes an *extensional* language as the basis for reconstruction. In any extensional language (e.g., *Principia Mathematica*) it is quite true that "Red = Square" (and even "Square is a color") would be accepted as true in the case that Red and Square are coextensive. (One can also say that I was defining the notion of a color *class* and not that of a color *property*.) But this is not necessarily serious: one can express what we ordinarily express by saying, "The *property*

Square is not a color property" by saying in the metalanguage: "Square is a color" is not *L*-true.

(b) In my paper, I did not define Red and Green in terms of particular objects (although it is true that I said one *could* do this; and I am quite convinced by Pap's objection). But the course I preferred was to take Red and Green as primitives and to take "Red and Green are different colors" as a meaning postulate.

The argument is this: it would not be plausible to take "Nothing is both red and green" as a direct linguistic stipulation, for reasons that have been excellently presented in Pap's book *Elements of Analytic Philosophy* (New York, 1949, p. 422). But it seems plausible to take "Red and Green are different colors" in this way ("Red" and "Green" are to be used to name different colors). And this does not evade the traditional problem, for the philosopher can still reply: "Even if I agree to use "Red" and "Green" as the names of different colors, how do you know nothing can be two different colors at once?" And to this I gave an answer.

Subsequently, I have discovered an argument which employs only the weaker postulates: "Red is a color" and "Green is a color." This argument does not, indeed, show that "Nothing is both red and green" is analytic; but it does show that it is *at least* entailed by an observation statement, which is enough to destroy the "mystery." Namely, from the fact that *one* red thing is not green, and the fact that Red and Green are colors, it follows analytically that Red and Green are different colors. And from this and *T,* which has been shown to be analytic in the narrower sense, it follows that nothing is both red and green.

**FURTHER READING**

Pap (7)
Pears (3)
Radford (1), (2)

# ∾ ARE LOGICAL TRUTHS ANALYTIC?

*Jaakko Hintikka*

The title of this paper may seem pointless. Nowadays the concept of analyticity is usually so characterized as to make all logical truths analytic by definition. Hence, why the question?

The purpose of the title is not only to ask a question but also to challenge the ways in which the concept of the analytic is currently defined. This concept was brought into philosophical prominence by Kant; I shall therefore examine some characterizations of this concept against the background of his use of it. It seems to me that the concept of analyticity as actually employed by philosophers like Kant is highly ambiguous and that most current definitions catch only one of the term's possible meanings.

I shall begin by listing a few of the ways in which the concept of the analytic (and, by implication, the concept of the synthetic) has been understood. The following explicit or implicit assertions have been made concerning analytic (analytically true) sentences:

I. They are true by sole virtue of the meanings of the terms they contain (analytic truth as conceptual truth).

From Jaakko Hintikka, "Are Logical Truths Analytic?", *The Philosophical Review*, LXXIV (1965), pp. 178–203. Reprinted by permission of the Editors of *The Philosophical Review*, and the author.

II. They do not convey any factual information (analytic truth as tautological truth).

III. They can be shown to be true by strictly analytic methods.

The first interpretation of the concept of the analytic is often elaborated by remarking that truths of logic are as clear-cut examples of truths based solely on meanings as we are likely to have. This has inspired attempts to obtain all analytic truths by starting from the truths of logic and suitably extending their range. The following definition is probably the best-known attempt of this sort:

I (a). Analytically true sentences comprise the truths of logic together with all sentences reducible to them by substituting synonyms for synonyms.

In this paper I shall disregard definitions of type I or I (a). Recent discussion has demonstrated, it seems to me, that they are unsatisfactory as they stand. Moreover, they make logical truths trivially analytic, and are therefore beside my present purpose.

But are there relevant senses of analyticity different from the one defined by I? I shall try to discover such senses by analyzing characterizations II and III. I shall first try to see somewhat more carefully what is implied by formulation III. Then I shall try to develop further characterization II so as to show that certain important truths of logic are analytic according to it. And finally I shall apply certain insights gained during the discussion to point out that the same truths are synthetic according to III, at least on one very natural interpretation of this characterization.

Let us therefore ask what can be said of sense III (that is, of the sense of analyticity defined by III). Here it is advisable to consider first the concept of an analytical argument-step instead of the concept of an analytic sentence. What can be said of the former can be subsequently extended to apply to the latter as well.

The basic idea of sense III seems to be expressible as follows:

III (a). All that is said by the conclusion of an analytic argument-step is already said in the premises.

This is admittedly very vague, largely owing to the vagueness of the notion of "saying" that is used here. For the purpose of definition III (a), this notion can be made somewhat clearer. In order to be able to speak of merely repeating or merely analyzing what is already said in the premises of an argument, we must restrict the sense of "saying" to what is in some sense actually or explicitly stated or mentioned in the premises. A traditional formulation of this idea was to say that the conclusion of an analytical argument-step merely repeats something already thought in the premises, although perhaps not yet with the same clarity and consciousness. Part of our task here is to see what objective explications such psychological or quasi-psychological formulations might have.

In spite of the vagueness which still remains in III (a), we can draw conclusions from it. The following criterion of analyticity will in any case follow from it:

III (b). In the conclusion of an analytic argument-step no more individuals are considered together at one and the same time than were already considered together in the premises.

For if more individuals are considered together in the conclusion than in the premises, some of them or some of their interrelations were not considered in the premises. Hence the conclusion does not consist in merely repeating what was already said in the premises, and the argument-step in question could not count as a case of "mere analysis."

Principle III (b) follows from III (a) no matter how the notion of "number of individuals considered together in a sentence" is to be understood. In the sequel I shall show how this notion can be clarified in the case of quantificational sentences.

A closely related consequence of criterion III (a) seems to be that the conclusion of an analytic argument cannot consider any individuals not already considered in the premises. Kant took this to imply the following principle:

III (c). An analytic argument never carries us from the existence of an object to the existence of a different object.

In short, according to Kant interindividual inferences concerning existence are impossible by analytic means.

It is not difficult to see how similar considerations might be applied to longer arguments, and hence to sentences established by means of such arguments. There is even more than one way of doing so. We might call a proof of $q$ from $p$ analytic if all its steps are analytic in one of the senses just indicated. This approach does not appear to be as interesting, however, as a slightly different one in which the proof in question is considered not only from the point of view of the premise $p$ but also from that of the conclusion $q$. Then a proof of $q$ from $p$ is analytic in sense III (b) if no more individuals are considered at any of the intermediate stages than are already considered either in $p$ or in $q$. This is the sense of analyticity as applied to proofs which I shall be using in what follows. A logically true sentence $p$ of quantification theory may then be called analytic if it can be proved analytically, in the sense just explained, from a propositional tautology in which no more individuals are considered together than in $p$. A sentence will be called analytically inconsistent if a propositional contradiction in which no more individuals are considered together can be derived from it analytically.

I shall return to these senses of analyticity later. Meanwhile, I shall stage my first main attack on analyticity in the direction of sense II. About forty years ago, a notion very much like this one was prominent. This was the notion of tautology of Wittgenstein's *Tractatus*. Unfortunately, the original form of this notion was satisfactorily defined only for propositional logic. Certain important generalizations have been suggested since, but for one reason or another they seem to have less philosophical interest than Wittgenstein's original notion.

I want to argue, nevertheless, that something like Wittgenstein's notion of tautology can be generalized in a natural and informative way so as to be applicable in quantification theory. In order to see what the generalization is, we have to see what makes his original notion so appealing.

It is made so, I think, by the fact that in propositional logic one can actually list all the "possible worlds" that we can describe by means of a given supply of atomic sentences.

If we are given the atomic sentences $p_i$ ($i = 1, 2, \ldots, k$), the descriptions of the possible worlds are conjunctions which for each $i$ contain either $p_i$ or its negation $\sim p_i$ (but not both) but which do not contain any other members. Following a time-honored precedent established by Boole, I shall call these con-junctions the *constituents* of propositional logic, and I shall designate an arbitrary constituent by $\prod\limits_{i=1}^{i=k} p_i$ or, more simply, by $\prod\limits_{i=1} p_i$. Different constituents may be distinguished from each other by attaching subscripts to $\prod$. These subscripts are assumed to run consecutively from one onward, so that the same notation can be applied repeatedly.

An arbitrary constituent $\prod\limits_{i=1}^{} {}_j\, p_i$ may also be said to be of the form

$$(\pm)\, p_1\ \&\ (\pm)\, p_2\ \&\ \ldots\ \&\ (\pm)\, p_k.$$

Here each symbol $(\pm)$ stands either for a negation sign or for nothing at all. For different patterns of negation signs a differ-ent subscript $j$ is chosen.

Why does the existence of the constituents make the notion of tautology appealing? Because each consistent sentence of propositional logic has a normal form which is a disjunction of some (perhaps all) of the constituents. In an obvious sense, every sentence considered in propositional logic thus admits some of the possibilities listed by the constituents, but excludes the rest. In an equally obvious sense, the more possibilities it excludes, the more informative it is.

A limiting case is that of a sentence admitting all the possibilities listed by the constituents, but excluding none of them. Such a sentence is empty in a very obvious sense of the word: it cannot convey any genuine information. And this limiting case is just that of the logically true sentences of propositional logic. They are undoubtedly true, but in the striking sense just explained they do not carry any information concerning the subject matter of which they apparently speak.

These are the facts, it seems to me, that make Wittgen-stein's notion of tautology so very appealing.

They immediately suggest a more general sense in which we may ask whether the truths of other parts of logic are also tautologous. This sense is not quite sharply defined yet, but we can nevertheless understand what is being asked. In any part of logic we may ask: is it always possible to list all the alternatives concerning the world in such a way that the truths of this part of logic are just the sentences admitting all these alternatives, but excluding none? If so, the truths of this part of logic are so many tautologies.

Let us study quantification theory as a test case. Can we list all the possibilities concerning the world that can be expressed by means of the resources employed in some given quantificational sentence?

The answer depends on the meaning we assign to the expression "by means of the resources employed in some given sentence." If this is taken to mean "by means of the predicates occurring in the given sentence" (plus quantifiers and propositional connectives, of course), then in most cases there is no hope of making a finite list of the desired kind.

But if we introduce further limitations, the answer is different. For each sentence which is considered in quantification theory, there is a maximum to the lengths of the sequences of nested quantifiers occurring therein. More popularly expressed, each quantificational sentence is characterized by the number of the layers of quantifiers it contains. This number will be called the *depth* of the sentence in question. In other words, the depth of a sentence is the maximum number of quantifiers whose scopes all overlap in it. Each sentence has, moreover, a finite number of free individual symbols (constants or free variables). The sum of this number and the depth of the sentence in question will be called its *degree*. If we now consider what can be expressed by means of sentences constructed from a given finite supply of predicates and free individual symbols plus quantifiers and having a degree smaller than a given positive integer, there is a way of listing all the different alternatives concerning our universe of discourse that can be expressed by means of these resources.

The limitation on the degree of the sentences is a natural one, for the notion of the degree of a sentence has a very simple intuitive meaning. The degree of a sentence is the maximum number of individuals we are considering at any one time in their relation to each other in the sentence.

Since this intuitive meaning of the notion of degree will be important in what follows, it is worth explaining carefully. For this purpose, we may ask: how are individuals introduced into our arguments? Part of an answer is obvious: individuals are introduced into our reasoning by free individual symbols. This gives us the first of the two addenda whose sum is the degree of a sentence. This answer is only a partial one, however, for individuals are introduced into our propositions also by quantifiers (bound individual variables). In order to see this, it suffices to recall the most accurate translations of quantifiers into more or less ordinary language: "$(Ex)$" is to be read "there is at least one individual (let us call it $x$) such that" and "$(x)$" is to be read "for each individual (call it $x$) it is the case that." Each quantifier thus invites us to consider exactly one new individual, however indefinite this individual may be. Two quantifiers whose scopes do not overlap cannot both be counted here, however, for there is no way of relating to each other the individuals which such quantifiers invite us to consider. Hence the contribution of quantifiers to the maximal number of individuals we are considering together in a certain sentence is the maximal number of quantifiers whose scopes overlap in it, exactly as was suggested.

Another way of seeing the intuitive meaning of the notion of a degree in quantification theory is to ask the question: what are the individuals whose properties and interrelations you are considering (or may consider) in a given part of a quantificational sentence, say between a certain pair of parentheses? Obviously, they include the individuals referred to by the free individual symbols of the sentence. They also include all the indefinite individuals introduced by the quantifiers within the scope of which we are moving. They do not include any other individuals. The maximum number of these individuals is just the degree of the sentence in question, which is therefore the maximum number of individuals we are considering together in the sentence.

This informal explanation has a neat formal counterpart. If it is required, as is natural, that quantifiers with overlapping scopes must have different variables bound to them, then the depth of a sentence is the least number of different bound variables one needs in order to write it out, and its degree is therefore the least number of different individual symbols (free or bound) one needs in it.

The intuitive meaning of the degree of a sentence is straightforward enough to have already caught the eye of C. S. Peirce, at least in a simple special case. (See his *Collected Papers,* 3.392: "The algebra of Boole affords a language by which anything may be expressed which can be said without speaking of more than one individual at a time.")

But does not a general sentence speak of all the individuals of the domain (universe of discourse)? Is not the number of individuals considered in such a sentence therefore infinite if the domain is infinite? Surely a general sentence does speak in some sense of all the individuals in the domain; but in such a sentence we are not considering all these individuals in their relations to each other. In a sentence like "All men admire Buddha" we are not considering the interrelations that obtain between any two men. We are, so to speak, considering each man at a time and saying something about *his* relation to the great Gautama. Hence the number of individuals considered in their relation to each other in this sentence is two, which is just its degree. In the first half of the sentence "John has at least one brother and John has at least one sister" we are considering John in his relation to an arbitrarily chosen brother of his, and in the second half we are considering him in his relation to one of his sisters. Nothing is said, however, of the relations between his brothers and his sisters. Hence the number of individuals considered together at any given time in the sentence is only two, which is again exactly its degree. This illustrates the fact that quantifiers with nonoverlapping scopes do not count in the total. By contrast, in the sentence "All John's sisters are older than his brothers" an arbitrary brother of John's is compared as to age with an arbitrary sister of John's; hence the number of individuals considered in their relations to each other is three, again equaling the degree of the sentence.

These examples illustrate the intuitive meaning of our notion of degree. Apart from this intuitive meaning, it plays an interesting role in quantification theory. If a limit is imposed on the degree of our sentences, we have in quantification theory a situation strongly reminiscent of propositional logic. Given a finite supply of predicates and free individual symbols, there is a finite number of constituents such that every consistent sen-

tence considered has a normal form in which it is a disjunction
of some (perhaps all) of the constituents. I shall not prove
this result here. I have done so in a number of other papers
in which I have also considered these "distributive normal
forms" in certain other respects.

It is not my purpose here to examine the structure of
distributive normal forms in any greater detail. There are two
questions concerning them which must nevertheless be discussed. First, we want to make sure that the constituents
occurring in them really list all the alternatives concerning the
world in as clear-cut a sense as do the constituents of propositional logic. Secondly, we have to ask whether the logical truths
of quantification theory are related to the constituents in the
same way as are the logical truths of propositional logic.

I think that the first point can be sufficiently established
by considering, by way of example, some of the simplest kinds
of quantificational constituents. If there are no free individual
symbols present and if we have merely a number of monadic
(one-place) predicates $P_i(x)$ $(i = 1, 2, \ldots, m)$, the constituents will have the following form:

(1)
$$\prod_{k=1}^{k=2^m} (Ex) \; \prod_{i=1}^{i=m} {}_k P_i(x)$$

This is in a clear-cut sense a description of one kind of a
"possible world." It is easy to see how this description is
accomplished. First, we list all the possible kinds of individuals
that can be specified by means of the predicates $P_i(x)$. This is
what the conjunctions

(2)
$$\prod_{i=1} {}_k P_i(x) = C_k(x)$$

$(k = 1, 2, \ldots, 2^m)$ do. Then we specify, for each such kind
of individuals, whether individuals of that kind exist or not.
It is perhaps not entirely surprising that everything we can say
by using only the predicates $P_i(x)$, quantifiers, and propositional connectives is a disjunction of such descriptions of kinds
of possible worlds.

A simple example perhaps makes the situation easier to
appreciate. Suppose that $m = 2$, that is to say, suppose that

we are given two monadic predicates, say "red" and "round." Then conjunctions (2) are of the form

$$(\pm) (x \text{ is red}) \& (\pm) (x \text{ is round}).$$

They specify all the different kinds of individuals that can be specified by means of the two predicates:

(2)*  
        *x* is red and round;  
        *x* is red but not round;  
        *x* is round but not red;  
        *x* is neither red nor round.

Each constituent of form (1) indicates, for each of the different kinds of individuals (2)*, whether such individuals exist or not. To take a random example of constituents of form (1), one of them will be the following sentence:

> There are individuals which are red and round;  
> there are no individuals which are red but not round;  
> there are no individuals which are round but not red;  
> there are individuals which are neither red nor round.

We can also see an interesting way of rewriting a constituent of form (1). Instead of listing all the different kinds of individuals that exist and also listing the kinds of individuals that do not exist, it suffices to list the kinds of existing individuals and simply to add that they are all the kinds of individuals in existence. This means that each constituent of form (1) can be rewritten so as to be of form

(3)        $(Ex)C_1(x) \& (Ex)C_2(x) \& \ldots \& (Ex)C_n(x) \&$  
           $(x) (C_1(x) \lor C_2(x) \lor \ldots \lor C_n(x)),$

where $\{C_i(x)\}$ $(i = 1, 2, \ldots, n)$ is some subset of the set of all conjunctions (2). It can be shown that all the constituents of quantification theory may be similarly rewritten.

For instance, the constituent which was formulated in words above could obviously be rewritten as follows:

> There are individuals which are red and round as well as individuals which are neither red nor round; and every individual is either red and round or neither red nor round.

In order to have more insight into the structure of our constituents, let us assume that we are given a number of dyadic (two-place) predicates $R_i(x, y)$ $(i = 1, 2, \ldots, r)$ but no other predicates nor any free individual symbols, and that the depth of our sentences is at most two. Then constituents are still of form (3). In fact, (3) may be said to be the general form of those constituents which do not contain free individual symbols. The definition of the conjunctions $C_i(x)$ has to be changed, however, from case to case. In the case at hand, each $C_i(x)$ is rather like (3):

(4)     $(Ey)C_1'(x, y)$ & $(Ey)C_2'(x, y)$ & $\ldots$ & $(Ey)C_s'(x, y)$
        & $(y)(C_1'(x, y) \lor C_2'(x, y) \lor \ldots \lor C_s'(x, y))$ &
$$\prod_{i=1}^{i=r} R_i(x, x)$$

Here each $C'(x, y)$ is of the form

$$\prod_{i=1}^{i=r} R_i(x, y) \ \& \ \prod_{i=1}^{i=r} R_i(y, x) \ \& \ \prod_{i=1}^{i=r} R_i(y, y).$$

The intuitive meaning of (4) is not very difficult to fathom. In effect, we first list all the different ways in which an individual $y$ may be related to a given individual $x$. Given a fixed $x$, this list is also a list of different kinds of individuals $y$ (in their relation to $x$). Then we specify which of these different kinds of $y$ exist for some fixed $x$. (We specify, furthermore, the ways in which $x$ is or is not related to itself.) What I am saying is that this gives us a list of all the possible kinds of individuals $x$ that we can specify by using only the dyadic predicates $R_i(x, y)$, quantifiers, and propositional connectives, provided we do not make use of sentences of a degree higher than one.

What happens in (4) may also be described as follows. We took a list of all the relations (two-place predicates) which may obtain between two individuals and which can be specified without using quantifiers, and we constructed out of them a list of all the possible complex attributes (one-place predicates) which an individual may have and which may be specified by means of just one layer of quantifiers. It is a straightforward task to generalize this: in the same way we may start from the list of all the possible relations which may obtain between $n + 1$ individuals and which can be specified by $m$ layers of quantifiers, and construct out of them a list of all the different relations which can obtain between $n$ individuals and which can be described by means of $m + 1$ layers of quantifiers. In this way we may in fact easily obtain an inductive definition of constituents in general, for in the case $m = 0$ we have simply constituents in the sense of propositional logic. (Such a definition is of course relative to a given finite list of predicates and free individual symbols.)

These examples and indications perhaps suffice to show that the constituents of quantification theory really give us a systematic list of all the different possibilities concerning reality which can be specified by the means of expression that we have at our disposal, in the same sense in which the constituents of propositional logic do so. We could also use these constituents in the same way as the constituents of propositional logic have sometimes been used, namely to develop measures of the information which a sentence carries. Tautologies would then be sentences with zero information. In other respects, too, the situation is exactly the same in quantification theory as it is in propositional logic, with but one important exception. This one difference between the two cases is that in quantification theory some constituents are inconsistent whereas no constituents of propositional logic are.

The question we have to ask is whether this makes the situation essentially different from what it is in propositional logic. It may appear that it does make a difference. The fact that there are inconsistent constituents implies that a sentence may be logically true even though its distributive normal form does not contain all the constituents, provided that the missing constituents are all inconsistent. Thus it may appear that the truths of quantification theory need not be tautologies in the sense of admitting all the alternatives that we can specify with respect to the world. It suffices for them to admit all the alternatives specified by the consistent constituents.

An answer lies close at hand. We suggested defining a tautology as a sentence which admits of all the possibilities that there are with respect to the world. Now it is perfectly natural to say that an inconsistent constituent does not specify a genuine possibility concerning the subject matter it seems to be speaking of, but only appears to describe one. Just because it is inconsistent, the state of affairs it purports to describe can never be realized, so there is no need for any sentence to exclude it. Hence a necessary and sufficient condition for a sentence of quantification theory to admit all the kinds of worlds which are really possible—that is to say, to be a tautology—is that its distributive normal form contain all the *consistent* constituents. And it is readily seen that all the truths of quantification theory really are tautologies in this sense.

This way out of the difficulty may seem far too simple. It can be strengthened, however, by means of further arguments.

I shall here give in the form of an analogy an argument which, although merely persuasive, can be converted into a stricter one. If we are given a constituent, we are not yet given a genuine picture of a possible state of affairs. We are given, rather, a way of constructing such a picture—as if we were given a jigsaw puzzle. In fact, (3) shows that being given a constituent is very much like being given an unlimited supply of a finite number of different kinds of pieces of a jigsaw puzzle, with two instructions: (*i*) at least one piece of each kind has to be used; (*ii*) no other kinds of pieces may be used. An attempt to construct "a picture of a possible state of affairs" in accordance with these instructions may fail. Then the jigsaw puzzle does not give any picture of reality: it cannot be used to convey information concerning the state of the world. We cannot give it to somebody and say "This is what the world is like" and hope to convey any real information to him as we could have done by giving him a ready-made picture of the world or even a jigsaw puzzle which might yield a genuine picture. Similarly, it may be suggested, an inconsistent constituent does not describe a genuine possibility as to what the world may be like but only appears to do so. Hence its presence or absence makes no difference to the normal forms: no knowledge of the subject matter of which the sentence in question speaks is needed to rule it out.

This analogy can be made stronger in two ways. It may be argued that what most directly specifies the structure of the world (and in this sense gives us the "real meaning" of a constituent) is not the constituent itself but rather the outcome of those operations that we have compared to the construction of a jigsaw puzzle. Such an argument might take the form of a defense of a rudimentary form of what is known as the picture theory of language. On this view, a constituent or a sentence of some other kind is not itself a "picture" of a possible state of affairs, but rather gives us a starting point for the construction of a picture or a set of alternative pictures. It would take us too far afield, however, to develop this idea here.

It will have to suffice to give a single reason for the aptness of the jigsaw puzzle analogy. This is the fact that it very well reproduces the reasons why inconsistent constituents are inconsistent. In order to see two such reasons, we may consider sentences (3) and (4) and assume that the latter occurs as a part of the former. Both (3) and (4) are lists of all the kinds of individuals that there are. In the first list these individuals are classified absolutely, in the second with respect to the given individual $x$. Nevertheless, the two lists have to be compatible for every $C_i(x)$—that is, for each sentence of the form (4) which occurs in (3). For, clearly, every individual that exists according to the absolute list has to find a place in the relative list of each existing individual, and vice versa. These two requirements are not always met. If they are not, (3) is inconsistent. If the first requirement is violated, (3) may be shown to be inconsistent by essentially one application of the exchange theorem $(Ex) (y) P (x, y) \supset (x) (Ey) P (y, x)$. If the second is violated, (3) may similarly be shown to be inconsistent by essentially one application of the exchange theorem $(Ex)(Ey) P (x, y) \supset (Ex)(Ey) P (y, x)$.

If I am right, these two are essentially the only ways in which a constituent can turn out to be inconsistent. Of course, this cannot mean that every constituent which is not inconsistent for one of these two reasons is thereby shown to be consistent. Often the failure of a constituent to meet the two requirements is implicit and becomes explicit only when the constituent in question is expanded into a disjunction of several constituents of a greater depth. At some finite depth, each of these deeper constituents will then be inconsistent for one of our two reasons.

Here the jigsaw puzzle analogy serves us remarkably well. I may sum up my explanation of the two reasons why a constituent may be inconsistent by comparing one of my inconsistent constituents to a jigsaw puzzle which can fail to yield a coherent picture, for two reasons. Either there are two pieces (or, rather, kinds of pieces) which are incompatible in the sense that they cannot be fitted into one and the same picture; or else one of the pieces leaves a gap which is such that it cannot be filled by any of the different kinds of pieces that are at our disposal. The former case arises when some member of the absolute list cannot find a niche in the relative list of one of its fellow members; then the two members of the absolute list are incompatible. The latter case arises when some member of the relative list of some fixed $C_i(x)$ does not fit into the absolute list; then this $C_i(x)$ "leaves a gap" which cannot be completed by any of the members of the absolute list of which we are allowed to make use. The fact that we sometimes have to expand the given constituent into a disjunction of several constituents of a greater depth may be compared to the fact that we sometimes have to carry an attempted construction of a jigsaw puzzle to a certain extent before it can be seen that it is impossible to complete for one of the two reasons which I just mentioned.

This success of the jigsaw puzzle analogy will reinforce the point which I made by its means: knowing that certain constituents are inconsistent does not give us any information concerning the reality which the constituents purport to speak of and hence does not interfere with the tautologicality of the logical truths of quantification theory.

Our observations thus strongly suggest that the truths of quantification theory are really analytic in sense II—that is, tautologies in the sense in which we have decided to use the term.

In the course of our discussion, we have already found indications that some of the logical truths of quantification theory are nevertheless *not* analytic in our sense III—that is, not provable by analytic methods. Now I shall argue more fully for this second main point.

For those truths of quantification theory that do not turn on the elimination of any constituents, it may be argued that they are analytic in sense III. But for the rest the situation is entirely different. The briefest glimpse already suggests that the inconsistency of some of the constituents is essentially connected with sense III of the analytic and the synthetic. If a constituent like (3) is inconsistent, then the following implication is provable.

(5)     $((Ex)C_1(x)$ & $(Ex)C_2(x)$ & ... & $(Ex)C_n(x)) \supset$
        $(Ex)(\sim C_1(x)$ & $\sim C_2(x)$ & ... & $\sim C_n(x))$.

This is clearly an instance of the kind of interindividual existential inference which for Kant constituted the paradigm of synthetic inferences (cf. criterion III[c] formulated above). In this case the difference between the different individuals that Kant speaks of is understood in the strongest possible sense, to wit, in the sense of logically necessary difference. Conversely, it may be argued (with certain qualifications) that in every logically valid inference from the existence of a number of individuals to the existence of another individual which is for logical reasons different from them there is implicit the inconsistency of at least one of our constituents. In short, inconsistencies of constituents would have been for Kant paradigmatic instances of synthetic truths of (modern) logic.

There are other ways of arguing that the elimination of the inconsistent constituents is a synthetic procedure in sense III of the analytic and the synthetic. An especially clear-cut one is given by criterion III(b). It was suggested earlier that one way of showing that a constituent is inconsistent is to transform it into a disjunction of constituents of a greater depth and therefore of a higher degree and to show that all of these are inconsistent for one of the two reasons I explained. Now the intuitive meaning of the notion of the degree of a sentence is, as I indicated, that of the maximum number of individuals that we are considering together at one and the same time in the sentence in question. According to criterion III(b), this number must not be greater in any of the sentences by means of which a given sentence $p$ is proved or disproved than it is in $p$ itself, if this proof or disproof is to be analytic. Since the procedure I just mentioned for eliminating an inconsistent constituent makes use of sentences of a degree higher than that of the constituent to be eliminated, it is a synthetic procedure in the sense of criterion III(b).

Is this perhaps an accidental peculiarity of my procedure? I do not think so; on the contrary, I think it an unavoidable feature of every complete proof procedure in quantification theory, in some fairly natural sense of "proof procedure." Every such proof procedure must make frequent use of sentences of higher degree than that of the sentence to be proved. This is made inevitable by the fact, noticed earlier, that only a finite number of nonequivalent sentences can be made by means of the predicates and free individual symbols occurring in a given sentence, if a limitation is imposed on the degree of these sentences. If our rules of inference do not affect this degree, they cannot lead us out of this finite set of sentences. If certain fairly natural limitations are imposed on these rules of inference, it will be possible to show that this would give us a decision procedure, which is known to be nonexistent in many cases. In order to give us a complete proof procedure, our rules of inference must therefore allow proofs of sentences by means of sentences of higher degrees. Such a proof procedure will then be synthetic in our sense III(b).

The limitations that have to be imposed on rules of inference in order for what was just said to be true have some interest in themselves. Sometimes a rule of inference in the most general sense of the word is essentially identified with a two-place recursive predicate of the Gödel numbers of sentences (or formulae, if you prefer). In this wide sense, we can indeed have rules of inference which are analytic in sense III(b) and which nevertheless enable us to prove all (and only all) the logical truths of quantification theory. I think this sense in any case far too broad, however, to constitute a natural explication of what we would naturally mean by a rule of inference. We have to require that the applicability of such a rule depends, intuitively speaking, only on what the sentences in question express or say and not on accidental features of their formulation. This requirement may seem too vague to be useful; nevertheless it has some very definite implications. For instance, it may be taken to imply that a rule of inference must be independent of the way in which truth functions are written out; and it must be independent of the particular free individual symbols which occur in the sentences in question. Hence only such two-place recursive predicates of Gödel numbers of sentences will qualify for a rule of inference as are invariant with respect to arbitrary replacements of truth functions by tautologously equivalent truth functions (of the same arguments) in the sentences in question (or which can be extended so as to become invariant in this sense without affecting provability relations). Such replacements must of course be admissible also inside larger sentences. Moreover, we must require symmetry with respect to the different free individual symbols.

If these natural restrictions are imposed on what we are willing to call a rule of inference, it may be shown that no set of rules of inference analytic in sense III(b) suffices to enable us to prove each logical truth of quantification theory from propositional tautologies of the same degree or to carry out analytically (in sense III[b]) all the proofs from premises which we would like to carry out.

It is easy to verify that most of the familiar proof procedures in quantification theory satisfy the two requirements, and also that they in fact allow proofs of sentences by means of higher-degree sentences, that is to say, proofs synthetic in the sense we are now considering. An innocent exception is constituted by some of the natural deduction methods, where the process known as existential instantiation does not depend solely on the existentially quantified sentence to be instantiated. Usually it has to be required that the instantiating free individual symbol is different from all the free individual symbols occurring earlier in the proof. This means that existential instantiation is not independent of the particular free singular terms occurring in the result of the process of existential instantiation. In deciding how many individuals are considered together in a step of a proof by natural deduction methods, we therefore have to count not only the free individual symbols which occur in the premises of this particular step but also all the ones that occur at earlier stages of the proof. We may, for example, consider the conjunction of all the sentences reached up to a certain point and consider its degree instead of the degree of the individual lines of proof. (It may be called the degree of the set of sentences so far reached.) But if we do this, we find that natural deduction methods also conform to the pattern we have found. In them, too, we frequently have to add to the number of individuals we are considering together in order to be able to carry out the proofs we want to carry out; in other words, we have to add to the degree of the sets of sentences we are considering.

Natural deduction methods are interesting from our point of view because the synthetic element in them may be reduced to a single rule. In a suitable formulation of these methods there is only one rule that is synthetic, that is, that adds to the number of individuals one is considering in the sense just explained. This is just the rule of existential instantiation. If the other rules are formulated in a suitable way, the rule of existential instantiation thus takes all the blame for increasing the degree of the sets of sentences we have to consider in order to establish a logical truth of quantification theory. (Universal instantiation need not increase the degree, for it may be restricted to the cases where the instantiating free individual symbol is an old one, that is, occurs earlier in the argument.)

I conclude, then, that the logical truths of quantification theory cannot all be captured by (natural) rules of inference which would be analytic. In this sense, quantification theory is a synthetic theory.

We might also try to spell out more clearly which particular logical truths of quantification theory are synthetic in the most natural sense of the word based on criterion III(b). Such an attempt would bring us back, it seems to me, to the distinction between logical truths depending on the elimination of inconsistent constituents and those not depending on it. Almost all the logical truths as well as almost all the usual logical arguments that one finds in ordinary textbooks of logic will then turn out to be analytic in the relevant sense of the term, the main exception probably being offered by the laws for exchanging adjacent quantifiers. The details need not detain us here, however, since the main point is clear enough. The fact that many logical truths of quantification theory turn out to be analytic in one sense of the word but synthetic in another sense shows the importance of the distinction between the different senses. It also shows that it does make sense to ask whether the logical truths of quantification theory are analytic.

It remains to make good my promise to relate our findings

to Kant's distinction between the analytic and the synthetic. I shall confine myself to a few general remarks only.

The basis of the connection may be expressed in terms of the history of the notions of the analytic and the synthetic. Like so many other important philosophical terms, they seem to have originated from the geometrical terminology of the Greeks. Traditionally, there were two main variants of the concepts of the analytic and the synthetic. In one of them, a synthetic argument was an ordinary step-by-step deductive argument, whereas in an analytic argument one started from what one wanted to prove and tried to reduce it to something known from which it could be proved. The other sense of the analytic and the synthetic was tied more closely to geometry, although these ties were by no means inseparable. Forgetting certain qualifications, we may say that a geometrical argument was called analytic in the second sense in so far as no constructions were carried out in it, that is, in so far as no new lines, points, circles, and the like were introduced during the argument. An argument was called synthetic if such new entities were introduced. Here we are interested in the second sense only.

Now it is well known that if the geometrical arguments of (say) Euclid's system are "formalized" in the sense of being converted into the form of explicit logical arguments, most of them are instances of quantificational arguments. It is also fairly obvious that the distinction between the two kinds of geometrical arguments largely coincides with the distinction between the two kinds of quantificational arguments that I have been discussing. A geometrical argument in the course of which no new geometrical entities are "constructed"—that is, introduced into the discussion—will normally be converted into a quantificational argument in the course of which no new free individual symbols are introduced and the degree of the sentences in question is not otherwise increased. The geometrical notion of analyticity definable in terms of the notion of a construction will thus virtually become a special case of the sense of analyticity that we characterized by means of the notion of degree. Elsewhere, I have argued that Kant's usage of the terms "analytic" and "synthetic" largely followed the mathematical paradigm. He made it clear, furthermore, that he had in mind only the second of the two variant senses of the analytic and the synthetic which were listed above. If I am right, Kant's usage therefore comes pretty close to the sense in which most logical truths of quantification theory were found above to be synthetic.

There is in the historical material also a half-implicit generalization of the geometrical notion of construction which may serve to establish an even closer connection between my suggested explication of the notion of analyticity and the meaning which the term "analytic" has actually had. The part of the demonstration of a Euclidean theorem in which figures were introduced (drawn for the first time) was called the *ecthesis* or "exposition." The same term was applied by Aristotle to a procedure, used in his syllogistic theory, that is very closely related to the rule of existential instantiation. (Indeed, on one interpretation it virtually is this rule.) It has been suggested that Aristotle was here borrowing from Greek mathematical terminology; but even if he was not, the two notions of *ecthesis* were frequently related to each other, as in fact may be done for perfectly good reasons. The result was a general but somewhat vague idea of something like the rule of existential instantiation. I have suggested elsewhere that something like this idea was what Kant had in mind when he described the synthetic method of mathematics. In fact, Kant indicates that mathematical truths are synthetic because they are based on the use of constructions. The general notion of a construction is explained by him as the introduction or "exhibition" of an individual idea (individual term, as we may equally well say) to represent a general concept, an explanation strongly reminiscent of existential instantiation. In the light of such explanations, we may safely say that for Kant something like the rule of existential instantiation was the paradigm of synthetic modes of reasoning in mathematics. Since we saw earlier that in a suitable system of quantification theory the rule of existential instantiation is the only one that increases the degree of the sets of sentences we are considering, this serves to relate Kant's notion of analyticity even more closely to the explication which can be given to this notion in terms of the degree of a sentence (or of a set of sentences). I think that in the light of this explication we can appreciate Kant's philosophy of mathematics and of logic much better than by means of any alternative explication of analyticity. In a sense, we may in this way even partially vindicate Kant's claim that most mathematical truths are synthetic. In certain other ways, too, we seem to have here a way of making certain parts of the traditional philosophy of mathematics more relevant to our own problems than modern philosophers sometimes think they are. What more can one ask of an explication of an old philosophical notion?

FURTHER READING

Hintikka (1), (4), (6), (9)

# ᐁ TWO DOGMAS
# OF EMPIRICISM

*W. V. Quine*

Modern empiricism has been conditioned in large part by two dogmas. One is a belief in some fundamental cleavage between truths which are *analytic,* or grounded in meanings independently of matters of fact, and truths which are *synthetic,* or grounded in fact. The other dogma is *reductionism:* the belief that each meaningful statement is equivalent to some logical construct upon terms which refer to immediate experience. Both dogmas, I shall argue, are ill-founded. One effect of abandoning them is, as we shall see, a blurring of the supposed boundary between speculative metaphysics and natural science. Another effect is a shift toward pragmatism.

## 1. Background for Analyticity

Kant's cleavage between analytic and synthetic truths was foreshadowed in Hume's distinction between relations of ideas and matters of fact, and in Leibniz's distinction between truths of reason and truths of fact. Leibniz spoke of the truths of reason as true in all possible worlds. Picturesqueness aside, this is to say that the truths of reason are those which could not possibly be false. In the same vein we hear analytic statements

From W. V. Quine, *From a Logical Point of View* (Cambridge: Harvard University Press, 1953), pp. 20–46. Reprinted by permission of the publisher.

defined as statements whose denials are self-contradictory. But this definition has small explanatory value; for the notion of self-contradictoriness, in the quite broad sense needed for this definition of analyticity, stands in exactly the same need of clarification as does the notion of analyticity itself. The two notions are the two sides of a single dubious coin.

Kant conceived of an analytic statement as one that attributes to its subject no more than is already conceptually contained in the subject. This formulation has two shortcomings: it limits itself to statements of subject-predicate form, and it appeals to a notion of containment which is left at a metaphorical level. But Kant's intent, evident more from the use he makes of the notion of analyticity than from his definition of it, can be restated thus: a statement is analytic when it is true by virtue of meanings and independently of fact. Pursuing this line, let us examine the concept of *meaning* which is presupposed.

Meaning, let us remember, is not to be identified with naming. Frege's example of 'Evening Star' and 'Morning Star', and Russell's of 'Scott' and 'the author of *Waverley*', illustrate that terms can name the same thing but differ in meaning. The distinction between meaning and naming is no less important at the level of abstract terms. The terms '9' and 'the number of the planets' name one and the same abstract entity but presumably must be regarded as unlike in meaning; for astronomical observation was needed, and not mere reflection on meanings, to determine the sameness of the entity in question.

The above examples consist of singular terms, concrete and abstract. With general terms, or predicates, the situation is somewhat different but parallel. Whereas a singular term purports to name an entity, abstract or concrete, a general term does not; but a general term is *true of* an entity, or of each of many, or of none. The class of all entities of which a general term is true is called the *extension* of the term. Now paralleling the contrast between the meaning of a singular term and the entity named, we must distinguish equally between the meaning of a general term and its extension. The general terms 'creature with a heart' and 'creature with kidneys', for example, are perhaps alike in extension but unlike in meaning.

Confusion of meaning with extension, in the case of general terms, is less common than confusion of meaning with naming in the case of singular terms. It is indeed a commonplace in philosophy to oppose intension (or meaning) to extension, or, in a variant vocabulary, connotation to denotation.

The Aristotelian notion of essence was the forerunner, no doubt, of the modern notion of intension of meaning. For Aristotle it was essential in men to be rational, accidental to be two-legged. But there is an important difference between this attitude and the doctrine of meaning. From the latter point of view it may indeed be conceded (if only for the sake of argument) that rationality is involved in the meaning of the word 'man' while two-leggedness is not; but two-leggedness may at the same time be viewed as involved in the meaning of 'biped' while rationality is not. Thus from the point of view of the doctrine of meaning it makes no sense to say of the actual individual, who is at once a man and a biped, that his rationality is essential and his two-leggedness accidental or vice versa. Things had essences, for Aristotle, but only linguistic forms have meanings. Meaning is what essence becomes when it is divorced from the object of reference and wedded to the word.

For the theory of meaning a conspicuous question is the nature of its objects: what sort of things are meanings? A felt need for meant entities may derive from an earlier failure to appreciate that meaning and reference are distinct. Once the theory of meaning is sharply separated from the theory of reference, it is a short step to recognizing as the primary business of the theory of meaning simply the synonymy of linguistic forms and the analyticity of statements; meanings themselves, as obscure intermediary entities, may well be abandoned.

The problem of analyticity then confronts us anew. Statements which are analytic by general philosophical acclaim are not, indeed, far to seek. They fall into two classes. Those of the first class, which may be called *logically true,* are typified by:

(1)             No unmarried man is married.

The relevant feature of this example is that it not merely is true as it stands, but remains true under any and all reinterpretations of 'man' and 'married'. If we suppose a prior inventory of *logical* particles, comprising 'no', 'un-', 'not', 'if', 'then', 'and', etc., then in general a logical truth is a statement which is true and remains true under all reinterpretations of its components other than the logical particles.

But there is also a second class of analytic statements, typified by:

(2)                    No bachelor is married.

The characteristic of such a statement is that it can be turned into a logical truth by putting synonyms for synonyms; thus (2) can be turned into (1) by putting 'unmarried man' for its synonym 'bachelor'. We still lack a proper characterization of this second class of analytic statements, and therewith of analyticity generally, inasmuch as we have had in the above description to lean on a notion of "synonymy" which is no less in need of clarification than analyticity itself.

In recent years Carnap has tended to explain analyticity by appeal to what he calls state-descriptions. A state-description is any exhaustive assignment of truth values to the atomic, or noncompound, statements of the language. All other statements of the language are, Carnap assumes, built up of their component clauses by means of the familiar logical devices, in such a way that the truth value of any complex statement is fixed for each state-description by specifiable logical laws. A statement is then explained as analytic when it comes out true under every state description. This account is an adaptation of Leibniz's "true in all possible worlds." But note that this version of analyticity serves its purpose only if the atomic statements of the language are, unlike 'John is a bachelor' and 'John is married', mutually independent. Otherwise there would be a state-description which assigned truth to 'John is a bachelor' and to 'John is married', and consequently 'No bachelors are married' would turn out synthetic rather than analytic under the proposed criterion. Thus the criterion of analyticity in terms of state-descriptions serves only for languages devoid of extralogical synonym-pairs, such as 'bachelor' and 'unmarried man' —synonym-pairs of the type which give rise to the "second class" of analytic statements. The criterion in terms of state-descriptions is a reconstruction at best of logical truth, not of analyticity.

I do not mean to suggest that Carnap is under any illusions

on this point. His simplified model language with its state-descriptions is aimed primarily not at the general problem of analyticity but at another purpose, the clarification of probability and induction. Our problem, however, is analyticity; and here the major difficulty lies not in the first class of analytic statements, the logical truths, but rather in the second class, which depends on the notion of synonymy.

## 2. Definition

There are those who find it soothing to say that the analytic statements of the second class reduce to those of the first class, the logical truths, by *definition;* 'bachelor', for example, is *defined* as 'unmarried man'. But how do we find that 'bachelor' is defined as 'unmarried man'? Who defined it thus, and when? Are we to appeal to the nearest dictionary, and accept the lexicographer's formulation as law? Clearly this would be to put the cart before the horse. The lexicographer is an empirical scientist, whose business is the recording of antecedent facts; and if he glosses 'bachelor' as 'unmarried man' it is because of his belief that there is a relation of synonymy between those forms, implicit in general or preferred usage prior to his own work. The notion of synonymy presupposed here has still to be clarified, presumably in terms relating to linguistic behavior. Certainly the "definition" which is the lexicographer's report of an observed synonymy cannot be taken as the ground of the synonymy.

Definition is not, indeed, an activity exclusively of philologists. Philosophers and scientists frequently have occasion to "define" a recondite term by paraphrasing it into terms of a more familiar vocabulary. But ordinarily such a definition, like the philologist's, is pure lexicography, affirming a relation of synonymy antecedent to the exposition in hand.

Just what it means to affirm synonymy, just what the interconnections may be which are necessary and sufficient in order that two linguistic forms be properly describable as synonymous, is far from clear; but, whatever these interconnections may be, ordinarily they are grounded in usage. Definitions reporting selected instances of synonymy come then as reports upon usage.

There is also, however, a variant type of definitional activity

which does not limit itself to the reporting of preëxisting synonymies. I have in mind what Carnap calls *explication*—an activity
to which philosophers are given, and scientists also in their
more philosophical moments. In explication the purpose is not
merely to paraphrase the definiendum into an outright synonym,
but actually to improve upon the definiendum by refining or
supplementing its meaning. But even explication, though not
merely reporting a preëxisting synonymy between definiendum
and definiens, does rest nevertheless on *other* preëxisting synonymies. The matter may be viewed as follows. Any word worth
explicating has some contexts which, as wholes, are clear and
precise enough to be useful; and the purpose of explication is
to preserve the usage of these favored contexts while sharpening
the usage of other contexts. In order that a given definition be
suitable for purposes of explication, therefore, what is required
is not that the definiendum in its antecedent usage be synonymous with the definiens, but just that each of these favored
contexts of the definiendum, taken as a whole in its antecedent
usage, be synonymous with the corresponding context of the
definiens.

Two alternative definientia may be equally appropriate for
the purposes of a given task of explication and yet not be synonymous with each other; for they may serve interchangeably
within the favored contexts but diverge elsewhere. By cleaving
to one of these definientia rather than the other, a definition of
explicative kind generates, by fiat, a relation of synonymy between definiendum and definiens which did not hold before. But
such a definition still owes its explicative function, as seen, to
preëxisting synonymies.

There does, however, remain still an extreme sort of definition which does not hark back to prior synonymies at all:
namely, the explicitly conventional introduction of novel notations for purposes of sheer abbreviation. Here the definiendum
becomes synonymous with the definiens simply because it has
been created expressly for the purpose of being synonymous
with the definiens. Here we have a really transparent case of
synonymy created by definition; would that all species of synonymy were as intelligible. For the rest, definition rests on synonymy rather than explaining it.

The word 'definition' has come to have a dangerously reassuring sound, owing no doubt to its frequent occurrence in logical and mathematical writings. We shall do well to digress now into a brief appraisal of the role of definition in formal work.

In logical and mathematical systems either of two mutually antagonistic types of economy may be striven for, and each has its peculiar practical utility. On the one hand we may seek economy of practical expression—ease and brevity in the statement of multifarious relations. This sort of economy calls usually for distinctive concise notations for a wealth of concepts. Second, however, and oppositely, we may seek economy in grammar and vocabulary; we may try to find a minimum of basic concepts such that, once a distinctive notation has been appropriated to each of them, it becomes possible to express any desired further concept by mere combination and iteration of our basic notations. This second sort of economy is impractical in one way, since a poverty in basic idioms tends to a necessary lengthening of discourse. But it is practical in another way: it greatly simplifies theoretical discourse *about* the language, through minimizing the terms and the forms of construction wherein the language consists.

Both sorts of economy, though prima facie incompatible, are valuable in their separate ways. The custom has consequently arisen of combining both sorts of economy by forging in effect two languages, the one a part of the other. The inclusive language, though redundant in grammar and vocabulary, is economical in message lengths, while the part, called primitive notation, is economical in grammar and vocabulary. Whole and part are correlated by rules of translation whereby each idiom not in primitive notation is equated to some complex built up of primitive notation. These rules of translation are the so-called *definitions* which appear in formalized systems. They are best viewed not as adjuncts to one language but as correlations between two languages, the one a part of the other.

But these correlations are not arbitrary. They are supposed to show how the primitive notations can accomplish all purposes, save brevity and convenience, of the redundant language. Hence the definiendum and its definiens may be expected, in each case, to be related in one or another of the three ways lately noted. The definiens may be a faithful paraphrase of the definiendum into the narrower notation, preserving a direct synonymy as of antecedent usage; or the definiens may, in the spirit of explication, improve upon the antecedent usage of the definiendum; or finally, the definiendum may be a newly created notation, newly endowed with meaning here and now.

In formal and informal work alike, thus, we find that definition—except in the extreme case of the explicitly conventional introduction of new notations—hinges on prior relations of synonymy. Recognizing then that the notion of definition does not hold the key to synonymy and analyticity, let us look further into synonymy and say no more of definition.

## 3. Interchangeability

A natural suggestion, deserving close examination, is that the synonymy of two linguistic forms consists simply in their interchangeability in all contexts without change of truth value —interchangeability, in Leibniz's phrase, *salva veritate*. Note that synonyms so conceived need not even be free from vagueness, as long as the vaguenesses match.

But it is not quite true that the synonyms 'bachelor' and 'unmarried man' are everywhere interchangeable *salva veritate*. Truths which become false under substitution of 'unmarried man' for 'bachelor' are easily constructed with the help of 'bachelor of arts' or 'bachelor's buttons'; also with the help of quotation, thus:

'Bachelor' has less than ten letters.

Such counterinstances can, however, perhaps be set aside by treating the phrases 'bachelor of arts' and 'bachelor's buttons' and the quotation ' 'bachelor' ' each as a single indivisible word and then stipulating that the interchangeability *salva veritate* which is to be the touchstone of synonymy is not supposed to apply to fragmentary occurrences inside of a word. This account of synonymy, supposing it acceptable on other counts, has indeed the drawback of appealing to a prior conception of "word" which can be counted on to present difficulties of formulation in its turn. Nevertheless some progress might be claimed in having reduced the problem of synonymy to a problem of wordhood. Let us pursue this line a bit, taking "word" for granted.

The question remains whether interchangeability *salva veritate* (apart from occurrences within words) is a strong enough condition for synonymy, or whether, on the contrary, some heteronymous expressions might be thus interchangeable. Now let us be clear that we are not concerned here with synonymy in the sense of complete identity in psychological associations or poetic quality; indeed no two expressions are synonymous in such a sense. We are concerned only with what may be called *cognitive* synonymy. Just what this is cannot be said without successfully finishing the present study; but we know something about it from the need which arose for it in connection with analyticity in §1. The sort of synonymy needed there was merely such that any analytic statement could be turned into a logical truth by putting synonyms for synonyms. Turning the tables and assuming analyticity, indeed, we could explain cognitive synonymy of terms as follows (keeping to the familiar example): to say that 'bachelor' and 'unmarried man' are cognitively synonymous is to say no more nor less than that the statement:

(3)      All and only bachelors are unmarried men

is analytic.

What we need is an account of cognitive synonymy not presupposing analyticity—if we are to explain analyticity conversely with help of cognitive synonymy as undertaken in §1. And indeed such an independent account of cognitive synonymy is at present up for consideration, namely, interchangeability *salva veritate* everywhere except within words. The question before us, to resume the thread at last, is whether such interchangeability is a sufficient condition for cognitive synonymy. We can quickly assure ourselves that it is, by examples of the following sort. The statement:

(4)    Necessarily all and only bachelors are bachelors

is evidently true, even supposing 'necessarily' so narrowly construed as to be truly applicable only to analytic statements. Then, if 'bachelor' and 'unmarried man' are interchangeable *salva veritate,* the result:

(5) Necessarily all and only bachelors are unmarried men

of putting 'unmarried man' for an occurrence of 'bachelor' in (4)

must, like (4), be true. But to say that (5) is true is to say that
(3) is analytic, and hence that 'bachelor' and 'unmarried man'
are cognitively synonymous.

Let us see what there is about the above argument that
gives it its air of hocus-pocus. The condition of interchangeability *salva veritate* varies in its force with variations in the richness
of the language at hand. The above argument supposes we are
working with a language rich enough to contain the adverb
'necessarily', this adverb being so construed as to yield truth
when and only when applied to an analytic statement. But can
we condone a language which contains such an adverb? Does the
adverb really make sense? To suppose that it does is to suppose
that we have already made satisfactory sense of 'analytic'. Then
what are we so hard at work on right now?

Our argument is not flatly circular, but something like it.
It has the form, figuratively speaking, of a closed curve in space.

Interchangeability *salva veritate* is meaningless until relativized to a language whose extent is specified in relevant respects.
Suppose now we consider a language containing just the following materials. There is an indefinitely large stock of one-place
predicates (for example, '*F*' where '*Fx*' means that *x* is a man)
and many-place predicates (for example, '*G*' where '*Gxy*' means
that *x* loves *y*), mostly having to do with extralogical subject
matter. The rest of the language is logical. The atomic sentences
consist each of a predicate followed by one or more variables
'*x*', '*y*', etc.; and the complex sentences are built up of the
atomic ones by truth functions ('not', 'and', 'or', etc.) and
quantification. In effect such a language enjoys the benefits
also of descriptions and indeed singular terms generally, these
being contextually definable in known ways. Even abstract singular terms naming classes, classes of classes, etc., are contextually definable in case the assumed stock of predicates includes
the two-place predicate of class membership. Such a language
can be adequate to classical mathematics and indeed to scientific
discourse generally, except in so far as the latter involves debatable devices such as contrary-to-fact conditionals or modal
adverbs like 'necessarily'. Now a language of this type is extensional, in this sense: any two predicates which agree extensionally (that is, are true of the same objects) are interchangeable
*salva veritate*.

In an extensional language, therefore, interchangeability *salva veritate* is no assurance of cognitive synonymy of the desired type. That 'bachelor' and 'unmarried man' are interchangeable *salva veritate* in an extensional language assures us of no more than that (3) is true. There is no assurance here that the extensional agreement of 'bachelor' and 'unmarried man' rests on meaning rather than merely on accidental matters of fact, as does the extensional agreement of 'creature with a heart' and 'creature with kidneys'.

For most purposes extensional agreement is the nearest approximation to synonymy we need care about. But the fact remains that extensional agreement falls far short of cognitive synonymy of the type required for explaining analyticity in the manner of §1. The type of cognitive synonymy required there is such as to equate the synonymy of 'bachelor' and 'unmarried man' with the analyticity of (3), not merely with the truth of (3).

So we must recognize that interchangeability *salva veritate,* if construed in relation to an extensional language, is not a sufficient condition of cognitive synonymy in the sense needed for deriving analyticity in the manner of §1. If a language contains an intensional adverb 'necessarily' in the sense lately noted, or other particles to the same effect, then interchangeability *salva veritate* in such a language does afford a sufficient condition of cognitive synonymy; but such a language is intelligible only in so far as the notion of analyticity is already understood in advance.

The effort to explain cognitive synonymy first, for the sake of deriving analyticity from it afterward as in §1, is perhaps the wrong approach. Instead we might try explaining analyticity somehow without appeal to cognitive synonymy. Afterward we could doubtless derive cognitive synonymy from analyticity satisfactorily enough if desired. We have seen that cognitive synonymy of 'bachelor' and 'unmarried man' can be explained as analyticity of (3). The same explanation works for any pair of one-place predicates, of course, and it can be extended in obvious fashion to many-place predicates. Other syntactical categories can also be accommodated in fairly parallel fashion. Singular terms may be said to be cognitively synonymous when the statement of identity formed by putting '=' between them is analytic.

Statements may be said simply to be cognitively synonymous when their biconditional (the result of joining them by 'if and only if') is analytic. If we care to lump all categories into a single formulation, at the expense of assuming again the notion of "word" which was appealed to early in this section, we can describe any two linguistic forms as cognitively synonymous when the two forms are interchangeable (apart from occurrences within "words") *salva* (no longer *veritate* but) *analyticitate*. Certain technical questions arise, indeed, over cases of ambiguity or homonymy; let us not pause for them, however, for we are already digressing. Let us rather turn our backs on the problem of synonymy and address ourselves anew to that of analyticity.

## 4. Semantical Rules

Analyticity at first seemed most naturally definable by appeal to a realm of meanings. On refinement, the appeal to meanings gave way to an appeal to synonymy or definition. But definition turned out to be a will-o'-the-wisp, and synonymy turned out to be best understood only by dint of a prior appeal to analyticity itself. So we are back at the problem of analyticity.

I do not know whether the statement 'Everything green is extended' is analytic. Now does my indecision over this example really betray an incomplete understanding, an incomplete grasp of the "meanings", of 'green' and 'extended'? I think not. The trouble is not with 'green' or 'extended', but with 'analytic'.

It is often hinted that the difficulty in separating analytic statements from synthetic ones in ordinary language is due to the vagueness of ordinary language and that the distinction is clear when we have a precise artificial language with explicit "semantical rules." This, however, as I shall now attempt to show, is a confusion.

The notion of analyticity about which we are worrying is a purported relation between statements and languages: a statement $S$ is said to be *analytic for* a language $L$, and the problem is to make sense of this relation generally, that is, for variable '$S$' and '$L$'. The gravity of this problem is not perceptibly less for artificial languages than for natural ones. The problem of making sense of the idiom '$S$ is analytic for $L$', with variable '$S$' and '$L$', retains its stubbornness even if we limit the range of the variable '*L*' to artificial languages. Let me now try to make this point evident.

For artificial languages and semantical rules we look naturally to the writings of Carnap. His semantical rules take various forms, and to make my point I shall have to distinguish certain of the forms. Let us suppose, to begin with, an artificial language $L_0$ whose semantical rules have the form explicitly of a specification, by recursion or otherwise, of all the analytic statements of $L_0$. The rules tell us that such and such statements, and only those, are the analytic statements of $L_0$. Now here the difficulty is simply that the rules contain the word 'analytic', which we do not understand! We understand what expressions the rules attribute analyticity to, but we do not understand what the rules attribute to those expressions. In short, before we can understand a rule which begins 'A statement *S* is analytic for language $L_0$ if and only if . . .', we must understand the general relative term 'analytic for'; we must understand '*S* is analytic for *L*' where '*S*' and '*L*' are variables.

Alternatively we may, indeed, view the so-called rule as a conventional definition of a new simple symbol 'analytic-for-$L_0$', which might better be written untendentiously as '*K*' so as not to seem to throw light on the interesting word 'analytic'. Obviously any number of classes *K*, *M*, *N*, etc., of statements of $L_0$ can be specified for various purposes or for no purpose; what does it mean to say that *K*, as against *M*, *N*, etc., is the class of the "analytic" statements of $L_0$?

By saying what statements are analytic for $L_0$ we explain 'analytic-for-$L_0$' but not 'analytic', not 'analytic for'. We do not begin to explain the idiom '*S* is analytic for *L*' with variable '*S*' and '*L*', even if we are content to limit the range of '*L*' to the realm of artificial languages.

Actually we do know enough about the intended significance of 'analytic' to know that analytic statements are supposed to be true. Let us then turn to a second form of semantical rule, which says not that such and such statements are analytic but simply that such and such statements are included among the truths. Such a rule is not subject to the criticism of containing the un-understood word 'analytic'; and we may grant for the sake of argument that there is no difficulty over the broader term 'true'. A semantical rule of this second type, a rule of truth, is not supposed to specify all the truths of the language; it merely stipulates, recursively or otherwise, a certain multitude of statements which, along with others unspecified, are to count as true. Such a rule may be conceded to be quite clear. Derivatively, afterward, analyticity can be demarcated thus: a statement is analytic if it is (not merely true but) true according to the semantical rule.

Still there is really no progress. Instead of appealing to an unexplained word 'analytic', we are now appealing to an unexplained phrase 'semantical rule'. Not every true statement which says that the statements of some class are true can count as a semantical rule—otherwise *all* truths would be "analytic" in the sense of being true according to semantical rules. Semantical rules are distinguishable, apparently, only by the fact of appearing on a page under the heading 'Semantical Rules'; and this heading is itself then meaningless.

We can say indeed that a statement is *analytic-for-$L_0$* if and only if it is true according to such and such specifically appended "semantical rules," but then we find ourselves back at essentially the same case which was originally discussed: '$S$ is analytic-for-$L_0$ if and only if. . . .' Once we seek to explain '$S$ is analytic for $L$' generally for variable '$L$' (even allowing limitation of '$L$' to artificial languages), the explanation 'true according to the semantical rules of $L$' is unavailing; for the relative term 'semantical rule of' is as much in need of clarification, at least, as 'analytic for'.

It may be instructive to compare the notion of semantical rule with that of postulate. Relative to a given set of postulates, it is easy to say what a postulate is: it is a member of the set. Relative to a given set of semantical rules, it is equally easy to say what a semantical rule is. But given simply a notation, mathematical or otherwise, and indeed as thoroughly understood a notation as you please in point of the translations or truth conditions of its statements, who can say which of its true statements rank as postulates? Obviously the question is meaningless—as meaningless as asking which points in Ohio are starting points. Any finite (or effectively specifiable infinite) selection of statements (preferably true ones, perhaps) is as much *a* set of postulates as any other. The word 'postulate' is significant only relative to an act of inquiry; we apply the word to a set of statements just in so far as we happen, for the year or the moment, to be thinking of those statements in relation to the statements which can be reached from them by some set of transformations to which we have seen fit to direct our attention. Now the notion of semantical rule is as sensible and meaningful as that of postulate, if conceived in a similarly relative spirit—relative, this time, to one or another particular enterprise of schooling unconversant persons in sufficient conditions for truth of statements of some natural or artificial language *L*. But from this point of view no one signalization of a subclass of the truths of *L* is intrinsically more a semantical rule than another; and, if 'analytic' means 'true by semantical rules', no one truth of *L* is analytic to the exclusion of another.

It might conceivably be protested that an artificial language *L* (unlike a natural one) is a language in the ordinary sense *plus* a set of explicit semantical rules—the whole constituting, let us say, an ordered pair; and that the semantical rules of *L* then are specifiable simply as the second component of the pair *L*. But, by the same token and more simply, we might construe an artificial language *L* outright as an ordered pair whose second component is the class of its analytic statements; and then the analytic statements of *L* become specifiable simply as the statements in the second component of *L*. Or better still, we might just stop tugging at our bootstraps altogether.

Not all the explanations of analyticity known to Carnap and his readers have been covered explicitly in the above considerations, but the extension to other forms is not hard to see. Just one additional factor should be mentioned which sometimes enters: sometimes the semantical rules are in effect rules of translation into ordinary language, in which case the analytic statements of the artificial language are in effect recognized as such from the analyticity of their specified translations in ordinary language. Here certainly there can be no thought of an illumination of the problem of analyticity from the side of the artificial language.

From the point of view of the problem of analyticity the notion of an artificial language with semantical rules is a *feu follet par excellence*. Semantical rules determining the analytic statements of an artificial language are of interest only in so far as we already understand the notion of analyticity; they are of no help in gaining this understanding.

Appeal to hypothetical languages of an artificially simple kind could conceivably be useful in clarifying analyticity, if the mental or behavioral or cultural factors relevant to analyticity—whatever they may be—were somehow sketched into the simplified model. But a model which takes analyticity merely as an irreducible character is unlikely to throw light on the problem of explicating analyticity.

It is obvious that truth in general depends on both language and extralinguistic fact. The statement 'Brutus killed Caesar' would be false if the world had been different in certain ways, but it would also be false if the word 'killed' happened rather to have the sense of 'begat'. Thus one is tempted to suppose in general that the truth of a statement is somehow analyzable into a linguistic component and a factual component. Given this supposition, it next seems reasonable that in some statements the factual component should be null; and these are the analytic statements. But, for all its a priori reasonableness, a boundary between analytic and synthetic statements simply has not been drawn. That there is such a distinction to be drawn at all is an unempirical dogma of empiricists, a metaphysical article of faith.

## 5. *The Verification Theory and Reductionism*

In the course of these somber reflections we have taken a dim view first of the notion of meaning, then of the notion of cognitive synonymy, and finally of the notion of analyticity. But what, it may be asked, of the verification theory of meaning? This phrase has established itself so firmly as a catchword of empiricism that we should be very unscientific indeed not to look beneath it for a possible key to the problem of meaning and the associated problems.

The verification theory of meaning, which has been conspicuous in the literature from Peirce onward, is that the meaning of a statement is the method of empirically confirming or infirming it. An analytic statement is that limiting case which is confirmed no matter what.

As urged in §1, we can as well pass over the question of meanings as entities and move straight to sameness of meaning, or synonymy. Then what the verification theory says is that statements are synonymous if and only if they are alike in point of method of empirical confirmation or infirmation.

This is an account of cognitive synonymy not of linguistic forms generally, but of statements. However, from the concept of synonymy of statements we could derive the concept of synonymy for other linguistic forms, by considerations somewhat similar to those at the end of §3. Assuming the notion of "word," indeed, we could explain any two forms as synonymous when the putting of the one form for an occurrence of the other in any statement (apart from occurrences within "words") yields a synonymous statement. Finally, given the concept of synonymy thus for linguistic forms generally, we could define analyticity in terms of synonymy and logical truth as in §1. For that matter, we could define analyticity more simply in terms of just synonymy of statements together with logical truth; it is not necessary to appeal to synonymy of linguistic forms other than statements. For a statement may be described as analytic simply when it is synonymous with a logically true statement.

So, if the verification theory can be accepted as an adequate account of statement synonymy, the notion of analyticity is saved after all. However, let us reflect. Statement synonymy is said to be likeness of method of empirical confirmation or infirmation. Just what are these methods which are to be compared for likeness? What, in other words, is the nature of the relation between a statement and the experiences which contribute to or detract from its confirmation?

The most naïve view of the relation is that it is one of direct report. This is *radical reductionism*. Every meaningful statement is held to be translatable into a statement (true or false) about immediate experience. Radical reductionism, in one form or another, well antedates the verification theory of meaning explicitly so called. Thus Locke and Hume held that every idea must either originate directly in sense experience or else be compounded of ideas thus originating; and taking a hint from Tooke we might rephrase this doctrine in semantical jargon by saying that a term, to be significant at all, must be either a name of a sense datum or a compound of such names or an abbreviation of such a compound. So stated, the doctrine remains ambiguous as between sense data as sensory events and sense data as sensory qualities; and it remains vague as to the admissible ways of compounding. Moreover, the doctrine is unnecessarily and intolerably restrictive in the term-by-term critique which it imposes. More reasonably, and without yet exceeding the limits of what I have called radical reductionism, we may take full statements as our significant units—thus demanding that our statements as wholes be translatable into sense-datum language, but not that they be translatable term by term.

This emendation would unquestionably have been welcome to Locke and Hume and Tooke, but historically it had to await an important reorientation in semantics—the reorientation whereby the primary vehicle of meaning came to be seen no longer in the term but in the statement. This reorientation, explicit in Frege . . . , underlies Russell's concept of incomplete symbols defined in use; also it is implicit in the verification theory of meaning, since the objects of verification are statements.

Radical reductionism, conceived now with statements as units, set itself the task of specifying a sense-datum language and showing how to translate the rest of significant discourse, statement by statement, into it. Carnap embarked on this project in the *Aufbau*.

The language which Carnap adopted as his starting point was not a sense-datum language in the narrowest conceivable sense, for it included also the notations of logic, up through higher set theory. In effect it included the whole language of pure mathematics. The ontology implicit in it (that is, the range of values of its variables) embraced not only sensory events but classes, classes of classes, and so on. Empiricists there are who would boggle at such prodigality. Carnap's starting point is very parsimonious, however, in its extralogical or sensory part. In a series of constructions in which he exploits the resources of modern logic with much ingenuity, Carnap succeeds in defining a wide array of important additional sensory concepts which, but for his constructions, one would not have dreamed were definable on so slender a basis. He was the first empiricist who, not content with asserting the reducibility of science to terms of immediate experience, took serious steps toward carrying out the reduction.

If Carnap's starting point is satisfactory, still his constructions were, as he himself stressed, only a fragment of the full program. The construction of even the simplest statements about the physical world was left in a sketchy state. Carnap's suggestions on this subject were, despite their sketchiness, very suggestive. He explained spatio-temporal point-instants as quadruples of real numbers and envisaged assignment of sense qualities to point-instants according to certain canons. Roughly summarized, the plan was that qualities should be assigned to point-instants in such a way as to achieve the laziest world compatible with our experience. The principle of least action was to be our guide in constructing a world from experience.

Carnap did not seem to recognize, however, that his treatment of physical objects fell short of reduction not merely through sketchiness, but in principle. Statements of the form 'Quality $q$ is at point-instant $x;y;z;t$' were, according to his canons, to be apportioned truth values in such a way as to maximize and minimize certain over-all features, and with growth of experience the truth values were to be progressively revised in the same spirit. I think this is a good schematization (deliberately oversimplified, to be sure) of what science really does; but it provides no indication, not even the sketchiest, of how a statement of the form 'Quality $q$ is at $x;y;z;t$' could ever be translated into Carnap's initial language of sense data and logic. The connective 'is at' remains an added undefined connective; the canons counsel us in its use but not in its elimination.

Carnap seems to have appreciated this point afterward; for in his later writings he abandoned all notion of the translatability of statements about the physical world into statements about immediate experience. Reductionism in its radical form has long since ceased to figure in Carnap's philosophy.

But the dogma of reductionism has, in a subtler and more tenuous form, continued to influence the thought of empiricists. The notion lingers that to each statement, or each synthetic statement, there is associated a unique range of possible sensory events such that the occurrence of any of them would add to the likelihood of truth of the statement, and that there is associated also another unique range of possible sensory events whose occurrence would detract from that likelihood. This notion is of course implicit in the verification theory of meaning.

The dogma of reductionism survives in the supposition that each statement, taken in isolation from its fellows, can admit of confirmation or infirmation at all. My countersuggestion, issuing essentially from Carnap's doctrine of the physical world in the *Aufbau,* is that our statements about the external world face the tribunal of sense experience not individually but only as a corporate body.

The dogma of reductionism, even in its attenuated form, is intimately connected with the other dogma—that there is a cleavage between the analytic and the synthetic. We have found ourselves led, indeed, from the latter problem to the former through the verification theory of meaning. More directly, the one dogma clearly supports the other in this way: as long as it is taken to be significant in general to speak of the confirmation and infirmation of a statement, it seems significant to speak also of a limiting kind of statement which is vacuously confirmed, *ipso facto,* come what may; and such a statement is analytic.

The two dogmas are, indeed, at root identical. We lately reflected that in general the truth of statements does obviously depend both upon language and upon extralinguistic fact; and we noted that this obvious circumstance carries in its train, not logically but all too naturally, a feeling that the truth of a statement is somehow analyzable into a linguistic component and a factual component. The factual component must, if we are empiricists, boil down to a range of confirmatory experiences. In the extreme case where the linguistic component is all that matters, a true statement is analytic. But I hope we are now impressed with how stubbornly the distinction between analytic and synthetic has resisted any straightforward drawing. I am impressed also, apart from prefabricated examples of black and white balls in an urn, with how baffling the problem has always been of arriving at any explicit theory of the empirical confirmation of a synthetic statement. My present suggestion is that it is nonsense, and the root of much nonsense, to speak of a linguistic component and a factual component in the truth of any individual statement. Taken collectively, science has its double dependence upon language and experience; but this duality is not significantly traceable into the statements of science taken one by one.

The idea of defining a symbol in use was, as remarked, an advance over the impossible term-by-term empiricism of Locke and Hume. The statement, rather than the term, came with Frege to be recognized as the unit accountable to an empiricist critique. But what I am now urging is that even in taking the statement as unit we have drawn our grid too finely. The unit of empirical significance is the whole of science.

## 6. *Empiricism without the Dogmas*

The totality of our so-called knowledge or beliefs, from the most casual matters of geography and history to the profoundest laws of atomic physics or even of pure mathematics and logic, is a man-made fabric which impinges on experience only along the edges. Or, to change the figure, total science is like a field of force whose boundary conditions are experience. A conflict with experience at the periphery occasions readjustments in the interior of the field. Truth values have to be redistributed over some of our statements. Reëvaluation of some statements entails reëvaluation of others, because of their logical interconnections—the logical laws being in turn simply certain further statements of the system, certain further elements of the field. Having reëvaluated one statement we must reëvaluate some others, which may be statements logically connected with the first or may be the statements of logical connections themselves. But the total field is so underdetermined by its boundary conditions, experience, that there is much latitude of choice as to what statements to reëvaluate in the light of any single contrary experience. No particular experiences are linked with any particular statements in the interior of the field, except indirectly through considerations of equilibrium affecting the field as a whole.

If this view is right, it is misleading to speak of the empirical content of an individual statement—especially if it is a statement at all remote from the experiential periphery of the field. Furthermore it becomes folly to seek a boundary between synthetic statements, which hold contingently on experience, and analytic statements, which hold come what may. Any statement can be held true come what may, if we make drastic enough adjustments elsewhere in the system. Even a statement very close to the periphery can be held true in the face of recalcitrant experience by pleading hallucination or by amending certain statements of the kind called logical laws. Conversely, by the same token, no statement is immune to revision. Revision even of the logical law of the excluded middle has been proposed as a means of simplifying quantum mechanics; and what difference is there in principle between such a shift and the shift whereby Kepler superseded Ptolemy, or Einstein Newton, or Darwin Aristotle?

For vividness I have been speaking in terms of varying distances from a sensory periphery. Let me try now to clarify this notion without metaphor. Certain statements, though *about* physical objects and not sense experience, seem peculiarly germane to sense experience—and in a selective way: some statements to some experiences, others to others. Such statements, especially germane to particular experiences, I picture as near the periphery. But in this relation of "germaneness" I envisage nothing more than a loose association reflecting the relative likelihood, in practice, of our choosing one statement rather than another for revision in the event of recalcitrant experience. For example, we can imagine recalcitrant experiences to which we would surely be inclined to accommodate our system by reëvaluating just the statement that there are brick houses on Elm Street, together with related statements on the same topic. We can imagine other recalcitrant experiences to which we would be inclined to accommodate our system by reëvaluating just the statement that there are no centaurs, along with kindred statements. A recalcitrant experience can, I have urged, be accommodated by any of various alternative reëvaluations in various alternative quarters of the total system; but, in the cases which we are now imagining, our natural tendency to disturb the total system as little as possible would lead us to focus our revisions upon these specific statements concerning brick houses or centaurs. These statements are felt, therefore, to have a sharper empirical reference than highly theoretical statements of physics or logic or ontology. The latter statements may be thought of as relatively centrally located within the total network, meaning merely that little preferential connection with any particular sense data obtrudes itself.

As an empiricist I continue to think of the conceptual scheme of science as a tool, ultimately, for predicting future experience in the light of past experience. Physical objects are conceptually imported into the situation as convenient intermediaries—not by definition in terms of experience, but simply as irreducible posits comparable, epistemologically, to the gods of Homer. For my part I do, qua lay physicist, believe in physical objects and not in Homer's gods; and I consider it a scientific error to believe otherwise. But in point of epistemological footing the physical objects and the gods differ only in degree and not in kind. Both sorts of entities enter our conception only as cultural posits. The myth of physical objects is epistemologically superior to most in that it has proved more efficacious than other myths as a device for working a manageable structure into the flux of experience.

Positing does not stop with macroscopic physical objects. Objects at the atomic level are posited to make the laws of macroscopic objects, and ultimately the laws of experience, simpler and more manageable; and we need not expect or demand full definition of atomic and subatomic entities in terms of macroscopic ones, any more than definition of macroscopic things in terms of sense data. Science is a continuation of common sense, and it continues the common-sense expedient of swelling ontology to simplify theory.

Physical objects, small and large, are not the only posits. Forces are another example; and indeed we are told nowadays that the boundary between energy and matter is obsolete. Moreover, the abstract entities which are the substance of mathematics—ultimately classes and classes of classes and so on up—are another posit in the same spirit. Epistemologically these are myths on the same footing with physical objects and gods, neither better nor worse except for differences in the degree to which they expedite our dealings with sense experiences.

The over-all algebra of rational and irrational numbers is underdetermined by the algebra of rational numbers, but is smoother and more convenient; and it includes the algebra of rational numbers as a jagged or gerrymandered part. Total science, mathematical and natural and human, is similarly but more extremely underdetermined by experience. The edge of the system must be kept squared with experience; the rest, with all its elaborate myths or fictions, has as its objective the simplicity of laws.

Ontological questions, under this view, are on a par with questions of natural science. Consider the question whether to countenance classes as entities. This, as I have argued elsewhere, is the question whether to quantify with respect to variables which take classes as values. Now Carnap . . . has maintained that this is a question not of matters of fact but of choosing a convenient language form, a convenient conceptual scheme or framework for science. With this I agree, but only on the proviso that the same be conceded regarding scientific hypotheses generally. Carnap . . . has recognized that he is able to preserve a double standard for ontological questions and scientific hypotheses only by assuming an absolute distinction between the analytic and the synthetic; and I need not say again that this is a distinction which I reject.

The issue over there being classes seems more a question of convenient conceptual scheme; the issue over there being centaurs, or brick houses on Elm Street, seems more a question of fact. But I have been urging that this difference is only one of degree, and that it turns upon our vaguely pragmatic inclination to adjust one strand of the fabric of science rather than another in accommodating some particular recalcitrant experience. Conservatism figures in such choices, and so does the quest for simplicity.

Carnap, Lewis, and others take a pragmatic stand on the question of choosing between language forms, scientific frameworks; but their pragmatism leaves off at the imagined boundary between the analytic and the synthetic. In repudiating such a boundary I espouse a more thorough pragmatism. Each man is given a scientific heritage plus a continuing barrage of sensory stimulation; and the considerations which guide him in warping his scientific heritage to fit his continuing sensory promptings are, where rational, pragmatic.

## FURTHER READING

Carnap (8), (11)
Goodman (1)
Lewis (1)
Quine (10), (11), (13)
Waismann (3)
Wang
White (1)

# IN DEFENSE
# OF A DOGMA

*H. P. Grice and P. F. Strawson*

In his article "Two Dogmas of Empiricism," Professor Quine advances a number of criticisms of the supposed distinction between analytic and synthetic statements, and of other associated notions. It is, he says, a distinction which he rejects. We wish to show that his criticisms of the distinction do not justify his rejection of it.

There are many ways in which a distinction can be criticized, and more than one in which it can be rejected. It can be criticized for not being a sharp distinction (for admitting of cases which do not fall clearly on either side of it); or on the ground that the terms in which it is customarily drawn are ambiguous (have more than one meaning); or on the ground that it is confused (the different meanings being habitually conflated). Such criticisms alone would scarcely amount to a rejection of the distinction. They would, rather, be a prelude to clarification. It is not this sort of criticism which Quine makes.

Again, a distinction can be criticized on the ground that it is not useful. It can be said to be useless for certain purposes, or useless altogether, and, perhaps, pedantic. One who criticizes in this way may indeed be said to reject a distinction, but in a sense which also requires him to acknowledge its existence. He

From H. P. Grice and P. F. Strawson, "In Defense of a Dogma", *The Philosophical Review*, LXV (1956), pp. 141–158. Reprinted by permission of the Editors of *The Philosophical Review* and the authors.

simply declares he can get on without it. But Quine's rejection of the analytic-synthetic distinction appears to be more radical than this. He would certainly say he could get on without the distinction, but not in a sense which would commit him to acknowledging its existence.

Or again, one could criticize the way or ways in which a distinction is customarily expounded or explained on the ground that these explanations did not make it really clear. And Quine certainly makes such criticisms in the case of the analytic-synthetic distinction.

But he does, or seems to do, a great deal more. He declares, or seems to declare, not merely that the distinction is useless or inadequately clarified, but also that it is altogether illusory, that the belief in its existence is a philosophical mistake. "That there is such a distinction to be drawn at all," he says, "is an unempirical dogma of empiricists, a metaphysical article of faith." It is the existence of the distinction that he here calls in question; so his rejection of it would seem to amount to a denial of its existence.

Evidently such a position of extreme skepticism about a distinction is not in general justified merely by criticisms, however just in themselves, of philosophical attempts to clarify it. There are doubtless plenty of distinctions, drawn in philosophy and outside it, which still await adequate philosophical elucidation, but which few would want on this account to declare illusory. Quine's article, however, does not consist wholly, though it does consist largely, in criticizing attempts at elucidation. He does try also to diagnose the causes of the belief in the distinction, and he offers some positive doctrine, acceptance of which he represents as incompatible with this belief. If there is any general prior presumption in favor of the existence of the distinction, it seems that Quine's radical rejection of it must rest quite heavily on this part of his article, since the force of any such presumption is not even impaired by philosophical failures to clarify a distinction so supported.

Is there such a presumption in favor of the distinction's existence? Prima facie, it must be admitted that there is. An appeal to philosophical tradition is perhaps unimpressive and is certainly unnecessary. But it is worth pointing out that Quine's objection is not simply to the words "analytic" and "synthetic," but to a distinction which they are supposed to express, and which at different times philosophers have supposed themselves to be expressing by means of such pairs of words or phrases as "necessary" and "contingent," "a priori" and "empirical," "truth of reason" and "truth of fact"; so Quine is certainly at odds with a philosophical tradition which is long and not wholly disreputable. But there is no need to appeal only to tradition; for there is also present practice. We can appeal, that is, to the fact that those who use the terms "analytic" and "synthetic" do to a very considerable extent agree in the applications they make of them. They apply the term "analytic" to more or less the same cases, withhold it from more or less the same cases, and hesitate over more or less the same cases. This agreement extends not only to cases which they have been *taught* so to characterize, but to new cases. In short, "analytic" and "synthetic" have a more or less established philosophical *use;* and this seems to suggest that it is absurd, even senseless, to say that there is no such distinction. For, in general, if a pair of contrasting expressions are habitually and generally used in application to the same cases, *where these cases do not form a closed list,* this is a sufficient condition for saying that there are *kinds* of cases to which the expressions apply; and nothing more is needed for them to mark a distinction.

In view of the possibility of this kind of argument, one may begin to doubt whether Quine really holds the extreme thesis which his words encourage one to attribute to him. It is for this reason that we made the attribution tentative. For on at least one natural interpretation of this extreme thesis, when we say of something true that it is analytic and of another true thing that it is synthetic, it simply never is the case that we thereby mark a distinction between them. And this view seems terribly difficult to reconcile with the fact of an established philosophical usage (i.e., of general agreement in application in an open class). For this reason, Quine's thesis might be better represented not as the thesis that there is *no difference at all* marked by the use of these expressions, but as the thesis that the nature of, and reasons for, the difference or differences are totally misunderstood by those who use the expressions, that the stories they tell themselves *about* the difference are full of illusion.

We think Quine might be prepared to accept this amendment. If so, it could, in the following way, be made the basis of something like an answer to the argument which prompted it. Philosophers are notoriously subject to illusion, and to mistaken theories. Suppose there were a particular mistaken theory about language or knowledge, such that, seen in the light of this theory, some statements (or propositions or sentences) appeared to have a characteristic which no statements really have, or even, perhaps, which it does not make sense to suppose that any statement has, and which no one who was not consciously or subconsciously influenced by this theory would ascribe to any statement. And suppose that there were other statements which, seen in this light, did not appear to have this characteristic, and others again which presented an uncertain appearance. Then philosophers who were under the influence of this theory would tend to mark the supposed presence or absence of this characteristic by a pair of contrasting expressions, say "analytic" and "synthetic." Now in these circumstances it still could not be said that there was no distinction at all being marked by the use of these expressions, for there would be at least the distinction we have just described (the distinction, namely, between those statements which appeared to have and those which appeared to lack a certain characteristic), and there might well be other assignable differences too, which would account for the difference in appearance; but it certainly could be said that *the* difference these philosophers supposed themselves to be marking by the use of the expressions simply did not exist, and perhaps also (supposing the characteristic in question to be one which it was absurd to ascribe to any statement) that these expressions, as so used, were senseless or without meaning. We should only have to suppose that such a mistaken theory was very plausible and attractive, in order to reconcile the fact of an established philosophical usage for a pair of contrasting terms with the claim that *the* distinction which the terms purported to mark did not exist at all, though not with the claim that there simply did not exist a difference of any kind between the classes of statements so characterized. We think that the former claim would probably be sufficient for Quine's purposes. But to establish such a claim on the sort of grounds we have indicated evidently requires a great deal more argument than is involved in showing that certain explanations of a term do not measure up to certain requirements of adequacy in philosophical clarification—and not only more argument, but argument of a very different kind. For it would surely be too harsh to maintain that the *general* presumption is that philosophical distinctions embody the kind of illusion we have described. On the whole, it seems that philosophers are prone to make too few distinctions rather than too many. It is their assimilations, rather than their distinctions, which tend to be spurious.

So far we have argued as if the prior presumption in favor of the existence of the distinction which Quine questions rested solely on the fact of an agreed *philosophical* usage for the terms "analytic" and "synthetic." A presumption with only this basis could no doubt be countered by a strategy such as we have just outlined. But, in fact, if we are to accept Quine's account of the matter, the presumption in question is not only so based. For among the notions which belong to the analyticity-group is one which Quine calls "cognitive synonymy," and in terms of which he allows that the notion of analyticity could at any rate be formally explained. Unfortunately, he adds, the notion of cognitive synonymy is just as unclarified as that of analyticity. To say that two expressions $x$ and $y$ are cognitively synonymous seems to correspond, at any rate roughly, to what we should ordinarily express by saying that $x$ and $y$ have the same meaning or that $x$ means the same as $y$. If Quine is to be consistent in his adherence to the extreme thesis, then it appears that he must maintain not only that the distinction we suppose ourselves to be marking by the use of the terms "analytic" and "synthetic" does not exist, but also that the distinction we suppose ourselves to be marking by the use of the expressions "means the same as," "does not mean the same as" does not exist either. At least, he must maintain this insofar as the notion of *meaning the same as,* in its application to predicate-expressions, is supposed to differ from and go beyond the notion of *being true of just the same objects as.* (This latter notion—which we might call that of "coextensionality"—he is prepared to allow to be intelligible, though, as he rightly says, it is not sufficient for the explanation of analyticity.) Now since he cannot claim this time that the

pair of expressions in question (viz., "means the same," "does
not mean the same") is the special property of philosophers,
the strategy outlined above of countering the presumption in
favor of their marking a genuine distinction is not available
here (or is at least enormously less plausible). Yet the denial
that the distinction (taken as different from the distinction between the coextensional and the non-coextensional) really
exists, is extremely paradoxical. It involves saying, for example,
that anyone who seriously remarks that "bachelor" means the
same as "unmarried man" but that "creature with kidneys"
does not mean the same as "creature with a heart"—supposing
the last two expressions to be coextensional—*either* is not in
fact drawing attention to any distinction at all between the
relations between the members of each pair of expressions *or*
is making a philosophical mistake about the nature of the
distinction between them. In either case, what he says, taken
as he intends it to be taken, is senseless or absurd. More
generally, it involves saying that it is always senseless or absurd
to make a statement of the form "Predicates $x$ and $y$ in fact
apply to the same objects, but do not have the same meaning."
But the paradox is more violent than this. For we frequently
talk of the presence or absence of relations of synonymy between kinds of expressions—e.g., conjunctions, particles of
many kinds, whole sentences—where there does not appear to
be any obvious substitute for the ordinary notion of synonymy,
in the way in which coextensionality is said to be a substitute
for synonymy of predicates. Is all such talk meaningless? Is all
talk of correct or incorrect *translation* of sentences of one
language into sentences of another meaningless? It is hard to
believe that it is. But if we do successfully make the effort to
believe it, we have still harder renunciations before us. If talk
of sentence-synonymy is meaningless, then it seems that talk of
sentences having a meaning at all must be meaningless too.
For if it made sense to talk of a sentence having a meaning,
or meaning something, then presumably it would make sense
to ask "What does it mean?" And if it made sense to ask
"What does it mean?" of a sentence, then sentence-synonymy
could be roughly defined as follows: Two sentences are synonymous if and only if any true answer to the question "What does
it mean?" asked of one of them, is a true answer to the same

question, asked of the other. We do not, of course, claim any clarifying power for this definition. We want only to point out that if we are to give up the notion of sentence-synonymy as senseless, we must give up the notion of sentence-significance (of a sentence having meaning) as senseless too. But then perhaps we might as well give up the notion of sense.—It seems clear that we have here a typical example of a philosopher's paradox. Instead of examining the actual use that we make of the notion of *meaning the same,* the philosopher measures it by some perhaps inappropriate standard (in this case some standard of clarifiability), and because it falls short of this standard, or seems to do so, denies its reality, declares it illusory.

We have argued so far that there is a strong presumption in favor of the existence of the distinction, or distinctions, which Quine challenges—a presumptio resting both on philosophical and on ordinary usage—and that this presumption is not in the least shaken by the fact, if it is a fact, that the distinctions in question have not been, in some sense, adequately clarified. It is perhaps time to look at what Quine's notion of adequate clarification is.

The main theme of his article can be roughly summarized as follows. There is a certain circle or family of expressions, of which "analytic" is one, such that if any one member of the circle could be taken to be satisfactorily understood or explained, then other members of the circle could be verbally, and hence satisfactorily, explained in terms of it. Other members of the family are: "self-contradictory" (in a broad sense), "necessary," "synonymous," "semantical rule," and perhaps (but again in a broad sense) "definition." The list could be added to. Unfortunately each member of the family is in as great need of explanation as any other. We give some sample quotations: "The notion of self-contradictoriness (in the required broad sense of inconsistency) stands in exactly the same need of clarification as does the notion of analyticity itself." Again, Quine speaks of "a notion of synonymy which is in no less need of clarification than analyticity itself." Again, of the adverb "necessarily," as a candidate for use in the explanation of synonymy, he says, "Does the adverb *really make sense?* To suppose that it does is to suppose that we have already *made satisfactory sense* of 'analytic.'" To make "satisfactory sense" of one of these expressions would seem to involve two things. (1) It would seem to involve providing an explanation which does not incorporate any expression belonging to the family-circle. (2) It would seem that the explanation provided must be of the same general character as those rejected explanations which do incorporate members of the family-circle (i.e., it must specify some feature common and peculiar to all cases to which, for example, the word "analytic" is to be applied; it must have the same general form as an explanation beginning, "a statement is analytic if and only if . . ."). It is true that Quine does not explicitly state the second requirement; but since he does not even consider the question whether any other kind of explanation would be relevant, it seems reasonable to attribute it to him. If we take these two conditions together, and generalize the result, it would seem that Quine requires of a satisfactory explanation of an expression that it should take the form of a pretty strict definition but should not make use of any member of a group of interdefinable terms to which the expression belongs. We may well begin to feel that a satisfactory explanation is hard to come by. The other element in Quine's position is one we have already commented on in general, before enquiring what (according to him) is to count as a satisfactory explanation. It is the step from "We have not made satisfactory sense (provided a satisfactory explanation) of $x$" to "$x$ does not make sense."

It would seem fairly clearly unreasonable to insist *in general* that the availability of a satisfactory explanation in the sense sketched above is a necessary condition of an expression's making sense. It is perhaps dubious whether *any* such explanations can *ever* be given. (The hope that they can be is, or was, the hope of reductive analysis in general.) Even if such explanations can be given in some cases, it would be pretty generally agreed that there are other cases in which they cannot. One might think, for example, of the group of expressions which includes "morally wrong," "blameworthy," "breach of moral rules," etc.; or of the group which includes the propositional connectives and the words "true" and "false," "statement," "fact," "denial," "assertion." Few people would want to say that the expressions belonging to either of these groups were senseless on the ground that they have not been formally defined (or even on the ground that it was impossible formally to define them) except in terms of members of the same group. It might, however, be said that while the unavailability of a satisfactory explanation in the special sense described was not a *generally* sufficient reason for declaring that a given expression was senseless, it was a sufficient reason in the case of the expressions of the analyticity group. But anyone who said this would have to advance a reason for discriminating in this way against the expressions of this group. The only plausible reason for being harder on these expressions than on others is a refinement on a consideration which we have already had before us. It starts from the point that "analytic" and "synthetic" themselves are technical philosophical expressions. To the rejoinder that other expressions of the family concerned, such as "means the same as" or "is inconsistent with," or "self-contradictory," are not at all technical expressions, but are common property, the reply would doubtless be that, to qualify for inclusion in the family-circle, these expressions have to be used in specially adjusted and precise senses (or pseudo-senses) which they do not ordinarily possess. It is the fact, then, that all the terms belonging to the circle are *either* technical terms *or* ordinary terms used in specially adjusted senses, that might be held to justify us in being particularly suspicious of the claims of members of the circle to have any sense at all, and hence to justify us in requiring them to pass a test for significance which would admittedly be too stringent if generally applied. This point has some force, though we doubt if the special adjustments spoken of are in every case as considerable as it suggests. (This seems particularly doubtful in the case of the word "inconsistent"— a perfectly good member of the nontechnician's meta-logical vocabulary.) But though the point has some force, it does not have whatever force would be required to justify us in insisting that the expressions concerned should pass exactly that test for significance which is in question. The fact, if it is a fact, that the expressions cannot be explained in precisely the way which Quine seems to require, does not mean that they cannot be explained at all. There is no need to try to pass them off as expressing innate ideas. They can be and are explained, though in other and less formal ways than that which Quine considers. (And the fact that they are so explained fits with the facts, first, that there is a generally agreed philosophical use for them, and second, that this use is technical or specially adjusted.) To illustrate the point briefly for one member of the analyticity family. Let us suppose we are trying to explain to someone the notion of *logical impossibility* (a member of the family which Quine presumably regards as no clearer than any of the others) and we decide to do it by bringing out the contrast between logical and natural (or causal) impossibility. We might take as our examples the logical impossibility of a child of three's being an adult, and the natural impossibility of a child of three's understanding Russell's Theory of Types. We might instruct our pupil to imagine two conversations one of which begins by someone (X) making the claim:

(1)  "My neighbor's three-year-old child understands Russell's Theory of Types,"

and the other of which begins by someone (Y) making the claim:

(1′)  "My neighbor's three-year-old child is an adult."

It would not be inappropriate to reply to X, taking the remark as a hyperbole:

(2)  "You mean the child is a particularly bright lad."

If X were to say:

(3)  "No, I mean what I say—he really does understand it,"

one might be inclined to reply:

(4)  "I don't believe you—the thing's impossible."

But if the child were then produced, and did (as one knows he would not) expound the theory correctly, answer questions on it, criticize it, and so on, one would in the end be forced to acknowledge that the claim was literally true and that the child was a prodigy. Now consider one's reaction to Y's claim. To begin with, it might be somewhat similar to the previous case. One might say:

(2′)  "You mean he's uncommonly sensible or very advanced for his age."

If Y replies:

(3′)   "No, I mean what I say,"

we might reply:

(4′)   "Perhaps you mean that he won't grow any more, or that he's a sort of freak, that he's already fully developed."

Y replies:

(5′)   "No, he's not a freak, he's just an adult."

At this stage—or possibly if we are patient, a little later—we shall be inclined to say that we just don't understand what Y is saying, and to suspect that he just does not know the meaning of some of the words he is using. For unless he is prepared to admit that he is using words in a figurative or unusual sense, we shall say, not that we don't believe him, but that his words have *no* sense. And whatever kind of creature is ultimately produced for our inspection, it will not lead us to say that what Y said was literally true, but at most to say that we now see what he meant. As a summary of the difference between the two imaginary conversations, we might say that in both cases we would tend to begin by supposing that the other speaker was using words in a figurative or unusual or restricted way; but in the face of his repeated claim to be speaking literally, it would be appropriate in the first case to say that we did not believe him and in the second case to say that we did not understand him. If, like Pascal, we thought it prudent to prepare against very long chances, we should in the first case know what to prepare for; in the second, we should have no idea.

We give this as an example of just one type of informal explanation which we might have recourse to in the case of one notion of the analyticity group. (We do not wish to suggest it is the only type.) Further examples, with different though connected types of treatment, might be necessary to teach our pupil the use of the notion of logical impossibility in its application to more complicated cases—if indeed he did not pick it up from the one case. Now of course this type of explanation does not yield a formal statement of necessary and sufficient conditions for the application of the notion concerned. So it does not fulfill one of the conditions which Quine seems to require of a satisfactory explanation. On the other hand, it does appear to fulfill the other. It breaks out of the family circle. The distinction in which we ultimately come to rest is that between not believing something and not understanding something; or between incredulity yielding to conviction, and incomprehension yielding to comprehension. It would be rash to maintain that *this* distinction does not need clarification; but it would be absurd to maintain that it does not exist. In the face of the availability of this informal type of explanation for the notions of the analyticity group, the fact that they have not received another type of explanation (which it is dubious whether *any* expressions *ever* receive) seems a wholly inadequate ground for the conclusion that the notions are pseudo-notions, that the expressions which purport to express them have no sense. To say this is not to deny that it would be philosophically desirable, and a proper object of philosophical endeavor, to find a more illuminating general characterization of the notions of this group than any that has been so far given. But the question of how, if at all, this can be done is quite irrelevant to the question of whether or not the expressions which belong to the circle have an intelligible use and mark genuine distinctions.

So far we have tried to show that sections 1 to 4 of Quine's article—the burden of which is that the notions of the analyticity group have not been satisfactorily explained—do not establish the extreme thesis for which he appears to be arguing. It remains to be seen whether sections 5 and 6, in which diagnosis and positive theory are offered, are any more successful. But before we turn to them, there are two further points worth making which arise out of the first two sections.

(1) One concerns what Quine says about *definition* and *synonymy*. He remarks that definition does not, as some have supposed, "hold the key to synonymy and analyticity," since "definition—except in the extreme case of the explicitly conventional introduction of new notations—hinges on prior relations of synonymy." But now consider what he says of these extreme cases. He says: "Here the definiendum becomes synonymous with the definiens simply because it has been expressly

created for the purpose of being synonymous with the definiens. Here we have a really transparent case of synonymy created by definition; would that all species of synonymy were as intelligible." Now if we are to take these words of Quine seriously, then his position *as a whole* is incoherent. It is like the position of a man to whom we are trying to explain, say, the idea of one thing fitting into another thing, or two things fitting together, and who says: "I can understand what it means to say that one thing fits into another, or that two things fit together, in the case where one was specially made to fit the other; but I cannot understand what it means to say this in any other case." Perhaps we should not take Quine's words here too seriously. But if not, then we have the right to ask him exactly what state of affairs he thinks *is* brought about by explicit definition, what relation between expressions *is* established by this procedure, and why he thinks it unintelligible to suggest that the same (or a closely analogous) state of affairs, or relation, should exist in the absence of this procedure. For our part, we should be inclined to take Quine's words (or some of them) seriously, and reverse his conclusions; and maintain that the notion of synonymy by explicit convention would be unintelligible if the notion of synonymy by usage were not presupposed. There cannot be law where there is no custom, or rules where there are not practices (though perhaps we can understand better what a practice is by looking at a rule).

(2) The second point arises out of [the following] paragraph. We quote:

> I do not know whether the statement "Everything green is extended" is analytic. Now does my indecision over this example really betray an incomplete understanding, an incomplete grasp, of the "meanings" of "green" and "extended"? I think not. The trouble is not with "green" or "extended," but with "analytic."

If, as Quine says, the trouble is with "analytic," then the trouble should doubtless disappear when "analytic" is removed. So let us remove it, and replace it with a word which Quine himself has contrasted favorably with "analytic" in respect of perspicuity—the word "true." Does the indecision at once disappear? We think not. The indecision over "analytic" (and equally, in this case, the indecision over "true") arises, of course, from a further indecision: viz., that which we feel when confronted with such questions as "Should we count a *point* of green light as *extended* or not?" As is frequent enough in such cases, the hesitation arises from the fact that the boundaries of application of words are not determined by usage in all possible directions. But the example Quine has chosen is particularly unfortunate for his thesis, in that it is only too evident that our hesitations are not *here* attributable to obscurities in "analytic." It would be possible to choose other examples in which we should hesitate between "analytic" and "synthetic" and have few qualms about "true." But no more in these cases than in the sample case does the hesitation necessarily imply any obscurity in the notion of analyticity; since the hesitation would be sufficiently accounted for by the same or a similar kind of indeterminacy in the relations between the words occurring within the statement about which the question, whether it is analytic or synthetic, is raised.

Let us now consider briefly Quine's positive theory of the relations between the statements we accept as true or reject as false on the one hand and the "experiences" in the light of which we do this accepting and rejecting on the other. This theory is boldly sketched rather than precisely stated. We shall merely extract from it two assertions, one of which Quine clearly takes to be incompatible with acceptance of the distinction between analytic and synthetic statements, and the other of which he regards as barring one way to an explanation of that distinction. We shall seek to show that the first assertion is not incompatible with acceptance of the distinction, but is, on the contrary, most intelligibly interpreted in a way quite consistent with it, and that the second assertion leaves the way open to just the kind of explanation which Quine thinks it precludes. The two assertions are the following:

(1) It is an illusion to suppose that there is any class of accepted statements the members of which are in principle "immune from revision" in the light of experience, i.e., any that we accept as true and must continue to accept as true whatever happens.

(2) It is an illusion to suppose that an individual statement, taken in isolation from its fellows, can admit of confirma-

tion or disconfirmation at all. There is no particular statement such that a particular experience or set of experiences decides once for all whether that statement is true or false, independently of our attitudes to all other statements.

The apparent connection between these two doctrines may be summed up as follows. Whatever our experience may be, it is in principle possible to hold on to, or reject, any particular statement we like, so long as we are prepared to make extensive enough revisions elsewhere in our system of beliefs. In practice our choices are governed largely by considerations of convenience: we wish our system to be as simple as possible, but we also wish disturbances to it, as it exists, to be as small as possible.

The apparent relevance of these doctrines to the analytic-synthetic distinction is obvious in the first case, less so in the second.

(1) Since it is an illusion to suppose that the characteristic of immunity in principle from revision, come what may, belongs, or could belong, to any statement, it is an illusion to suppose that there is a distinction to be drawn between statements which possess this characteristic and statements which lack it. Yet, Quine suggests, this is precisely the distinction which those who use the terms "analytic" and "synthetic" suppose themselves to be drawing. Quine's view would perhaps also be (though he does not explicitly say this in the article under consideration) that those who believe in the distinction are inclined at least sometimes to mistake the characteristic of strongly resisting revision (which belongs to beliefs very centrally situated in the system) for the mythical characteristic of total immunity from revision.

(2) The connection between the second doctrine and the analytic-synthetic distinction runs, according to Quine, through the verification theory of meaning. He says: "If the verification theory can be accepted as an adequate account of statement synonymy, the notion of analyticity is saved after all." For, in the first place, two statements might be said to be synonymous if and only if any experiences which contribute to, or detract from, the confirmation of one contribute to, or detract from, the confirmation of the other, to the same degree; and, in the

second place, synonymy could be used to explain analyticity. But, Quine seems to argue, acceptance of any such account of synonymy can only rest on the mistaken belief that individual statements, taken in isolation from their fellows, can admit of confirmation or disconfirmation at all. As soon as we give up the idea of a set of experiential truth-conditions for each statement taken separately, we must give up the idea of explaining synonymy in terms of identity of such sets.

Now to show that the relations between these doctrines and the analytic-synthetic distinction are not as Quine supposes. Let us take the second doctrine first. It is easy to see that acceptance of the second doctrine would not compel one to abandon, but only to revise, the suggested explanation of synonymy. Quine does not deny that individual statements are regarded as confirmed or disconfirmed, are in fact rejected or accepted, in the light of experience. He denies only that these relations between single statements and experience hold independently of our attitudes to *other* statements. He means that experience can confirm or disconfirm an individual statement, only given certain assumptions about the truth or falsity of other statements. When we are faced with a "recalcitrant experience," he says, we always have a choice of what statements to amend. What we have to renounce is determined by what we are anxious to keep. This view, however, requires only a slight modification of the definition of statement-synonymy in terms of confirmation and disconfirmation. All we have to say now is that two statements are synonymous if and only if any experiences which, *on certain assumptions about the truth-values of other statements,* confirm or disconfirm one of the pair, also, *on the same assumptions,* confirm or disconfirm the other to the same degree. More generally, Quine wishes to substitute for what he conceives to be an oversimple picture of the confirmation-relations between particular statements and particular experiences, the idea of a looser relation which he calls "germaneness". . . . But however loosely "germaneness" is to be understood, it would apparently continue to make sense to speak of two statements as standing in the same germaneness-relation to the same particular experiences. So Quine's views are not only consistent with, but even suggest, an amended account of statement-synonymy along these lines. We are not, of course, concerned to defend such an account, or even to state it with any precision. We are only concerned to show that acceptance of Quine's doctrine of empirical confirmation does not, as he says it does, entail giving up the attempt to define statement-synonymy in terms of confirmation.

Now for the doctrine that there is no statement which is in principle immune from revision, no statement which might not be given up in the face of experience. Acceptance of this doctrine is quite consistent with adherence to the distinction between analytic and synthetic statements. Only, the adherent of *this* distinction must also insist on another; on the distinction between that kind of giving up which consists in merely admitting falsity, and that kind of giving up which involves changing or dropping a concept or set of concepts. Any form of words at one time held to express something true may, no doubt, at another time, come to be held to express something false. But it is not only philosophers who would distinguish between the case where this happens as the result of a change of opinion solely as to matters of fact, and the case where this happens at least partly as a result of a shift in the sense of the words. Where such a shift in the sense of the words is a necessary condition of the change in truth-value, then the adherent of the distinction will say that the form of words in question changes from expressing an analytic statement to expressing a synthetic statement. We are not now concerned, or called upon, to elaborate an adequate theory of conceptual revision, any more than we were called upon, just now, to elaborate an adequate theory of synonymy. If we can make sense of the idea that the same form of words, taken in one way (or bearing one sense), may express something true, and taken in another way (or bearing another sense), may express something false, then we can make sense of the idea of conceptual revision. And if we can make sense of this idea, then we can perfectly well preserve the distinction between the analytic and the synthetic, while conceding to Quine the revisability-in-principle of everything we say. As for the idea that the same form of words, taken in different ways, may bear different senses and perhaps be used to say things with different truth-values, the onus of showing that this is somehow a mistaken or confused idea rests squarely on Quine. The point of substance (or one of them) that Quine is making, by this emphasis on revisability, is that there is no absolute necessity about the adoption or use of any conceptual scheme whatever, or, more narrowly and in terms that he would reject, that there is no analytic proposition such that we *must* have linguistic forms bearing just the sense required to express that proposition. But it is one thing to admit this, and quite another thing to say that there are no necessities within any conceptual scheme we adopt or use, or, more narrowly again, that there are no linguistic forms which do express analytic propositions.

The adherent of the analytic-synthetic distinction may go further and admit that there may be cases (particularly perhaps in the field of science) where it would be pointless to press the question whether a change in the attributed truth-value of a statement represented a conceptual revision or not, and correspondingly pointless to press the analytic-synthetic distinction. We cannot quote such cases, but this inability may well be the result of ignorance of the sciences. In any case, the existence, if they do exist, of statements about which it is pointless to press the question whether they are analytic or synthetic, does not entail the nonexistence of statements which are clearly classifiable in one or other of these ways and of statements our hesitation over which has different sources, such as the possibility of alternative interpretations of the linguistic forms in which they are expressed.

This concludes our examination of Quine's article. It will be evident that our purpose has been wholly negative. We have aimed to show merely that Quine's case against the existence of the analytic-synthetic distinction is not made out. His article has two parts. In one of them, the notions of the analyticity group are criticized on the ground that they have not been adequately explained. In the other, a positive theory of truth is outlined, purporting to be incompatible with views to which believers in the analytic-synthetic distinction either must be, or are likely to be, committed. In fact, we have contended, no single point is established which those who accept the notions of the analyticity group would feel any strain in accommodating in their own system of beliefs. This is not to deny that many of the points raised are of the first importance in connection with the problem of giving a satisfactory general account of analyticity and related concepts. We are here only criticizing the contention that these points justify the rejection, as illusory, of the analytic-synthetic distinction and the notions which belong to the same family.

**FURTHER READING**

Mates (2)
Sommers
R. Taylor

# ༺ ANALYTIC-SYNTHETIC

## Jonathan Bennett

## 1. Introductory

The aim of this paper is to attack Quine's views on the analytic-synthetic distinction (ASD), but more than half of it will be devoted to arguing that an attack is still required. This preliminary thesis is based on the claim that what Quine presents as (1) an attack on the ASD, followed by (2) some remarks about confirmation and disconfirmation, offers a more formidable obstacle to the adherent of the traditional ASD if (2) is built into (1) as a positive but unwelcome theory of the ASD.

I shall argue that a proponent of this broadly Quinean theory of the ASD has a crucial advantage over most of Quine's critics who have so far published, namely that if the Quinean theory is correct then it is possible clearly and cogently to explain the ASD to someone who does not yet understand any intensional terminology at all. I shall try to give such an explanation in terms of the Quinean theory, and to show that there are some grounds for pessimism as to the chances of the rival theory's being able to do as well. Formal definitions of intensional terms always involve other intensional terms, of

From Jonathan Bennett, "Analytic-Synthetic", *Proceedings of the Aristotelian Society*, LIX (1958–59), pp. 163–188. Reprinted by permission of the Honorary Secretary and Editor of the Aristotelian Society.

course, but I shall argue that *any* of the usual non-Quinean ways of explaining intensional terminology, however informally, essentially involve a prior understanding of other intensional terms.

Grice and Strawson . . . offer one such explanation, freely admit that it is not a *full* explanation of the intensional term concerned, but claim that at least 'it breaks out of the family circle [of intensional terms]'. I shall argue that this is not true. But this leaves open the question whether they would grant that the provision of explanations which break out of the family circle is a necessary condition of the acceptability of intensional terminology as a whole (and the related question, whether they grant that the *way* in which one breaks out of the circle must determine what theoretical remarks one permits oneself about intensional terminology). An assumption which will underlie the whole of this paper is that such explanations *are* required. One may of course understand a group of words without being capable in practice of explaining their meaning in terms of words outside the group; but if one believes that such explanations are not even in principle available, then I do not see how one can justifiably hold to the claim to understand the words concerned, unless one can indicate how their meaning could be learned non-verbally (presumably through some sort of ostensive procedure), an option which I do not think anyone regards as open in the case of the intensional family circle. Reading between the lines of 'In Defense of a Dogma' . . . I suspect that Grice and Strawson share this assumption that there would be something radically suspect about a family of intensional words of which no extra-familiar explanation *could* be given. But I may be wrong about this.

## 2. *A Quinean Analysis of the ASD*

Any given person at any given time has a corpus of belief which is registered in a class of sentences which he calls or is disposed to call true (or, for brevity, 'sentences which he accepts'). In the light of experience, he from time to time alters the membership of his class of accepted sentences, because some experiences put him in a position such that if he is to be rational he *must* deny something he has hitherto accepted (or, for brevity, 'because some experiences are recalcitrant [relative to his class of accepted sentences]'). In making a linguistic adjustment in face of a recalcitrant experience, any given sentence *may* be retained in the class of accepted sentences; and any given sentence *may* be banished from that class in face of some re- calcitrant experience.

Some comments: (1) The notion of recalcitrance may be broken down further into the notions of an 'observation sen- tence', of 'having to accept an observation sentence in the light of experience', and of 'inconsistency between an observation sentence and a totality of other accepted sentences'. This kind of inconsistency can be unproblematical for someone who nev- ertheless does have a problem about inconsistency between non-observation-sentences or about inconsistency between an observation-sentence and a small class of non-observation-sen- tences. Of course, anyone who believes himself to possess inde- pendent reasons for denying that any sentence can function just to report on a present experience, will not accept this elab- oration of the notion of recalcitrance: the debate on *that* issue has only a terminological relevance to the problems here under discussion. The main thing to notice is that if one does believe that there is a class of present-tense sentences which do nothing but report on present experience then one will locate them in the way just indicated: one will say that these sentences are simply forced on us by experience, but that in the reconciling of any accepted sentences of this sort with a hitherto accepted totality of other sentences, any other sentence may be retained and any may be rejected. (2) The fact that any sentence may be retained becomes obvious upon consideration of the ways in which counter-evidence can be explained away by the acceptance of hitherto rejected sentences (as in 'The barometer must have been playing up'); and upon consideration of the fact that a sentence can always be retained by changing its meaning appropriately. (I here use intensional terminology, but only to point to an uncontroversial aspect of a familiar phenomenon.) (3) Similarly, the fact that experience may lead us to reject any given sentence is just the fact that any synthetic sentence may be falsified by the empirical facts, and that any analytic sentence may become false through a meaning-change which is brought about by the occur- rence of recalcitrant experiences. Some people who grant that any sentence could be rendered false by a meaning-change nevertheless claim that with only a small class of sentences is it possible to describe a state of affairs which would invite a meaning-change such as to render the sentence false. I see no reason to believe this, and as an indication of how to look for such a description in a given case, I suggest the following: associated with any analytic sentence there is a range of synthetic sentences stating facts about the world in virtue of which it is convenient that the words in the analytic sentence should have the meanings they do have; suppose a falsification of a judiciously selected sub-set of these synthetic sentences, and you are well on the way to describing a state of affairs which invites the falsification of the analytic sentence.

To return to our description of a range of linguistic facts which could be known and understood by someone who had no understanding of any intensional words: If two different adjustments in the face of a recalcitrant experience are envisaged, one of which produces a totality of accepted sentences which is a very great deal simpler than that resulting from the other adjustment, then the former will be chosen. The notion of simplicity used here cannot be made very precise: sometimes the greater simplicity of one totality will consist in its greater adaptability to mathematical handling; sometimes in its relative economy of basic vocabulary; sometimes in its being able to say in fewer words than the other anything that the other can say. Other criteria than simplicity also operate in these decisions, but it seems clear that wherever this criterion applies decisively in favour of one totality against another, an acceptance of the latter totality will be condemned as irrational. In some such cases it is said that the former embodies a more satisfactory conceptual scheme than the latter; in others, that certain members of the latter totality are being retained only at the cost of arbitrary and implausible saving devices of various sorts; and sometimes one would not know which of these descriptions to adopt. In the meantime we need only note the plain kind of fact which is pointed to by either description. There is a further plain fact. If someone is confronted with a recalcitrant experience, the various alternative adjustments which he may make to his hitherto accepted totality may be compared not only in respect of the simplicity of the resultant totality in each case, but also in respect of the extensiveness of the adjustment necessary to reach the resultant totality in each case. Often, if not always, the least extensive adjustment consists in dismissing the recalcitrant experience as illusory; but if this way out is taken often enough the resultant totality will be more complex—because less thoroughly organised—than would have been a totality which was more trouble to arrive at. I take an adjustment to be more extensive than another if it involves the acceptance of more hitherto rejected sentences than the other, or the rejection of more hitherto accepted sentences than the other. The two halves of this criterion do not conflict in the cases with which I am concerned.

Further: A person at a given time can have a certain amount of information about individual members of his set of accepted sentences, information as to the extensiveness of *any* adjustment of which their rejection formed a part. He will have such information about, say, the sentence *S* if he knows that in his currently accepted set there are many sentences his acceptance of which he justifies by arguments in which *S* occurs and which he cannot justify by arguments using only sentences he now accepts but not using *S*. For in such a case he will know that any adjustment in which *S* is rejected will lead to a resultant totality of accepted sentences in which either (a) membership is denied to the sentences whose present defence requires *S*, or (b) membership is accorded to new sentences which provide alternative ways of justifying the continued acceptance of the sentences in question.

For example: Accepted sentences of the form (i) 'The temperature of such-and-such a star is such-and-such' depend, for those who accept them, on sentences of the form (ii) 'Temperature correlates with light-emission in such-and-such ways', and these depend on sentences of the form (iii) 'Temperature correlates with mercury-column readings in such-and-such ways', and these in their turn depend on sentences along the lines of (iv) 'Temperature has to do with the obtaining of such-and-such sensations.' Rejection of (ii) jeopardises (i) and all that depends on it; rejection of (iii) jeopardises (i) and (ii); rejection of (iv) jeopardises all the other three.

This example brings out the fact that the most straightforward cases of commensurability of two or more sentences in respect of how much depends on them are those cases where the sentences have a general term (or an abstract noun) in common and where one sentence is said to have more depending on it than another simply because the second sentence itself depends on the first. The example also helps to bring out the fact that where $S_1$ and $S_2$ both involve a general term $F$, and where $S_1$ depends on $S_2$, the situation can be described as one in which $S_2$ states necessary and/or sufficient conditions for $F$ness which are employed in establishing $S_1$. In what follows, when I wish to say that one sentence shares a general term with another and has more depending on it than depends on the other, I shall say that it is *less dispensable* than the other.

Now the point of all this is that a candid observer of the linguistic scene, having noted all these facts and having listened to uses of intensional terminology, might very well conclude that to call a sentence 'analytic' is to register a conviction that it is highly indispensable—less dispensable than any sentence which shares a general term with it and which is called 'synthetic'. It might be argued that such a belief about the meaning of 'analytic' *must* be wrong, on the grounds that if that were what people intend by their use of intensional terminology then they would not make the theoretical remarks *about* intensional terminology which in fact they do make. But if the holder of the belief were led by it to draw the analytic-synthetic line just where everyone else draws it, and if his critics were unable to challenge his account of intensional terminology by producing a counter-theory, then most of us would grant that he was entitled to be satisfied with his theory and to remain unconvinced by opponents' protests that his story, though extensionally adequate, was wrong in some way which they were unable to express except in words which would be intelligible only to the already converted (*i.e.*, to those who already claimed to understand intensional terminology, and agreed that this account of it was wrong).

In fact, I cannot prove that this theory is extensionally adequate. But I do claim that it is, at least, fairly plausible: any discovery about all the $F$'s presupposes one or more tests for $F$ness (one or more answers to questions of the form 'How do you know it *was* an $F$?') and provides a new test which could be used in the establishing of yet further generalisations about the $F$'s. It therefore seems reasonable to envisage a hierarchy of all the accepted sentences about the $F$'s: with the upper regions occupied by synthetic generalisations which have seldom or never provided tests for $F$ness in the establishment of other generalisations; the middle regions occupied by generalisations which are still synthetic but which—because they are better established, or longer established, or in some way more versatile—have more often been used as tools in the establishment of other generalisations; and the lower regions occupied by the analytic generalisations on which the establishment of all the others depends.

Quine does not talk about the comparative indispensability of sentences; but he does compare sentences in respect of their 'distance from the periphery' of our totality of accepted sentences, and I offer 'indispensability' as a literal version of what (I think) he is getting at with this metaphor.

Two features of the theory at present under discussion appear to give some difficulty:

(1) It has been objected that on this theory of the ASD a sentence may be analytic though false. For although 'analytic at $t_1$' is defined only for sentences accepted at $t_1$, the theory seems to allow that one might accept a sentence at $t_1$, correctly call it 'analytic' at $t_1$, reject it at $t_2$, and claim (at $t_2$) that it was false, though accepted and indeed highly indispensable, at $t_1$; whence it follows that at $t_2$ it was both analytic and false. But this whole argument rests upon the distinction between '$S$ was true but is now false' and '$S$ was false all the time, though we thought it to be true.' This is a perfectly good distinction, of course, but it is a thoroughly intensional one: to the best of my knowledge, it can be elucidated only by means of standard intensional terminology, in such phrases as 'true with the meaning it then had, false with the meaning it now has'. An objection based on this distinction is thus illegitimate unless the objector is prepared to claim that the distinction is in some way so much clearer and plainer than the other intensional notions that once we have shown their relations with it (and they can indeed be defined in terms of it) there is nothing more that needs to be said. On the Quinean theory I am now exploring, furthermore, this distinction will be made just as everyone makes it; it will have the standard formal relations with the ASD, and thus it will *not* be the case that any sentence is analytic and false. I

shall show in a more convenient place (in the next section) just how this conclusion fails to be derivable.

(2) The theory defines the ASD only for sets of sentences having a general term in common. It draws a line, for instance, between 'Obligatory actions are permissible' on the one hand, and 'Bigamy is sometimes permissible' and 'Obligatory actions are tiresome' on the other, while cheerfully admitting that the first sentence is incommensurable with 'Some mammals are oviparous.' It has been objected that this is a difference between the ASD according to this theory and the ASD as usually drawn; for, it is said when one says that 'Obligatory actions are permissible' is analytic while 'Some mammals are oviparous' is synthetic, one is making a distinction based on a direct comparison between these two sentences. How one takes this objection must depend upon what is meant by 'direct' comparison. Is a 'direct' contrast made between a mouse and a hamster when a nutrition researcher reports that after the first six weeks of an experiment the mouse was overgrown (*i.e.,* larger than most mice of its age and type) while the hamster was not overgrown (*i.e.,* not larger than most hamsters of its age and type)? If so, then the Quinean theory now under discussion *does* admit of 'direct' comparison between the members of any analytic/synthetic pair. If not, then what *is* meant by 'direct'? It seems unlikely that this point could be pressed further except as the conclusion of an argument most of which would range over more familiar territory. That is, it seems to me to be a dangerous procedure for anyone to try to take a *basic* stand on the dubious notion of directness, just as it would be dangerous to take a basic stand on the undubious but equally peripheral notion of the distinction between 'was true, is false' and 'was false all along, though accepted'.

The theory I am trying to elaborate appears to be unacceptable to most if not all of those who regard themselves as in a general way opponents of Quine's views on these matters. I think it is fair to say that the crucial feature to which they object is the theory's claim that the ASD marks a difference (in a quite straightforward sense) of *degree,* whereas they claim that it marks a difference (in some sense) of *kind.* Perhaps the most concrete result of this disagreement is that, according to the Quinean theory, a great deal of talk about *deciding* whether something is to be analytic or not is simply out of place. Sometimes we genuinely do not know whether a given sentence has the required degree of indispensability, and then talk about *discovery* is in order. But there is, on the Quinean theory, a large class of cases where we cannot say whether a sentence is analytic or not simply because the analytic/synthetic borderline is an indeterminate one—there just is no way of stating an exact measure of *how* much more indispensable $S$ (containing $F$) must be than most of the other sentences containing $F$ for one to call it 'analytic'—and in these cases, the Quinean theorist will say, it is inappropriate to talk (with the naïve) of discovery, and equally inappropriate to talk (with the sophisticated) of decision. There is nothing to discover, and nothing to decide.

For expository purposes I shall adopt the label 'PQ' for an imaginary proponent of the Quinean theory. PQ, then, is a man who defends the positive thesis that *the workaday employment of the ASD and related intensional terminology can be understood in terms of degrees of indispensability,* and the negative thesis that *none of the arguments which have so far appeared in the literature succeeds in showing that there is any reason for treating the ASD in quite a different way, notably in such a way that it can be called a distinction in kind rather than in degree.*

The next section will be primarily concerned with the second, negative thesis; but some of its points will be made through discussions of various sorts of challenge to PQ's positive thesis.

## 3. Quinean Theory v. Traditional Theory

The most obvious criticism to make of PQ's theory is that it is simply false, in that 'analytic' registers recognition not of some unspecified but high degree of indispensability but rather recognition that denial is not rationally possible *at all* in respect of the sentence called analytic.

This takes us over old territory. PQ's reply would be: 'But sentences universally called analytic have come to be denied in face of the facts, and any sentence now called analytic might come to suffer the same fate.' The proper response would be something like this: 'Certainly, analytic sentences have come to be said with "It is not the case that . . ." put in front of them. But in calling them analytic in the first place we were talking about the sentences with the meanings they then had; for denial to be rationally possible, the meanings had to change. Or, to put it another way, the word "analytic" strictly applies to propositions rather than to sentences; when we seem to call a sentence analytic, we are really applying the word to the proposition *then* expressed by the sentence.'

Taking up the part of this which uses the phrase 'change of meaning' and its cognates, could not PQ answer somewhat as follows: 'You have added to my theory, but you have not contradicted it. For, what is it for a meaning to change? Surely, it is for a sentence, to the effect that a word applies to certain sorts of things, to have once had and no longer to have a high degree of indispensability: thus change of meaning shades into unexpectedness of application, the borderline between the two corresponding to the ASD in such a way that it is true, as you say, that the denial of a hitherto analytic sentence is the changing of a meaning. But what makes this a *criticism* of what I have been saying?'

In dealing with the part of his critic's remarks which depends on the word 'proposition', PQ could say something like this: 'So far as I can work out this "proposition" terminology, the proposition expressed by $S_1$ at $t_1$ is different from the proposition expressed by $S_1$ at $t_2$ if and only if an appropriate set of sentences of the form "$S_1$ is true if and only if $S_n$ is true" which are highly indispensable at $t_1$ are not highly indispensable at $t_2$. So that a hitherto analytic sentence can be denied only if it comes to express a different proposition from the one it formerly expressed—a conclusion which I welcome as a perfectly consistent addition to my original theory.'

This dialogue is essentially a discussion of the ASD in terms of the formal relationships holding amongst certain intensional terms. Many more could be given, threading through the network from 'proposition' to 'synonymous' to 'necessary' to 'impossible', and so on. We know that this will achieve nothing to our present purpose for, as Quine has shown, the family is such a tightly knit one that someone who had trouble over one of its members would be likely to have trouble over all of them. In the light of PQ's positive thesis (his analysis of the ASD), however, the moral to be drawn from the smoothness of passage around the family circle is not so much that trouble with one involves trouble with all as that a theory which is (arguably) extensionally adequate for one will be (arguably) extensionally adequate for all. And with respect to PQ's negative thesis (his, and my, critique of the standard attempts to elucidate intensional terminology as a whole), the moral is that this kind of approach will be *entirely* unhelpful to someone who does not already understand some members of the circle: if the inter-relations had to be stated in a series of biconditionals which *almost* held—so that room was left for explanations, not involving intensional terminology, of some or all of the ways in which the biconditionals failed to hold exactly—then it might be useful to look to these formal relations for help. As it is, we must turn to explanatory devices of a different sort—to what we can loosely call informal explanations.

Before doing so, mention should be made of one sort of compromise of the smoothness with which intensional terms can be related to one another by simple biconditionals, namely the debates which break out from time to time over these biconditionals themselves: arguments over the equation of 'possibly possible' with 'possible', of '*a priori*' with 'analytic', of entailment with the analytic conditional, of propositional identity with reciprocal entailment, and so on. But the existence of these need not embarrass PQ, for they contain nothing on which the participants agree and the acceptance of which would create difficulties for PQ in respect of his positive thesis. Nor could such arguments be claimed to provide any illumination at all for someone who did not understand any intensional terms. Indeed, PQ could with some justice claim that the inconclusiveness of these debates points directly to the need for some such clarification of the ASD as he has offered.

I propose to consider four sorts of informal locution which are frequently used to explain in a non-question-begging way something about the way in which intensional terminology is to be used and, in particular, to give explanations which will result in the ASD's being a distinction in *kind*, in some sense incompatible with PQ's theory of the ASD. Discussion of these ways of talking will therefore be relevant to both PQ's positive and his negative theses.

(1) The whole problem would be settled in favour of PQ's opponents if a distinction in kind could be established between

*factual revision* and *conceptual revision;* and it has been suggested that such a distinction begins to emerge if we consider factual *disagreements* and conceptual *disagreements*—the latter being understood as disagreements over the practical problem of which conceptual scheme to adopt—and notice that the former are always in principle capable of settlement while the latter may well go on for ever without any lack of candour or energy on the part of the disputants. This suggestion, though, could well be snatched at by PQ as offering the basis for a point in his favour. For the one way in which a factual disagreement may steadily and stubbornly resist resolution is by one disputant's insisting on accommodating any evidence which tells against his thesis by the adoption of supplementary postulates of some appropriate sort; but if he does this to an enormous degree of complexity and arbitrariness, while his opponent can defend *his* view without being driven to such shifts, it would usually be said that the former was being unreasonable and that he *should* allow the disagreement to be settled against him. And a conceptual disagreement can be settled (for all reasonable men) in all and only those situations where the adoption of one conceptual scheme has no advantage over the adoption of the other, and has the disadvantage of involving a much greater degree of complexity in what is said about the facts. The criteria for settlement of the two sorts of dispute are, in brief, identical.

It is true that when one party to a dispute persistently refuses (in the elaborate and perverse way just indicated) to lose the argument, he is often said to have turned the dispute into a 'merely conceptual' one. This way of talking suggests that in conceptual disputes the criteria for the reasonableness of a party to a factual dispute do not apply in the same way; and PQ is obliged to account for this use of 'merely conceptual'.

On his own showing, PQ is entitled to point out that someone who seems to depart from the usual criteria of reasonableness in one area of debate may naturally be assumed either to be unreasonable or to have in mind the ramifications of what he is saying into other areas altogether, and thus very likely to be concerned with the long-range benefits to be gained from the denial of one or more sentences which his opponent calls analytic. But such a man might be hoping to derive long-range benefits of simplicity at the cost of complexity in this one area, by

propounding a new *scientific* theory, *i.e.*, one which challenges
only sentences which would be called synthetic. If the latter is
the case, then PQ must say that we are simply wrong to say 'He
is turning the dispute into a merely conceptual one', and there is
an onus upon him to explain why it is that we are so ready to
say this when there is always the other possibility.

An explanation, however, seems to be available: As a rule,
when one is faced with a recalcitrant experience there is no time
for conceptual revision (the long, hard route to an outcome)
even when in the long run a conceptual revision would be the
most rational move to make; and thus the standard case of conceptual revision is the situation in which there is an accommodation of all the known facts, but its degree of complexity is such
as to suggest (in a quiet hour) that it might be worth while to
try to simplify it, if necessary the hard way. There is a tendency
therefore to think of conceptual revision in terms of a move from
one accommodation to another, and of factual revision in terms
of the situation where one is faced with a recalcitrant experience,
*i.e.*, where one does not have an accommodation of all the facts.
But there is no reason in principle why a recalcitrant experience
should not be given an on-the-spot accommodation which
involves conceptual revision, or why an accommodation of all
the known facts should not be turned quietly into something
simpler by means of a factual revision.

If it be claimed that the point of the remark 'He is turning it
into a merely conceptual dispute' is simply to say that he is not
*going* to back down in the light of *anything* else that may happen, then the remark is a simple, though possibly justified, accu-
sation of irrationality. If it doesn't sound accusatory to the casual
ear, then so much the worse (PQ might add) for the effect on
the casual ear of bad theories of confirmation and of the ASD.

(2) An elucidatory and anti-Quinean power is often
claimed for such locutions as this: 'The world can't make me
wrong about that, whereas with this other it is always *possible*
that something will happen which will make me withdraw it.'
But PQ can reply: 'The first half of what you have just said is
true only if you fail to take into account certain sorts of possibility of falsification, namely, all the possibilities the simplest
accommodations of which would involve the denial of highly

indispensable sentences now called analytic. *Of course* there is a bump in the scale if you cut part of it off; but if you take the whole situation into account, the continuity is still there. And if your remarks of the form "I can't be shown wrong about *that*" refer not to sentences but to the propositions they express, then you have indeed established a discontinuity between "analytic" and "synthetic" when these words are applied to propositions; but this is of no interest, since the "proposition" terminology itself is built out of the "sentence" terminology (in my theory, anyway, and I am still waiting to be shown that it is wrong) in such a way that propositional identity shades smoothly into propositional non-identity; so that the discontinuity which you seem to have established is illusory.'

One comment: This line of argument invites the hostile question 'Are you saying that until we know whether later developments are going to lead us to withdraw an analytic sentence, we can't be confident that it is true *now*?' This question's hostility derives from its tacit assumption of the distinction, mentioned earlier, between 'was true, is false' and 'was false all along, though accepted'. There are countless ways in which this distinction can insinuate itself into the debate, but perhaps this one should be dealt with, for its own sake and as an example of the way in which, it seems, we must handle 'true' if we wish to beg no questions about intensional terminology. What PQ must say is that, if $S$ is accepted at $t_1$, and rejected at $t_2$, the way to settle at $t_2$ whether $S$ was false at $t_1$ is to find out whether its rejection came about as part of an over-all adjustment which included the rejection of sentences which were at $t_1$ indispensable enough to warrant the label 'analytic'. If $S$ was rejected without going as deep as the rejection of anything analytic, then it is proper to describe $S$ as having been false, though accepted; but if its rejection was, or was accompanied by, the rejection of an analytic sentence, then there is no reason at $t_2$ for saying that $S$ was false at $t_1$. The upshot of this is that to be false is to be due for what we might call superficial rejection; and it follows that if a sentence is analytic at $t_1$ it will never be proper to say that it was false at $t_1$; if it is synthetic at $t_1$ it may become proper to say that it was false at $t_1$; both of which are just the results we should expect if PQ's theory is to be viable at all. And, as regards his negative thesis, it is simply a mistake to think that these results can be used to *make* the ASD in the first place.

(3) 'I base my acceptance of that simply on my knowledge of the use of words, but no one is rationally entitled to accept this other just on such a slim basis as the use of words.' To this PQ can reply: 'The trouble with that sort of talk is that it draws the line you wish to draw only by construing the phrase "use of words" in a highly special way. Is it a fact about how words are used that the word "non-human" applies to everything to which the phrase "born in Antarctica" applies? You will have to say "No"; and if the enquirer into the meaning of intensional terminology then asks you what you *do* count as being "about the use of words", you will presumably have to follow all the others who have travelled this route and refer him to rules of *meaning* or something of the sort. You cannot avoid the use of "meaning" by appealing to dictionaries: they give all sorts of information which you wouldn't want to regard as analytic; and if you appeal not to dictionaries as they sit there on the shelf, but to dictionaries considered as fulfilling the characteristic lexicographic function, then we are back at "meaning" again. So your appeal to "use of words" seems to be just another *instance* of what I am saying in my negative thesis. And if your original pair of remarks is appropriately amended by substituting "meanings" for "use", it becomes manifestly harmless to my positive thesis.'

(4) 'If you denied that, I shouldn't have any idea of what you were getting at—I should be simply bewildered—but if you denied this other, I should be surprised but I should know what to expect.' PQ can reply: 'That is true only because of the way you have selected your cases. If you take some sentence which we both regard as synthetic and which we both have, and know each other to have, powerful reasons for regarding as true and none worth mentioning for regarding as false; and if I then deny that sentence; you will be just as bewildered as you would be if I said that I had drawn a square circle. If I say "It will rain this afternoon" you will take an umbrella; if I say "It will both rain and be fine all afternoon" you won't know what to do—agreed; but if, as we look out of the window at the sunshine, I say "It is

raining so hard that you shouldn't go out", which of the other two situations is this more like?'

This fourth example is the one given by Grice and Strawson, and I am indebted to Mr. Grice for, amongst much else, some comments on my treatment of it. He grants that 'It is raining so hard that you shouldn't go out' may be bewildering *in some circumstances,* but says that it is not *prima facie* bewildering as is 'It will both rain and be fine all afternoon.' But what does '*prima facie*' mean here? The only relevant sense I can attach to it is 'bewildering whatever one does or does not happen to know about the world', and even this is relevant only if one excludes that set of facts to which adherents of the traditional ASD constantly appeal—the behavioural facts determining what is to be said about meanings. If this set of facts can be located in a non-question-begging way, then we can save example (4), or even by-pass it and perform the more useful task of saving example (3). But *can* it be located in the way required? The fact that Grice and Strawson select an approach through bewilderingness suggests, perhaps misleadingly, that they are pessimistic about the chances of making a successful frontal attack on 'meaning'; such a pessimism would certainly be justified by the literature. In brief, then, it seems that the difference-in-kind alleged in example (4) to constitute a partial elucidation of the ASD has to be understood in terms of the notion of a sentence's being bewildering to anyone who knows the *meanings* of its constituent terms even if that is all he knows. Indeed, this fact is explicitly recognised by Grice and Strawson when they say, rightly, that the denial of an analytic sentence will be bewildering only if one assumes that the words involved are not being used in 'a figurative or unusual sense'. This is a use of intensional terminology in defence of 'Denials of analytic sentences are bewildering' which is exactly parallel to the use of intensional teminology which I have just tried to show to be necessary in defence of 'Denials of synthetic sentences are not bewildering.' In each case it seems that the explanation of intensional terminology—granted that it is intended to be only partial and (perhaps) approximate—cannot be given *at all* without the use of intensional terminology. In the light of all this, it is not clear to me what Grice and Strawson wish to claim when they say that their explanation 'breaks out of the family circle'. Certainly, it does not 'break out' in the sense of that phrase presupposed in the first section of the present paper.

Nor of course do examples (2) and (3). They, like (4) and like every attempt I have met at an informal but non-question-begging explanation of all or part of the intensional family circle, simply do beg the question. I do not maintain that the family circle cannot be broken out of: indeed, the next section of the present article will constitute an attempt to break out of it. But I have tried to establish that it is not an easy circle to break out of, that a number of plausible attempts to do so fail, and that some case can be made for breaking out of it in the sort of way suggested by Quine's work on confirmation-theory, *i.e.,* along the lines of the 'indispensability' theory expounded above.

## 4. A Non-Quinean Theory of the ASD

A rough account of what is to be attempted in this section may be given as follows: Instead of taking the statement that some sentences are traditionally analytic (*i.e.,* in a sense such that the Quinean analysis is not adequate) in every confirmation-situation and then forlornly trying to qualify it, putting 'proposition' for 'sentence' and the like, in such a way as to make it true, I shall make an independent attempt to establish the weaker statement that in every confirmation-situation some sentence (meaning *sentence*) is traditionally analytic. Just what this means should emerge in the course of the argument.

As a starting-point, let us consider a story of the sort told in illustration of Quine's thesis that no sentence undergoes, solo, confirmation or disconfirmation at the hands of any experience. For example: We find in Australia those birds which in fact led people to say that there are black swans; and the finding of them is a recalcitrant experience, in the sense that now that this has happened *something* of what we have been accustomed to saying must be denied. In this particular case, easily the best thing to sacrifice is 'All swans are white' and a few others; but we could save this and instead sacrifice 'Birds which are thus and so are swans' together with a good deal of our taxonomy and the natural history depending on it; or we could save all that too, and sacrifice instead 'Nothing is black all over and white all over' together with very large stretches of talk which depend upon certain features of our use of colour-terminology; or . . . etc., etc. There are many intermediate possibilities, such as the introduction of geographical qualifications into the laws of optics, and an acceptance of consequent revisions of physics and neurophysiology; and no remark about the consequences of any particular sacrifice is absolute: we can drive a wedge between any sentence and any other sentence so long as we are prepared to pay an appropriate price.

It is of first importance to notice that this pattern of disconfirmation does not ever allow us to say 'Well, if I *can* save S, then I *shall* save it and there's an end of the matter': the end of the matter always comes just after a sacrifice, not just after a save. If this were not so, there would be no such thing as recalcitrance.

A question which can be raised after the saving of any sentence—say of $S_1$—is 'Why must I make some other sacrifice?' The answer must be of the form 'Because the set of sentences you now accept is inconsistent with the occurrence of the experience $E$'; but Quine must give this answer in the special form 'Because you accept the sentence $S_2$ which compels you, now that $E$ has occurred, to sacrifice $S_1$.' One could save $S_2$ as well, but then some other sacrifice must be made, 'Because you accept $S_3$ which compels you, now that $E$ has occurred, to reject either $S_1$ or $S_2$.' Now, the trouble with this is that Quine must refuse to allow the process to come to an end. For the only way in which he can call a halt at, say the $n$th step is to answer the $n$th asking of 'Why must I make some other sacrifice?' with 'Because it just *is* the case, whatever else you may be given to saying, that in the light of experience $E$ you cannot retain the conjunction $S_1.S_2$ . . . $S_n$'; and this would be tantamount to admitting that there is a sentence (albeit a long one) which is, in isolation, strongly disconfirmed by an experience.

There is no logical objection to this infinite regress. The most likely form for it to take would be for members of a small group of logical laws to appear repeatedly, first 'neat', then in instances of ever-increasing length, each instance being formed by the substitution *of* laws which have already occurred in the regress *in* laws which have already occurred in the regress. This could go on for as long as one liked, without its becoming simply repetitious.

But although the question 'Why must some other sacrifice be made?' can always be answered without repetition—*i.e.*, without appealing to any member of the group of sentences whose joint saving is in question—it is not at all clear that it can always be answered also with truth. Certainly, it is true for only a finite number of distinct values of *s* that *s* is in a literal sense a sentence which Smith calls true: Smith has considered at most a few million sentences, many of those he calls false, and of the rest only a few dozen are likely to be relevant in a given confirmation-situation. So we must look for some sense in which we can say that each sacrifice is forced upon Smith by a sentence which he already regards as true, without our having to admit that the relevant sentence has in fact ever been explicitly considered by Smith.

It might seem possible to avoid the difficulty by construing 'Smith calls *S* true' at least sometimes as 'Smith calls true something which leads by logic to *S*', thus making it possible for Smith to call true an infinity of sentences, gathered into bundles each of which consists of the logical consequences of some sentence which Smith *explicitly* calls true. But this device does not solve the problem, for the conditions under which something 'follows by logic' from something else are precisely what the Quinean theory is about anyway. Whether we give the centre of our attention to the possibility of gathering sentences into bundles, or to the more general problem of sacrifices and saves, it remains true wherever Quine says that one sentence follows by logic from another he must allow each step in the 'following from' to be the locus of a possible sacrifice of something called true. Therefore, no attempt of this sort to tie 'sentences called true' into bundles can effect any reduction in the number of sentences *explicitly* called true, for (to put it another way) in each bundle there can be no more member-sentences than there are sentences holding the bundle together, and each of the latter sentences must be either explicitly called true or be a member of a further bundle which is held together by further sentences each of which is either . . . and so on, *ad infinitum*.

Consider Achilles and the Tortoise in Lewis Carroll's story. Their trouble had its origin in the Tortoise's refusal to allow any sort of move from premise to conclusion—his tacit departure from the usual convention whereby any move from antecedent to consequent of an analytic conditional is deemed legitimate, without replacing this convention by either a more or a less liberal one. The result of this is, so to speak, a refusal to treat anything as analytic: every step must be explicitly justified before it can be taken and, since *justifying* is itself *taking a step,* this means that no step can be taken at all.

This relates closely to the difficulty confronting Quine. Although his stress is not upon the alleged need explicitly to justify each step in an argument but rather on the alleged possibility of making any step illegitimate by the taking of appropriate avoiding action, the former implies the latter and therefore shares its difficulties: for the only way in which it can be the case (as Quine seems committed to saying it is) that any logical move from one sentence to another can be avoided by the denial of some other sentence the assertion of which is necessary for the legitimacy of the move, is for it to be the case (as the Tortoise pretends it is) that for any logical move from one sentence to another there is some sentence the assertion of which is necessary for the legitimacy of the move.

Another suggestion for the required sense of 'calls true' is simply that of 'is disposed to call true', which would solve the problem of finitude at once. Following out the consequences of this suggestion: Smith registers $E$'s recalcitrance; decides (perhaps) to retain every relevant sentence he has ever formulated; but then—being honest and energetic—casts around to formulate and then reject some sentence which he has never explicitly considered before but which has the following two properties: (i) If it *had* been put to him before $E$ occurred he *would* have called it true (and thus it is, in the sense of this paper, a sentence which was until $E$'s occurrence a member of the set of sentences 'accepted by' Smith); (ii) Formulation and rejection of it provides an accommodation of $E$—*i.e.,* modifies Smith's set of accepted sentences in such a way that $E$ is no longer recalcitrant with respect to it.

Suppose, though, that Smith's energy is not equal to his honesty, and that his reaction to the recalcitrant experience goes like this instead: he decides to retain every relevant sentence he has ever formulated; he acknowledges that there must be some sentence which he has never thought about but (a) which he would in the past have called true if it had been put to him, and (b) which he must not in future call true if he does ever confront it in an explicit form; he decides not to go hunting for it now but to forget the whole matter until such a sentence does turn up; but even then he does not guarantee to reject the *first* such sentence to turn up. Can he not claim that by thus disposing himself to recognise and reject some such sentence he is, *a fortiori,* disposing himself to reject some such sentence? And is not this all that is required for him to have effected an accommodation of *E*? It is clear that if this pattern of 'accommodation' is followed often enough, we shall begin to question Smith's honesty: it will before long be fair to say 'He doesn't back down on *anything:* he keeps saying that he *could* straighten it all out by means of [no doubt] a conceptual revision, but he never produces the conceptual revision.' But, while it seems clear that this would be a legitimate charge, it is not easy to see why it should be so if the original suggestion—that the recalcitrance-producing pressure could come from a sentence Smith has been disposed to call true but has never formulated —is correct. For if we combine the Quinean claim that whatever sentences we retain in the face of *E* there is always some remaining way of accommodating *E*, with the current proposal that recalcitrance may be created by a combination of sentences-thought-of-but-still-retained with sentences-still-unformulated, there seems to be no reason at all why the ever-possible saving adjustments in face of *E* should not remain in the latter category of sentences-still-unformulated.

Someone who combines these two views is, of course, entitled to a natural suspicion of Smith's forever unsubstantiated claims to be able in practice to carry out the required formulations and rejections; but there is no reason why Smith should make such claims in the first place. On the view I am now considering, there is no reason why Smith should not admit that *he* cannot *show* that it is all right for him to say the things that he does say, and simply adduce general Quinean theory as his reason for saying that nevertheless there must always *be* some way in which this *could* be shown. In brief: We have here two kinds of generosity—Quine's about our freedom of choice in making adjustments, and the other about our right to keep silent—

which *together* produce the result that there is nothing theoretically wrong with refusing to let experience modify anything we actually say.

I conclude that neither the 'follows by logic' nor the 'disposed to call true' approaches will solve the difficulty with which this section has been concerned; and the apparent absence of any viable alternative solution leads to the conclusion that in any experiential situation, if the experiences involved are to offer a challenge to *any* sentences then there must be some sentences to which they offer no challenge at all—some sentences which simply are not up for possible revision in the particular situation concerned. This is what was meant by the declaration with which this section began: in every confirmation-situation, some sentence is traditionally analytic.

It may look as though this claim is weak not only in respect of its placing of the crucial quantifier, but also in respect of the way in which that quantifier is to be understood; that is, it might be suggested that the *only* force of saying that in any confirmation situation there are sentences which are not up for revision is simply to deny that there are no such sentences, not to suggest any way in which we could sometimes *find* one. But although the arguments so far used have been of the form 'There are such sentences, because we cannot allow that there are not', more can be said than this. I have come to it by a route through the enemy's camp—through general objections to Quinean theory rather than by the positive development of a contrary theory—primarily because the statement that there are sentences of this sort can be argued for without providing a way for finding any, relative merely to confirmation *situations;* while to be able to say of a given sentence that *it* is of the required sort we must be able to relate it not just to a confirmation situation but to an individual person propounding an *argument* about that situation.

A constructive account of 'analytic in the argument' must proceed through an account of 'involved in the argument'. To discover what sentences are involved in the argument whereby Smith concludes 'Because $E$ has occurred, $S_1$ is true', we must ask Smith, for there is always a choice of routes for any given experience-sentence pair. How does Smith decide that, say, $S_2$ is involved in his argument? Surely, by seeing that his reason for saying 'If $E$ has occurred, $S_1$ is true' is that he accepts as true both $S_2$ and 'If $S_2$ is true then if $E$ has occurred then $S_1$ is true'; and he accepts this last as true because he accepts both $S_3$ and 'If $S_3$ is true then if $S_2$ is true, then . . .'; and so on backwards, but not *ad infinitum*. For at some stage he will say something like 'I accept $S_n$ as true and $S_n$ *says that* if $S_{n-1}$ is true then . . .' The phrase 'says that' does not matter; what *is* important is Smith's arrival at a stopping-place (or at stopping-places; but for brevity I shall deal only with cases where the 'involvement' sequence does not ramify) at which he says 'There is nothing more to say. Accepting $S_n$ is accepting . . . , and not through the mediation of anything else, either.'

The terminal sentence in the 'involvement' sequence could be said to be analytic in that argument. Normally it will not be stated in the argument, but if it is stated it will be labelled as a rule of inference or in some other way which would make it clear that no further-back sentences are admitted by Smith to be in need of statement at all in this argument. As a rule, Smith will choose the terminus which most people would choose in such an argument, because as a rule he will wish to use words in their normal senses and not propose any conceptual revisions. This way of putting things presupposes—what I should wish to defend—a definition of 'analytic' as 'analytic in most arguments', and a consequent development of the rest of the standard intensional terminology on this basis.

A sentence may fall short of Smith's terminus and still not be considered by him as on the cards for possible revision; but his terminal sentence and all that lie behind it are *put* off the cards for possible revision by the very shape of Smith's argument—*i.e.,* by his insistence that once he has worked back to $S_n$ *there is* nothing more to say—and it is with this *impossibility* of revision that I am here concerned. Of course, $S_n$ might be considered for revision, or at least located short of the terminus, in another argument; but sensible criteria for the identity of arguments would demand that it be considered *another* argument. I grant that this is an elementary definitional matter, but it is not a definitional matter that this definition has application. It can be cashed only because we have a straightforwardly empirical sense for the notion of a *complete argument* (and a set of logical considerations to confute those who take the line that the appearance of completeness is always misleading and that no actually occurring argument is really complete in the required sense), and this gives us a straightforwardly empirical sense for the notion of argument non-identity. Contrast this with what happens when PQ's theory is applied to standard remarks about 'different meaning', 'different use', 'different proposition' and the rest.

The conclusions so far reached in this section have a certain tameness, stemming particularly from the fact that the identification of any given sentence as analytic in a given argument may well lack the confidence of the claim that *some* sentence must be analytic in the argument. But there are lessons to be learned from the development of a doctrine of analyticity in this way. For brevity, I shall state them in an assured and unqualified fashion which may well not be warranted by the arguments which I have presented.

The situation is this: Quine claims that sentences are never used in the way in which his critics say that analytic sentences are used, *viz.,* in such a way that they are not capable of revision in the light of the facts. The standard reply to this is that there are two sorts of revision, conceptual and factual, a claim which (as the device of PQ has been used to show) cannot in any obvious way be made good. The upshot of the arguments advanced in the present paper is that Quine is wrong—that there is, and indeed must be, an analytic use of sentences in a traditional sense of 'analytic'—but that Quine's critics, while underestimating the force of his arguments and the strength of his position, have granted him too much. In particular, they have apparently granted him that any sentence is at all times capable of revision of one sort or the other; and this has put them in the position of having to establish an important difference of kind between the situation where an analytic sentence is denied and that in which a synthetic sentence is denied. On the basis of the arguments I have offered, all that is required is the establishment of an important difference of kind between the argument in which a sentence is up for possible revision of some sort and the argument in which it cannot be up for revision *at all*. If the arguments of this section are in order, the difference between the two arguments is absolute—it is, for instance, not capable of analysis in PQ's way—and if Quine or PQ should object that sensible people never treat sentences in such a way as to rule out the question of their possible falsification, we are in a position to reply that sensible people must sometimes treat sentences in this way if they are to be capable of constructing arguments at all.

[I stand by this paper's attempt (a) to re-interpret Quine's doctrine of the ASD, (b) to defend it against certain attacks, and (c) to show that 'recalcitrance' raises a problem for Quine. But I don't now think (d) that Quine's doctrine founders on this problem: a Quinean *can* explain recalcitrance as is implied by my 1961 paper listed below. And I am embarrassed by (e) the attempt to put the ASD on a non-Quinean footing: even if (d) were right, those final pages would be a failure.] *

FURTHER READING

Bennett (4)
Putnam (4)

---

\* Added by the author in this edition.

# ᘒ SOME REMARKS ON QUINE ON ANALYTICITY

*Jerrold J. Katz*

## 1. Introduction

This paper is neither another exposition of my account of the analytic-synthetic distinction nor a popularization of my previous expositions, but, rather, an attempt to show how Quine's criticisms in "Two Dogmas of Empiricism" can be answered on my account of the distinction. I presuppose the technical expositions of my account and here address myself to showing why Quine's criticisms do not apply to them. In no sense is this paper a reply or rejoinder to Quine. In my opinion, his arguments are sound objections to Carnap's treatment of analyticity, against which they were, of course, directed. Rather, this paper is an attempt to prevent others from the too easy assumption, unfortunately encouraged by Quine himself, that Quinean arguments are conclusive against any basis for drawing the analytic-synthetic distinction.

## 2. Analyticity and Logical Truth

Quine's working characterization of an analytic statement is as follows. He first defines a *logical truth* as a statement that is true under any reinterpretation of any of its components ex-

From Jerrold J. Katz, "Some Remarks on Quine on Analyticity", *The Journal of Philosophy*, LXIV (1967), pp. 36–52. Reprinted by permission of the Editors of *The Journal of Philosophy*.

cept its logical particles and, then, defines an *analytic statement* as one that can be converted into a logical truth by substituting synonyms for synonyms. Accordingly,

(1) Bachelors are unmarried men

is shown to be analytic if the terms 'unmarried men' and 'bachelors' are synonymous, and the substitution of the former for the latter in (1) converts (1) into a logical truth, viz.

(2) Unmarried men are unmarried men

By way of contrasting Quine's approach with mine, it is important to notice that, in this connection, Quine is talking about the logical truths of English, for if he were here assuming only the logical truths of quantification theory, his way of characterizing analyticity would provide only a proper subset of the analytic statements of a language. A sentence such as

(3) Bachelors are males

which is analytic, but whose predicate term is not synonymous with its subject, would not appear among the analytic sentences. Although 'unmarried adult males' and 'bachelors' are synonymous, the substitution of the former for the latter in (3) does not yield a logical truth of quantification theory, nor even, as in the case of (2), something that is an obvious instance of such. The substitution yields the debatable case:

(4) Unmarried adult males are males

Formally, 'unmarried adult males' and 'males' are distinct terms, so that, from this viewpoint, there is no basis for claiming that (4) is an instance of $(x)(Ux \cdot Ax \cdot Mx \supset Mx)$ rather than $(x)(Px \supset Qx)$. We cannot treat (4) as an instance of $(x)(Ux \cdot Ax \cdot Mx \supset Mx)$ on the grounds that 'males' is one of the terms in 'unmarried adult males', since, without some independent considerations, this approach, by parity of reasoning, would lead to the absurd consequence that

(5) Wooden indians are indians
(6) Decoy ducks are ducks

are both cases of logical truth and, hence, truths. Moreover, it is of no use to reply that 'wooden indians' and 'decoy ducks' are somehow idiomatic, as illustrated by the contrast of (7) and (8) with, say, (9):

(7) Indians who are wooden are indians
(8) Ducks who are decoys are ducks
(9) Males who are adult and unmarried are males

since treating (9) as an instance of $(x)(Mx \cdot Ax \cdot Ux \supset Mx)$ would permit us to treat the sentence

(10) Heathens converted to Christianity are heathens

as an instance of $(x)(Hx \cdot Cx \supset Hx)$ and, thus, as a truth, insofar as the expression 'heathens converted to Christianity' is in no way idiomatic in the manner of 'wooden indian' or 'decoy duck'.

But, of course, Quine's use of the term 'logical truths' refers to the logical truths of English rather than to those of quantification theory. And certainly Quine was in his rights to assume the logical truths of English in this connection, since he was conceding a specification of the logical truths of English only in order to make the further critical point that, even with such a specification, there is no characterization of analyticity within Carnap's framework. Were one to say that significant semantic questions are begged by the assumption that logical truths in quantification theory can be antecedently paired with sentences of English so as to pick out the logical truths of English, Quine could happily agree and say that this criticism merely undermines Carnap's approach to analyticity at an earlier point than his own.

My approach, however, is constructive, not critical like Quine's. Since it is an attempt to construct a definition of analyticity, rather than to refute one, we can make no assumption that allows us to start with the logical truths of English. Such an assumption, as the examples cited above show, does involve far more about the semantics of English than one might first think if one conceives the assumption as tantamount to just taking the logical truths of quantification theory and generating the logical truths of English by substituting words or expressions from English for predicate variables in the direct, simple-minded way. As we have seen, this would require us to know quite a bit about the semantics of certain types of English constructions in order to avoid treating false statements as true ones. Moreover, it is not at all clear what must be known about the semantics of English, nor, for that matter, what semantic concepts we might have to have—perhaps even a definition of synonymy might be necessary—in order to avoid such undesirable consequences.

Accordingly, in my treatment of analyticity, I have avoided using Quine's approach, which starts with the notion of logical truth and seeks a definition of analyticity in terms of it. Instead, I start with a relation more general than synonymy, viz., *inclusion of meaning,* of which synonymy, or mutual inclusion of meaning, is a special case, and I seek to define it on the basis of features of the semantic analyses of sentences in natural languages. A theory of analyticity of this sort, then, will claim that it is this relation of inclusion of meaning between 'unmarried adult males' and 'males' (which does not hold between 'heathens converted to Christianity' and 'heathens') by virtue of which (3) and (4) are analytic.

My reason for avoiding Quine's approach is that I reject the extensionalist view that underlies it: the view that sentences of a natural language can be directly translated into substitution instances of formulas in quantification theory. I accept instead the intensionalist view that such translation must be mediated by a representation of the meaning of sentences and must thus be indirect. The view that translation is indirect can be regarded as a version (in the formal mode) of the traditional intensionalist thesis that meaning (or intension) determines extension. The meaning of a sentence is represented by the readings assigned to it by the semantic component of a grammar. On the other hand, the extension of a sentence is represented by an appropriate substitution instance of a formula in quantification theory (I will ignore the fact that there is actually an equivalence class of these). This is what Quine is saying in claiming that quantification is the "idiom of objective reference." In these terms, the issue on which the traditional intensionalist-extensionalist controversy turns is whether translation into the idiom of quantification must be indirect in the sense that features of the readings of a sentence must be taken into account to obtain a substitution instance of a quantification formula that correctly translates that sentence.

I cannot argue for the intensionalist thesis here, but I can mention some considerations supporting the intensionalist side in this controversy. One is that expressions and sentences are often semantically ambiguous, so that the translation cannot be one-one from sentences to substitution instances of quantification formulas but must be one-one from readings (i.e., representations of their senses) to substitution instances of quantification formulas (i.e., representations of their extension). Another is that some sentences that are grammatically well formed are, nevertheless, semantically anomalous (i.e., meaningless) and, thus, should not receive any translation. This difficulty can be met only in an ad hoc way if translation goes from sentences to substitution instances of quantification formulas, since there are no differences among grammatically well-formed sentences on which to base this distinction between the translatable and the nontranslatable ones. It will be met automatically and naturally if translation goes from readings to substitution instances of quantification formulas, since semantically anomalous sentences have no readings. Still another consideration follows from the fact that we require of the substitution instance of a quantification formula which is the translation of a sentence that it be optimal. That is, its orthography must formally mark every feature on which valid inferences from it depend. We can obtain an optimal translation of a sentence only by introducing a distinct term into the substitution instance of the quantification formula for each distinct semantic marker in its reading. If we merely formalize the conceptual distinctions that are marked out by the words (or morphemes) in the sentence (i.e., introduce a term for each distinct word or morpheme and no more), then the translation will not be optimal because valid inferences depending on conceptual distinctions within the broader conceptual distinctions marked out by the words (or morphemes) cannot be drawn from that translation. To put the point in Quine's terms, the choice of an adequate canonical paraphrase—from which the translation *is* direct—itself presupposes that the orthography of the chosen canonical paraphrase mark each of the conceptual distinctions marked by the semantic markers in the reading for the sentence in question. For example, taking (4) to be a canonical paraphrase of (3)—or close enough to one for our purposes—presupposes a factoring of the appropriate sense of 'bachelor' into the concepts expressed by 'unmarried', 'adult', and 'male', and presupposes further that the combination of these words forming the subject of (4) does not eliminate any of these concepts, say in the way in which some of the semantic content of 'heathen' is eliminated in combination with 'converted to Christianity' in the subject of (10). Note that, although the intensionalist can utilize both the readings of a sentence and the semantic properties and relations defined in terms of them to guide him in determining an optimal translation, it is not at all clear how the steadfast extensionalist is to proceed, since he must eschew both in order to translate directly from sentences to substitution instances of quantification formulas. Thus, for example, he cannot justify taking (4) as the canonical paraphrase of (3) on the grounds that 'bachelor' and 'unmarried adult male' are synonymous, because he cannot appeal to semantic relations such as synonymy, as Quine does in "Two Dogmas of Empiricism."

## 3. Definition

Another respect in which my approach differs from Quine's concerns definition. Three types of definition are discussed in "Two Dogmas of Empiricism" . . . : *lexical definition,* which provides a paraphrase of an appropriate sort; *explication,* which preserves aspects of the meaning of the definiendum but improves upon its meaning in some way or another; and *notational definition,* which merely introduces a new notational convention for purposes of abbreviation. According to Quine—and I concur fully—the former two depend on prior relations of synonymy. Since lexical definitions and, in the relevant respects, explications too, report antecedent synonymy relations, they are, by themselves, no answer to the question of what such reports are really reports of. I agree also that notational definition has nothing whatever to do with the problem of analyticity. But Quine's catalogue of types of definition omits the very type that my account of analyticity uses. The type of definition I proposed for deriving the analytic sentences of a natural language and for explaining what is predicated of them by marking them analytic is what I shall refer to as *theoretical definition.*

Theoretical definition comes closest to lexical definition. Like the latter, it avoids the inherent difficulty with explications: that no way has yet been devised to determine when a departure from the meaning of the explicandum is a genuine improvement and when it is simply a failure on the part of the explicatum to capture a significant aspect of the meaning of the explicandum. Also, like lexical definition, it is an attempt to describe empirical facts about a natural language by expressing them in the form of confirmable hypotheses. But, unlike lexical definition, theoretical definition does not define a term by other terms or expressions in the same language, with which it is synonymous. Rather—and this is the significant difference— theoretical definitions define terms *on the basis of constructs from linguistic theory,* that theory in empirical linguistics which expresses what is common to natural languages in the form of a definition of the notion 'natural language'. That is, a term from a natural language is defined by a dictionary entry which represents each of its senses in the form of a theoretical construction, called a 'reading', that is composed, not of words from that language, but of symbols expressing language-independent constructs, called 'semantic markers', drawn from the theoretical vocabulary of empirical linguistics.

There are several reasons why the semantic component of a grammar must employ theoretical definition rather than lexical definition. One is that defining words by pairing them with synonymous expressions in the same language (or even a different one; it makes no difference here) cannot provide an account of their meaning. Such pairings say no more than that the meaning of this or that word is the same as the meaning of some expression without at all saying what the meaning of either is. They are thus no more illuminating about meaning than the statement that two species have the same sensory organ is about the nature of that organ. Another reason is this. Being expressions in the same natural language (or a different one; again it makes no difference), the definientia of lexical definitions will have, in general, the same semantic properties and relations that other words and expressions do. In particular, given the fact that practically every word in a natural language is ambiguous, which one can easily verify by consulting any standard reference dictionary like Webster's, practically every definiens of a lexical definition will be ambiguous, too. Accordingly, lexical definitions cannot give *the* meaning of their definienda. To do this would require some way of disambiguating the definiens antecedently, some way of identifying the proper sense from among the various senses of the definiens and indicating that it alone is the sense of the definiendum; and this cannot be done by further lexical definitions for just the reason that requires such disambiguation in the first place. Consequently, a semantic component based on lexical definition must beg the significant questions in semantics, for it is capable of accounting for semantic properties like synonymy and ambiguity only if they are independently accounted for on the basis of some other means of representing and marking them. These and other reasons make it necessary to resist the extension of lexical definition, which has its proper place in ordinary reference dictionaries, to theoretical semantics. These reasons also show, though I cannot argue it here, that Quine's basis for endorsing lexical definition, viz., his view that all talk about meaning can be dispensed with in favor of just talk about meaningfulness (significance) and synonymy, is inadequate. Therefore, theoretical definition is employed instead of lexical definition because it defines a sense of a word in terms of a vocabulary of theoretical constructs (semantic markers) each of which is devised to represent uniquely a specific component in the senses of words and to combine with other such constructs to form semantic representations (readings) that unequivocally specify a sense of a word, phrase, clause, or sentence.

This has the following consequence. Synonymy relations are not affirmed by the institution of a definitional connection between one term or expression from a natural language and another, as is the case in lexical definition. Rather, synonymy relations are affirmed on the basis of sameness of semantic representation, i.e., where the readings correlated with the two terms or expressions are formally identical. A case of meaning inclusion, such as 'male' and 'bachelor', is affirmed when the semantic markers in the reading that represents one item all appear in the reading that represents the meaning of the other. Conversely, such formal relations, on the basis of which we affirm or deny that a particular linguistic construction has one or another semantic property or relation, provide the abstract conditions that serve as definienda for the general semantic concepts *is synonymous with, has its meaning included in that of, is analytic,* and so on.

## 4. Interchangeability and Circularity

Quine's remarks on the possibility of defining synonymous constructions as constructions that are interchangeable *salva veritate* are, in my opinion, quite correct. Something stronger is needed, and it is interchangeability *salva analyticitate.* But, since the notion of analyticity is what we sought to explain in studying the notion of synonymy, we cannot accept a proposal to define synonymy that rests on the unexplained notion of analyticity. So, according to Quine, we are back where we started, having learned only that the two notions are interdefinable.

The consequence of employing theoretical definition referred to at the end of the previous section enables us to avoid the circularity of trying to define analyticity in terms of logical truth and synonymy, and synonymy in terms of interchangeability *salva analyticitate.* For now 'analytic', 'synonymous', 'meaning inclusion', etc. do not themselves appear as terms in the definienda of any such semantic concepts. As indicated, each such semantic concept is defined in terms of certain formal features of the readings for sentences and their constituents—more precisely, in terms of formal conditions on semantically interpreted underlying phrase markers. For example, with no appeal to such terms as 'synonymous', we might define an analytic sentence as a sentence whose semantically interpreted underlying phrase marker (generated by the optimal grammar for the language) is such that every semantic marker in the reading for its predicate also occurs in the reading for its subject.

It is important to notice that this method of defining semantic properties and relations is general, by which I mean that every semantic property and relation will be defined on the same basis, i.e., in terms of a configuration of symbols in semantically interpreted underlying phrase markers. Thus, semantic theory defines a sentence or constituent as semantically anomalous just in case it receives no readings, as semantically ambiguous just in case it receives two or more readings, and so forth. Of course, as things presently stand, there are semantic properties and relations that have not been so defined within semantic theory, but my claim is not that semantic theory is now complete. My claim is that my conception of semantic theory offers a sufficiently rich conceptual apparatus for representing semantic structure to enable us, with sufficient ingenuity, to set up adequate definitions for all semantic properties and relations.

Even though semantic properties and relations are not defined in terms of one another, because they are defined on a common basis (i.e., formal features of semantically interpreted underlying phrase markers), different semantic properties and relations are interconnected by virtue of interrelated formal features of semantically interpreted underlying phrase markers (which reflect uniformities in the semantic structure of the sentences these semantically interpreted phrase markers describe). For example, the lexical reading of 'shadow' that enables us to mark

(11)  The shadow hit the ground (with a loud thud)

as semantically anomalous also enables us to mark

(12)  A shadow is not a physical object

as analytic. This type of interconnection between semantic concepts makes it possible to obtain indirect evidence for a prediction about a given sentence having a given semantic property or relation by considering successful predictions about other semantic properties and relations that can be derived from the same representations of semantic structure. We shall return to this point later.

## 5. *Semantical Rules*

Carnap's conception of semantical rules (and meaning postulates) is criticized by Quine on essentially two counts. First, there is what I shall refer to as the *generality criticism*: that the notion which should be defined is '*S* is analytic for *L*' for variable '*S*' and '*L*', but that Carnap does not define this. Second, there is what I shall call the *explanation criticism*:

that, besides a specification of the analytic statements of a language, we require some account of just what is attributed to them by marking them as analytic. These criticisms establish the inadequacy of Carnap's treatment of analyticity.

Neither of these criticisms carry over to my treatment of analyticity, synonymy, etc. The generality criticism does not carry over because, on my account, semantic properties and relations are defined within linguistic theory. Accordingly, their definitions have the status of hypotheses about what all languages have in common, and, hence, each semantic property or relation is defined for variable '$L$'. Furthermore, unlike Carnap's account, where some analytic statements qualify as such by virtue of being listed under the heading 'analytic', on my account, the concept 'analytic' is defined in terms of a formal condition such that *any* sentence whose semantically interpreted underlying phrase marker satisfies it is analytic. The same is true of other semantic properties and relations, and, hence, semantic concepts are defined for variable '$S$', too.

The explanation criticism does not carry over either. Quine rightly says of Carnap's semantical rules that ". . . the rules contain the word 'analytic', which we do not understand! We understand what expressions the rules attribute analyticity to, but we do not understand what the rules attribute to those expressions". . . . On my treatment, however, 'analytic' is defined in a way that tells us what is attributed to a sentence so marked: linguistic truth by virtue of definitionally guaranteed correct predication. That is, since a sentence is true if its predicate attributes to its subject a property or properties that that subject has, an analytic sentence, on my definition, is true by virtue of meaning alone, since semantic considerations, presented in its semantically interpreted underlying phrase marker, suffice to determine that its subject has the property or properties that its predicate attributes to its subject. In other words, because the property or properties attributed by the predicate are contained in the meaning of the subject, anything that qualifies as a case of the subject will by so qualifying necessarily have the property or properties in question.

Our approach eliminates the need for such ad hoc devices as meaning postulates and semantic rules of the Carnapian variety. The reason why Carnap originally proposed them is clear. Logic reconstructs inferences formally on the basis of rules governing manipulation with "logical symbols," propositional connectives, quantifiers, etc. But some inferences also depend on the meaning of the "descriptive symbols" of a natural language, for which no formal representation is available. Thus, the inference from (13) to (14):

(13)   Someone is a bachelor
(14)   Someone is male

is formalized improperly by the invalid argument schema:

(15)                    $(\exists x)(Bx)$
              $\therefore (\exists x)(Mx)$

unless the meanings of 'bachelor' and 'male' are somehow taken into consideration. Accordingly, Carnap introduces the meaning postulate:

(16)                    $(x)(Bx \supset Mx)$

But, as we have already seen, this way of taking the meaning of descriptive symbols into consideration is not adequate. Our approach renders such ad hoc and inadequate devices unnecessary, because it provides a formal representation of the inherent semantic structure of descriptive symbols, i.e., morphemes, words, and expressions. Thus, the semantic markers in the readings for 'bachelor' and 'male' break up their meaning into component concepts, representing each separate component by a distinct formal symbol in the readings. On this basis, the inference from (13) to (14) can be properly reconstructed as an entailment according to that condition in the definition of 'entailment' which specifies that a sentence $S_1$ entails a sentence $S_2$ just in case the reading for $S_1$'s subject contains the reading for $S_2$'s subject and the reading for $S_1$'s predicate contains the reading for $S_2$'s predicate, since the reading for 'male' will be included in that of 'bachelor'.

The introduction of meaning postulates and semantical rules constitutes a recognition, on Carnap's part, of the need for formally distinguishing the inherent semantic features of different words in a language in order that the representation of inferences be able to incorporate aspects of the meaning of words on which the validity of the inferences depend. But the device of meaning postulates and semantical rules is ad hoc because it provides a basis for dealing only with certain special cases of semantic properties and relations, in particular 'analytic', 'entails', and some other logically related notions, whereas representing the inherent semantic features of words on the basis of the lexical readings in a dictionary provides a basis for dealing with all semantic properties and relations, relations and properties such as 'semantic anomaly', 'semantic ambiguity', etc., in addition to 'analytic', 'entails', etc. As an example, consider a case such as (11) and (12), where Carnap can lay down a meaning postulate to mark (12) as analytic but where that meaning postulate does not suffice to mark (11) as semantically anomalous, and contrast Carnap's approach to that case with ours, where the dictionary characterizes 'shadow', 'mirror image', etc. as perceptual but not physical objects and where this characterization suffices to mark (11) as semantically anomalous and (12) as analytic. Moreover, the device of meaning postulates and semantical rules does not meet the need for which it was originally introduced, because, as Quine has shown, the meaning postulates and semantical rules are given only for a particular language and then just stipulated under one or another empty label. Our approach, on the other hand, dispenses entirely with such pointless, relativized notions by proposing a general, language-independent concept of analyticity and by providing, for each distinct language, a semantic component (for its grammar) that assigns a semantically interpreted underlying phrase marker to each sentence in the language. These semantic representations of sentences formally mark the inherent semantic features of these sentences, and so they provide a domain for the application of the definitions for 'analytic' and other semantic concepts. Consequently, the needs of formal logic are met in a far more natural and adequate a fashion.

## 6. The Evidential Basis

So as not to attribute to Quine a position that he does not actually hold, let us distinguish between "Quine of the printed word" and "Quine of legendary fame." Henceforth, unless otherwise indicated, I will be talking only about the latter Quine.

This Quine is reputed to deny any analytic-synthetic distinction. One of his arguments might be put as follows: "Insofar as one can construct semantic interpretations for sentences of natural languages, as envisaged, one can make a sharp analytic-synthetic distinction *in linguistic theory,* but the definitions for 'analytic', 'synonymous', etc. in linguistic theory are of use only if such semantic interpretations can be set up on a sound empirical basis. Otherwise they are merely empty exercises in definition. But there is no such basis for them." Thus, the focus of Quine's skepticism shifts from the general concepts 'analytic', 'synonymous', etc. to the semantic representations of the sentences and constituents on the basis of which these general concepts are to be applied. In terms of a specific case, the point can be put as follows. If the readings for the subject and predicate of (3) are the way they are alleged to be, then (3) is analytic, but what is the evidential basis for the claim that these readings are the way they are alleged to be?

The general question is how we tell whether a reading correctly represents the meaning of the construction to which it is assigned. Let us start with a straightforward answer. A semantic description, as part of a generative grammar, is a theory about the semantic structure of a language. The readings given in the semantic description for sentences and other syntactically complex constituents come from the readings that the dictionary provides for their component morphemes. Thus, the question is basically about how we decide on the correctness of these lexical readings. Now, a lexical reading is a hypothesis about the structure of a sense of a morpheme, and as such, one part of the evidential basis for a lexical reading will be considerations to the effect that it helps us state true empirical regularities at the lexical level. "Should one reading for 'bachelor' contain the semantic marker (Male)?" becomes the question "Does a reading for 'bachelor' that contains (Male) help us state an empirical regularity?"

The inclusion of a semantic marker in lexical readings for different morphemes is the manner in which a grammar states a regularity over those morphemes, for those lexical items whose readings contain this semantic marker are *ipso facto* grouped together as semantically similar in the respect indicated by the semantic marker. If (Male) is included in one reading for 'bachelor' as well as in a reading for 'uncle', 'bull', 'priest', 'father', etc., and it is excluded from the readings for 'parent', 'animal', 'spinster', 'classmate', etc., we thereby succeed in stating an empirical regularity about the semantic similarity of the members of the former set. Moreover, the inclusion of (Male) in the lexical reading for the "unmarried-adult-man" sense of 'bachelor' and its exclusion from the lexical reading for the "person-having-a-degree-for-completion-of-the-first-four-years-of-college" sense enables us to state one of the empirical differences between these senses.

Again, hypotheses worked into a theory as integrated parts of the theory can be tested in various indirect ways by virtue of the ways in which they are systematically interconnected with other parts of the theory. Whenever the theory makes essential use of a hypothesis to predict data successfully, the hypothesis receives confirmation. Accordingly, we may ask how a dictionary and set of projection rules might use a reading for 'bachelor' that contained the semantic marker (Male) to predict facts about the semantics of English. In particular, how this reading for 'bachelor' can be used to obtain, by projection rules, readings for sentences that permit us to mark their semantic properties and relations correctly. For example, since (Male) and (Female) are antonymous semantic markers, we can use this reading for 'bachelor' to mark

(17)  My mother is a bachelor

as contradictory on one of its senses. Furthermore, because (Male) helps to distinguish different senses of 'bachelor', it helps to mark (17) as semantically ambiguous. Also, it helps us mark (14) as entailed by (13). Since this lexical reading helps us mark these and other types of semantic properties and relations, there is certainly empirical evidence for the claim that one reading of 'bachelor' should have (Male) occur in it, and this evidence is, in turn, also evidence that (3) is analytic.

We might suppose that we can rest our case with the observation that the above treatment of 'bachelor' can serve as a model for the treatment of any other examples about which the same methodological question is raised. But for the Quine of legendary fame this straightforward answer will not do. He will not allow us to take the facts that were assumed for

granted. "How do you know," he will ask, "that (17) is semantically ambiguous and contradictory on one of its senses, or
that (13) entails (14), or that (3) is analytic?" To this, we
would answer that such facts are obtained from intuitive judgments speakers make about the sentences; these judgments constitute our data. Now, Quine's rejoinder will concern how we
obtain such data, and he will ask two questions about the claim
to have such data.

First, he will want to know how we deal with cases that
are unclear because speakers are unable to make definite judgments about them. For example, we can expect speakers to be
somewhat confused about whether or not

(18) Whales are fish

is analytic, or even expect that they might make a wrong judgment about this case. But here we can reply that, as indicated
in the last paragraph of section 4, we do not need to have
clear-cut judgments about a given case to have sound evidence
on which to assert its analyticity, since we can bring indirect
evidence to bear on it. That is, the virtue of semantic theory
is that it interrelates semantic concepts and, thus, permits us
to decide on the character of an unclear case by theoretical
triangulation from clear cases of sentences having other semantic properties or relations. Let us give an example of this in
connection with (18). We assume that "fishing" and "whaling"
are, respectively, an activity in which one tries to catch fish and
an activity in which one tries to catch whales, so that 'fishing'
and 'whaling' differ semantically in just the way that 'fish' and
'whale' do. Now, 'but'-conjunction is governed by a semantic
restriction that the conjoined expressions contrast semantically
if the whole conjunction is to avoid semantic anomaly. For
example,

(19) I went fishing but caught a fish (bass, pike, etc.) instead
(20) I went whaling but caught a whale (baleen, sperm, etc.)
     instead

are both semantically anomalous because the object of the
second clause in each makes what was caught some type that
is the same as that which the speaker was trying to catch, or a
subtype of that type. To avoid semantic anomaly, the type in-

dicated by the object in the second clause must be a contrasting type. Thus,

(21) I went fishing but caught an old shoe instead
(22) I went whaling but caught an octopus instead

are both nonanomalous sentences. But (23) and (24):

(23) I went fishing but caught a whale instead
(24) I went whaling but caught a fish instead

are also nonanomalous, from which we can conclude that whales are not a type of fish, from the viewpoint of English. This can be reflected in the lexical reading for 'whale' only if that reading does not contain the semantic markers that represent the concept of a fish, and, hence, (18) will be marked as not analytic, even though there may be no clear-cut judgment to this effect about (18) *per se*.

Second, Quine will want to know whether, in clear cases, we have to ask speakers whether (17) is semantically ambiguous and contradictory on one sense, whether (13) entails (14), and whether (3) is analytic. "Must speakers understand what such technical terms as 'semantically ambiguous', 'contradictory', 'entails', and 'analytic' mean before they can answer reliably?" The answer to this question is a categorical 'no'. It is possible to obtain the relevant data without invoking such technical terms in framing the questions that are put to speakers. One test that avoids such circularity is this. We present speakers with short lists of sentences. List A contains only sentences that are clear cases of what we would regard as analytic. Lists B, C, D, etc. contain clear cases of sentences that are not analytic, but, say, respectively, synthetic, contradictory, anomalous, etc. Then, we give the speakers a batch of sentences of all sorts and ask them to place these on the lists to which they belong. Each sentence is to be put on the list with whose members it is similar. If this experiment is conducted properly and if the predictions that the semantic component of the grammar makes match the actual sorting performed by the speakers (cases that are put on list A are those and only those that are predicted to be analytic, and so on), then we can claim that we have evidence, obtained in a quite unobjectionable fashion, in favor of the semantic component, as a result of its successful predictions about the data. However, the qualification that the experiment be conducted properly is extremely important. If the controls used in the experiment ensure that the members of the short lists A, B, C, etc. are sufficiently different from one another in the appropriate respects, then there will be no spurious common features that might lead speakers to classify sentences on the basis of irrelevant linguistic properties (e.g., in the case of list A, on the basis of some linguistic property other than analyticity). Positive results in this experiment can be interpreted to mean that the judgments of the speakers reflect a recognition of the analyticity of the sentences concerned. We can say, then, that our definition of analyticity, which enabled us to predict the outcome of the experiment, describes the concept of analyticity employed by the speakers as their implicit criterion for identifying analytic sentences, i.e., for differentiating those of the test sentences that are similar to the members on list A from those that are not similar to them. We can say this on the grounds that assuming that this is their criterion provides us with the best explanation of the behavioral data obtained in the experiment. Since these grounds are the same as those on which theories in other sciences are justified, they should satisfy even the Quine of legendary fame.

## 7. Analyticity and Analyticity

In contrast to the Quine of legendary fame, Quine of the printed word wrote, "One quickly identifies certain seemingly transparent cases of synonymy, such as 'bachelor' and 'man not married', and senses the triviality of associated sentences such as 'No bachelor is married.' Conceivably the mechanism of such recognition, when better understood, might be made the basis of a definition of synonymy and analyticity in terms of linguistic behavior. . . . I can see no reason to expect that the full-width analyticity which Carnap and others make such heavy demands upon can be fitted to such a foundation in even an approximate way." Quine is, I believe, one hundred per cent right in this, and my account of analyticity supports him in two ways. First, it shows that a precise, well-explained, unobjectionable definition of analyticity does not grant analytic status to the philosophically significant cases for which the full-width notion of analyticity was sought. Consequently, what their epistemological status is becomes a more acute question for empiricists. Second, although such cases do not come under analyticity in the narrow sense, the obvious cases of analytic sentences, such as (3), do, and this shows that whatever empirical support there seemed to be for the existence of a full-width analytic-synthetic distinction on the basis of these obvious cases is no longer available. This casts further doubt on the empiricist claim that linguistic considerations suffice to account for the epistemological status of alleged necessary truths.

Thus, there are two notions of analyticity, the one with which I have been concerned, which derives from Kant, and the one that Quine refers to as "full-width analyticity," which is sought by Carnap and other logical empiricists. The latter was intended to serve as the basis for a linguistic account of necessary truth and so to divide necessary truths from truths of contingent fact as to leave no middle ground upon which the metaphysician could take a stand. But, although the former concept of analyticity is well defined and empirically motivated, it will not serve the empiricist's purposes, because the analytic-synthetic distinction it draws gives the metaphysician much too much ground on which to stand, whereas the latter notion is not only a mere promissory note but one whose redemption is made far less likely by the fact that obvious cases of analytic sentences cannot now be construed as evidence for the existence of an analytic-synthetic distinction in this wide sense. One loses confidence that someone can pay back the money he owes after learning that all the money he's been flashing about is really someone else's.

**FURTHER READING**

Katz (1), (2), (4)

# ❧ ON A SUGGESTION
## OF KATZ

*W. V. Quine*

Analyticity is a supposed trait of certain sentences, or of certain uses of them. I have felt the notion to be insufficiently empirical. A notion having to do with language seems peculiarly unpromising if its relation to observable behavior is obscure, for language is first and last a system of dispositions to observable behavior. The very learning and teaching of a language rests on socially observable responses to socially observable circumstances. It is ironical that empiricists have so seldom mistrusted the notion of analyticity for its want of behavioral criteria, and the irony is double in the case of empiricists with a bias toward language.

Katz, unlike so many, evidently agrees with me that a satisfactory version of analyticity would have to carry with it some approximate behavioral criterion. Let us look to his. Some of the apparatus that surrounds his account of analyticity, in this paper or elsewhere, can be set aside as inessential to the central issue. This is true of his devices for coping with homonymy, since our analyticity problem would remain even if our language were miraculously pruned of homonyms. Again it seems desirable to by-pass, if we can, the system of classification which he calls "semantic markers." For, even if it were

From W. V. Quine, "On a Suggestion of Katz", *The Journal of Philosophy*, LXIV (1967), pp. 52–54. Reprinted by permission of the Editors of *The Journal of Philosophy*.

possible by superimposing these classes to determine every meaning, there might still be argument as to the arbitrariness of the classes used.

In a passage near the end of his paper, Katz happily cuts through all this and epitomizes his approach by suggesting a direct test of analyticity with a minimum of auxiliary constructions. The informant is presented with lists of sentences. List A contains 'No bachelor is married', 'Black swans are black', and others. Such a sentence as 'Some dogs are black' would appear only in another list. The informant is then called upon to sort further sentences into the lists.

Even if this test brings results that are uniform from informant to informant, it affords at best a criterion for analyticity in English. For another language new lists would be needed, and no linguistically general method is offered for making such lists. To offer one would be to define analyticity for languages generally. Not to offer one is to fall afoul of what Katz has called my "generality criticism."

Still it would be ungrateful not to prize a criterion for analyticity-in-English. Even if less general than could be wished, analyticity-in-English is far more to the point than analyticity-in-$L_0$, where $L_0$ is merely some newly invented language whose very definition includes a stipulation of what sentences to call analytic.

Katz's proposed criterion of analyticity-in-English is that native informants generally put the sentence into list A. Degrees of analyticity could be measured, I suppose, in terms of the amount of agreement among informants and the average swiftness of decision. Also some refinement might be introduced into the definition to allow for chains of reasoning on the informant's part in the case of complex examples.

Sentences that informants do not pretty generally agree to put into list A have low analyticity on the imagined scale. Roughly speaking, they do not count as analytic. Therefore, in the really interesting regions—notably in scientific theories—where philosophers have trouble sorting out the analytic sentences, none would count as analytic. Such point as the notion of analyticity was once supposed to have for the philosophy of science would in this way be largely forfeited. This I have long thought inevitable. But then we must recognize that Katz's criterion, like my own criterion of stimulus analyticity, defines something other than the analyticity notion I have criticized. This he seems to appreciate.

The fact remains that, if evidence should accumulate to suggest that there is an impressively broad range of sentences which nearly all informants would put into list A, this would be a uniformity worth studying. A study of common traits of such sentences, and of psychological mechanisms behind them, might help us on some semantical points which have been ill served by the uncritically posited dichotomy between analytic and synthetic. But it must be said that experiments already carried out in 1956 along somewhat these lines, by Apostel, Mays, and others, do not give us to expect so impressive a uniformity.*

In conclusion I turn briefly to some remarks of Katz's on synonymy. He represents me as "endorsing lexical definition," i.e., definition of words by synonymous words or phrases. I have repeatedly stressed the contrary. "Knowing words is knowing how to work out the meanings of sentences containing them. Dictionary definitions are mere clauses in recursive definitions of the meaning of sentences." "Synonymy in the small is no primary concern of the lexicographer; lame synonyms plus stage directions are quite satisfactory insofar as they expedite his primary business of explaining how to translate or paraphrase long speeches. We may continue to characterize the lexicographer's domain squarely as synonymy, but only by recognizing synonymy as primarily a relation of sufficiently long segments of discourse."

Katz voices two objections to explaining meanings by equating expressions. One of them has to do with ambiguity; but ambiguity dwindles as we move out to sentences and longer sentences. The other is that the equating of expressions in respect of meaning does not say "what the meaning of either is." But this, if true, seems of little consequence as long as we understand one of the pair of equated expressions.

---

* This sentence added by the author in this reprinting.

# BIBLIOGRAPHY

Ajdukiewicz, K. "Le problème du fondement des propositions analytiques", *Studia Logica,* 1958.

Aldrich, V. C. (1) "The Last Word on Being Red and Blue All Over", *Philosophical Studies,* 1954.

——. (2) "The Origin of the *A Priori*", *Journal of Philosophy,* 1954.

Alexander, H. G. "Necessary Truth", *Mind,* 1957.

Allaire, E. B. "Tractatus 6.3751", *Analysis,* 1959.

Alston, W. P., and G. Nakhnikian, eds. *Readings in Twentieth-Century Philosophy,* 1963.

Ambrose, A. (1) "Finitism in Mathematics", *Mind,* 1935.

——. (2) "Self-Contradictory Suppositions", *Mind,* 1944.

——. (3) "Wittgenstein on Some Questions in the Foundations of Mathematics", *Journal of Philosophy,* 1955.

——. (4) "On Entailment and Logical Necessity", *Proceedings of the Aristotelian Society,* 1955–56.

Ammerman, R., ed. *Classics of Analytic Philosophy,* 1965.

Anderson, A. R. "Mathematics and the 'Language Game'", *Review of Metaphysics,* 1958; reprinted in Benacerraf and Putnam.

——, et al. "Modal and Many-Valued Logics", *Acta Philosophica Fennica,* 1963.

Apostel, L., et. al. *Les liaisons analytiques et synthétiques dans les comportements du sujet,* 1957.

Aune, B. (1) "Is There an Analytic A Priori?", *Journal of Philosophy,* 1963.

——. (2) "Reply to Skyrms and Sosa", *Philosophical Studies,* 1965–67.

Austin, J. L. (1) "Are There *A Priori* Concepts?", *Proceedings of the Aristotelian Society, Supplementary Volume,* 1939; reprinted in Austin (3).

——. (2) "The Meaning of a Word", in Austin (3).

——. (3) *Philosophical Papers,* 1961.

Ayer, A. J. (1) "Internal Relations", *Proceedings of the Aristotelian Society,* 1935.

————. (2) *Language, Truth and Logic,* 1936; chapter 4 reprinted in this collection, in Benacerraf and Putnam, in Canfield and Donnell, in Edwards and Pap, and in Feinberg.

————. (3) "Truth by Convention", *Analysis,* 1936–37.

————. (4) "Meaning and Intentionality", *Proceedings of the XIIth Congress of Philosophy,* 1958.

Ayer, A. J., ed., *Logical Positivism,* 1959.

Bar-Hillel, Y. "Bolzano's Definition of Analytic Propositions", *Theoria,* 1950; also in *Methodos,* 1950.

————, and R. Carnap. "Semantic Information", *British Journal for the Philosophy of Science,* 1953–54.

Barker, S. F. *Philosophy of Mathematics,* 1964.

Beard, R. W. "Analyticity, Informativeness and the Incompatibility of Colors", *Logique et Analyse,* 1967.

Beck, L. W. (1) "Remarks on the Distinction Between Analytic and Synthetic", *Philosophy and Phenomenological Research,* 1948–49.

————. (2) "Can Kant's Synthetic Judgements Be Made Analytic?", *Kant-Studien,* 1955–56; reprinted in Beck (5).

————. (3) "Kant's Theory of Definition", *Philosophical Review,* 1956; reprinted in Beck (5).

————. (4) "On the Meta-Semantics of the Problem of the Synthetic A Priori", *Mind,* 1957; reprinted in Beck (5).

————. (5) *Studies in the Philosophy of Kant,* 1965.

Behmann, H. "Sind die mathematischen Urteile synthetisch?", *Erkenntnis,* 1934.

Benacerraf, P., and H. Putnam, eds. *Philosophy of Mathematics,* 1964.

Benardete, J. A. "The Analytic A Posteriori . . .", *Journal of Philosophy,* 1958.

Bennett, J. F. (1) "Meaning and Implication", *Mind,* 1954.

————. (2) "Analytic-Synthetic", *Proceedings of the Aristotelian Society,* 1958–59; reprinted in this collection.

————. (3) "A Myth About Logical Necessity", *Analysis,* 1961.

————. (4) "On Being Forced to a Conclusion", *Proceedings of the Aristotelian Society, Supplementary Volume,* 1961.

Bergmann, G. (1) "Two Cornerstones of Empiricism", *Synthese,* 1950–51; reprinted in Bergmann (2).

————. (2) *The Metaphysics of Logical Positivism,* 1954.

————. (3) "Analyticity", *Theoria,* 1958; reprinted in Bergmann (4).

————. (4) *Meaning and Existence,* 1959.

————. (5) "The Philosophical Significance of Modal Logic", *Mind,* 1960.

Berkeley, G. *A Treatise Concerning the Principles of Human Knowledge,* 1710.

Bird, G. H. "Analytic and Synthetic", *Philosophical Quarterly*, 1961.

Black, M. (1) *The Nature of Mathematics*, 1933.

――――. (2) "Truth by Convention", *Analysis*, 1936–37.

――――. (3) "Certainty and Empirical Statements", *Mind*, 1942.

――――. (4) "Conventionalism in Geometry and the Interpretation of Necessary Statements", *Philosophy of Science*, 1942.

――――. (5) "The Analysis of a Simple Necessary Statement", *Journal of Philosophy*, 1943.

――――. (6) "Necessary Statements and Rules", *Philosophical Review*, 1958; reprinted in Black (7).

――――. (7) *Models and Metaphors*, 1962.

Black, M., ed. (1) *Philosophical Analysis*, 1950.

――――. (2) *The Importance of Language*, 1962.

Blanshard, B. (1) *The Nature of Thought*, 1939.

――――. (2) *Reason and Analysis*, 1962.

Bolzano, B. *Wissenshaftslehre*, 1837.

Bosanquet, B. *Logic*, 1888; partially reprinted in Nagel and Brandt.

Bradley, R. D. "Geometry and Necessary Truth", *Philosophical Review*, 1964.

Brandt, R., and E. Nagel, eds. *Meaning and Knowledge*, 1965.

Britton, K. (1) *Communication—A Philosophical Study of Language*, 1939.

――――. (2) "Are Necessary Truths True by Convention?", *Proceedings of the Aristotelian Society, Supplementary Volume*, 1947.

――――. (3) "The Nature of Arithmetic—A Reconsideration of Mill's Views", *Proceedings of the Aristotelian Society*, 1947.

Broad, C. D. (1) "Are There Synthetic A Priori Truths?", *Proceedings of the Aristotelian Society, Supplementary Volume*, 1936.

――――. (2) "Kant's Theory of Mathematical and Philosophical Reasoning", *Proceedings of the Aristotelian Society*, 1941–42.

Brodbeck, M., and H. Feigl, eds. *Readings in the Philosophy of Science*, 1953.

Brower, R. A., ed. *On Translation*, 1959.

Brown, D. G. "What the Tortoise Taught Us", *Mind*, 1954.

Bunge, M. "Analyticity Redefined", *Mind*, 1961.

Butler, R. J. "Language Strata and Alternative Logics", *Australasian Journal of Philosophy*, 1955.

Butler, R. J., ed., *Analytical Philosophy*, Second Series, 1965.

Campbell, C. A. "Contradiction: 'Law' or 'Convention'?", *Analysis*, 1958.

Canfield, J. V., and F. H. Donnell, eds. *Readings in the Theory of Knowledge*, 1964.

Carnap, R. (1) "Die Alte und die Neue Logik", *Erkenntnis*, 1930–31; reprinted, in translation, in Ayer (5).

————. (2) *Logische Syntax der Sprache*, 1934; translated *The Logical Syntax of Language*, 1937.

————. (3) "Formalwissenschaft und Realwissenschaft", *Erkenntnis*, 1935–36; reprinted, in translation, in Feigl and Brodbeck.

————. (4) "Testability and Meaning", *Philosophy of Science*, 1936–37; partially reprinted in Feigl and Brodbeck; revised version reprinted in Ammerman.

————. (5) *The Foundations of Logic and Mathematics*, 1939.

————. (6) *Introduction to Semantics*, 1942.

————. (7) "Modalities and Quantification", *Journal of Symbolic Logic*, 1946.

————. (8) *Meaning and Necessity*, 1947; second edition, with supplements, 1956.

————. (9) *Logical Foundations of Probability*, 1950.

————. (10) "Meaning Postulates", *Philosophical Studies*, 1952; reprinted in Carnap (8), second edition.

————. (11) "Meaning and Synonymy in Natural Languages", *Philosophical Studies*, 1955; reprinted in Hook (2) and in Nagel and Brandt.

————, and Y. Bar-Hillel. "Semantic Information", *British Journal for the Philosophy of Science*, 1953–54.

Carroll, L. "What the Tortoise Said to Achilles", *Mind*, 1895.

Castaneda, H-N. (1) "Analytical Propositions, Definitions and the A Priori", *Ratio*, 1959.

————. (2) "Arithmetic and Reality", *Australasian Journal of Philosophy*, 1959; reprinted in Benacerraf and Putnam.

————. (3) " '7 + 5 = 12' as a Synthetic Proposition", *Philosophy and Phenomenological Research*, 1960–61.

————. (4) "On Mathematical Proofs and Meaning", *Mind*, 1961.

Chihara, C. S. (1) Wittgenstein and Logical Compulsion", *Analysis*, 1960–61.

————. (2) "Mathematical Discovery and Concept Formation", *Philosophical Review*, 1963.

Chisholm, R. M. (1) "Reason and the A Priori", in Chisholm, et al.

————. (2) *Theory of Knowledge*, 1966.

————. (3) "Identity Through Possible Worlds: Some Questions", *Nous*, 1967.

————, et al. *Philosophy*, 1964.

Church, A. "Intentional Isomorphism and Identity of Belief", *Philosophical Studies*, 1954.

Cobitz, J. L., and J. Wild. "On the Distinction Between the Analytic and the Synthetic", *Philosophy and Phenomenological Research*, 1947–48.

Cohen, L. J. *The Diversity of Meaning*, 1962.

Copi, I. M. (1) "Modern Logic and the Synthetic A Priori", *Journal of Philosophy*, 1949.

————. (2) "Gödel and the Synthetic A Priori", *Journal of Philosophy*, 1950.

————. (3) "Analytical Philosophy and Analytical Propositions", *Philosophical Studies*, 1953.

————, and J. A. Gould, eds. *Contemporary Readings in Logical Theory*, 1967.

Crossley, J. N., and M. Dummett, eds. *Formal Systems and Recursive Functions*, 1965.

Davidson, D. (1) "Theories of Meaning and Learnable Languages", *Proceedings of the 1964 International Congress for Logic, Methodology, and Philosophy of Science*, 1964.

————. (2) "Truth and Meaning", *Synthese*, 1967.

Daya, K. "The Synthetic A Priori", *Philosophy*, 1961.

Donnell, F. H., and J. V. Canfield, eds. *Readings in the Theory of Knowledge*, 1964.

Donnellan, K. S. "Necessity and Criteria", *Journal of Philosophy*, 1962.

Dubislav, W. *Über die sogenannten analytischen und synthetischen Urteile*, 1926.

Dummett, M. "Wittgenstein's Philosophy of Mathematics", *Philosophical Review*, 1959; reprinted in Benacerraf and Putnam and in Pitcher.

Dummett, M., and J. N. Crossley, eds. *Formal Systems and Recursive Functions*, 1965.

Ebersole, F. B. "On Certain Confusions in the Analytic-Synthetic Distinction", *Journal of Philosophy*, 1956.

Edwards, P. (1) "Do Necessary Propositions 'Mean Nothing'?", *Journal of Philosophy*, 1949.

————. (2) "Necessary Propositions and the Future", *Journal of Philosophy*, 1949.

Edwards, P., and A. Pap, eds. *A Modern Introduction to Philosophy*, 1957.

Einstein, A. *Sidelights of Relativity*, 1922.

Emmet, D. " 'That's that': or Some Uses of Tautology", *Philosophy*, 1962.

Ewing, A. C. (1) "The Linguistic Theory of A Priori Propositions", *Proceedings of the Aristotelian Society*, 1939–40; reprinted in H. D. Lewis.

————. (2) *The Fundamental Problems of Philosophy*, 1951.

Feigl, H., and M. Brodbeck, eds. *Readings in the Philosophy of Science*, 1953.

————, and G. Maxwell, eds. *Minnesota Studies in the Philosophy of Science*, Volume III, 1962.

————, and W. Sellars, eds. *Readings in Philosophical Analysis*, 1949.

Feinberg, J., ed. *Reason and Responsibility*, 1965.

Ferré, F. "Colour Incompatibility and Language-Games", *Mind*, 1961.

Fitch, F. B. (1) "The Problem of the Morning Star and the Evening Star", *Philosophy of Science*, 1949; reprinted in Copi and Gould.

——. (2) "A Theory of Logical Essences", *Monist*, 1967.

Flew, A., ed. (1) *Logic and Language, First Series*, 1951.

——. (2) *Logic and Language, Second Series*, 1953.

Fodor, J. A., and J. J. Katz, eds. *The Structure of Language*, 1964.

Frege, G. *Die Grundlagen der Arithmetik*, 1884; translated *The Foundations of Arithmetic*, 1950.

Gahringer, R. E. "Analytic Propositions and Philosophical Truths", *Journal of Philosophy*, 1963.

Garver, N. "Analyticity and Grammar", *Monist*, 1967.

Gasking, D. A. T. "Mathematics and the World", *Australasian Journal of Philosophy*, 1940; reprinted in Flew (2) and in Benacerraf and Putnam.

Geach, P. T. "Necessary Propositions and Entailment Statements", *Mind*, 1948.

Gewirth, A. "The Distinction Between Analytic and Synthetic Truths", *Journal of Philosophy*, 1953.

Glassen, P. "Reds, Greens and the Synthetic *A Priori*", *Philosophical Studies*, 1958.

Goldstein, L. J. "On Anything Whatever", *Mind*, 1965.

Goodman, N. (1) "On Likeness of Meaning", *Analysis*, 1949–50; reprinted in Macdonald (2); revised version reprinted in Linsky.

——. (2) "On Some Differences About Meaning", *Analysis*, 1952–53; reprinted in Macdonald (2).

——, and W. V. Quine. "Steps Toward a Constructive Nominalism", *Journal of Symbolic Logic*, 1947.

Gould, J. A., and I. M. Copi, eds. *Contemporary Readings in Logical Theory*, 1967.

Grice, H. P. "Meaning", *Philosophical Review*, 1957.

——, and P. F. Strawson. "In Defense of a Dogma", *Philosophical Review*, 1956; reprinted in this collection and in Ammerman; partially reprinted in Nagel and Brandt.

Hackett, S. C. "Contemporary Philosophy and the Analytic-Synthetic Dichotomy", *International Philosophical Quarterly*, 1967.

Hacking, I. "Possibility", *Philosophical Review*, 1967.

Hahn, H. *Logik, Mathematik und Naturerkennen*, 1933; partially reprinted, in translation, in Ayer (5).

Hamlyn, D. W. (1) "Analytic Truths", *Mind*, 1956.

——. (2) "On Necessary Truth", *Mind*, 1961.

Hampshire, S. (1) "Logical Necessity", *Philosophy*, 1948.

————. (2) "Mr. Strawson on Necessary Propositions and Entailment Statements", *Mind,* 1948.

Hanson, N. R. (1) "Mr. Pap on Synonymity", *Mind,* 1951.

————. (2) "The Very Idea of a Synthetic-Apriori", *Mind,* 1962; reprinted in this collection.

————. (3) "Justifying Analytic Claims", *Analysis,* 1963.

Hanson, W. H. "On Formalizing the Distinction Between Logical and Factual Truth", *Journal of Symbolic Logic,* 1966.

Hardie, C. D. "The Necessity of A Priori Propositions", *Proceedings of the Aristotelian Society,* 1937–38.

Harman, G. "Quine on Meaning and Existence", *Review of Metaphysics,* 1967.

Hausman, A., and F. Wilson. *Carnap and Goodman: Two Formalists,* 1967.

Hay, W. H., and J. R. Weinberg. "Concerning Allegedly Necessary Nonanalytic Propositions", *Philosophical Studies,* 1951.

Heinemann, F. H. (1) "Truths of Reason and Truths of Fact", *Philosophical Review,* 1948.

————. (2) "Are There Only Two Kinds of Truth?", *Philosophy and Phenomenological Research,* 1956.

Hempel, C. G. (1) "Geometry and Empirical Science", *American Mathematical Monthly,* 1945; reprinted in Feigl and Sellars.

————. (2) "The Nature of Mathematical Truth", *American Mathematical Monthly,* 1945; reprinted in Feigl and Sellars, in Feigl and Brodbeck, and in Benacerraf and Putnam.

————. (3) "Implications of Carnap's Work for the Philosophy of Science," in Schilpp.

Henkin, L. "Are Logic and Mathematics Identical?", *Science,* 1962.

Henle, P. (1) "On the Certainty of Empirical Statements", *Journal of Philosophy,* 1947.

————. (2) "Do We Discover Our Uses of Words?" *Journal of Philosophy,* 1957.

Herburt, G. K. "The Analytic and the Synthetic", *Philosophy of Science,* 1959.

Hilton, J. "Red and Green All Over Again", *Analysis,* 1961.

Hintikka, J. (1) "Distributive Normal Forms in the Calculus of Predicates", *Acta Philosophica Fennica,* 1953.

————. (2) "Identity, Variables, and Impredicative Definitions", *Journal of Symbolic Logic,* 1956.

————. (3) "Kant's Theory of Mathematics" (in Finnish), *Ajatus,* 1959.

————. (4) "Distributive Normal Forms and Deductive Interpolation", *Zeitschrift für mathematische Logik und Grundlagen der Mathematik,* 1964.

————. (5) "Are Logical Truths Analytic?", *Philosophical Review,* 1965; reprinted in this collection.

————. (6) "Distributive Normal Forms in First-Order Logic", in Crossley and Dummett.

————. (7) "Kant on the Mathematical Method", *Monist,* 1967.

————. (8) "A Program and a Set of Concepts for Philosophical Logic", *Monist,* 1967.

————. (9) "Semantic Information", in Yourgrau.

Hirst, R. J. "Mathematics and Truth", *Philosophical Quarterly,* 1953.

Hofstadter, A. (1) "Causality and Necessity", *Journal of Philosophy,* 1949.

————. (2) "Explanation and Necessity", *Philosophy and Phenomenological Research,* 1950–51.

————. (3) "The Myth of the Whole", *Journal of Philosophy,* 1954.

————. (4) "Six Necessities", *Journal of Philosophy,* 1957.

Hook, S., ed. (1) *John Dewey: Philosopher of Science and Freedom,* 1950.

————. (2) *American Philosophers at Work,* 1956.

Hospers, J. *Introduction to Philosophical Analysis,* 1953; second edition, 1967.

Hume, D. (1) *A Treatise of Human Nature,* 1739–40.

————. (2) *An Inquiry Concerning Human Understanding,* 1748.

Jackson, R. (1) "Are There Synthetic A Priori Truths?", *Proceedings of the Aristotelian Society, Supplementary Volume,* 1936.

————. (2) "Are There Analytic Propositions?", *Proceedings of the Aristotelian Society,* 1938–39.

Johnson, O. A. "Denial of the Synthetic A Priori", *Philosophy,* 1960.

Johnson, W. E. *Logic,* 1921.

Kant, I. (1) *Critique of Pure Reason,* 1781; second edition, 1787; partially reprinted in this collection, in Canfield and Donnell, and in Edwards and Pap.

————. (2) *Prolegomena to Any Future Metaphysics,* 1783.

Katz, J. J. (1) "Analyticity and Contradiction in Natural Language", in Fodor and Katz.

————. (2) *The Philosophy of Language,* 1966.

————. (3) "Some Remarks on Quine on Analyticity", *Journal of Philosophy,* 1967; reprinted in this collection.

————. (4) "Unpalatable Recipes for Buttering Parsnips", *Journal of Philosophy,* 1968.

Katz, J. J. and J. A. Fodor, eds. *The Structure of Language,* 1964.

Kaufman, A. S. "The Analytic and the Synthetic", *Philosophical Review,* 1953.

Keene, G. B. "Analytic Statements and Mathematical Truth", *Analysis,* 1956.

Kemeny, J. G. (1) "A New Approach to Semantics", *Journal of Symbolic Logic,* 1956.

――――. (2) "Analyticity versus Fuzziness", *Synthese,* 1963.

Kenner, L. "The Triviality of the Red-Green Problem", *Analysis,* 1965.

Kneale, W. C. (1) "Truths of Logic", *Proceedings of the Aristotelian Society,* 1945–46.

――――. (2) "Are Necessary Truths True by Convention?", *Proceedings of the Aristotelian Society, Supplementary Volume,* 1947; reprinted in H. D. Lewis.

――――, and M. Kneale. *The Development of Logic,* 1962.

Körner, S. (1) "On Entailment", *Proceedings of the Aristotelian Society,* 1946.

――――. (2) "Are Philosophical Questions, Questions of Language?", *Proceedings of the Aristotelian Society, Supplementary Volume,* 1948.

――――. (3) "Entailment and the Meaning of Words", *Analysis,* 1949–50.

――――. (4) "Reference, Vagueness and Necessity", *Philosophical Review,* 1957.

――――. (5) "On Determinables and Resemblance", *Proceedings of the Aristotelian Society, Supplementary Volume,* 1959.

――――. (6) *The Philosophy of Mathematics,* 1960.

Krikorian, Y. H., ed. *Naturalism and the Human Spirit,* 1944.

Kripke, S. "A Completeness Theorem in Modal Logic", *Journal of Symbolic Logic,* 1959.

Kuhnemann, E. "Analytisch und Synthetisch", *Archiv für Systematische Philosophie,* 1895.

Lachièze-Rey, P. "Reflexions historiques et critiques sur la possibilité des jugements synthétiques a priori", *Revue Internationale de Philosophie,* 1954.

Lake, B. "Necessary and Contingent Statements", *Analysis,* 1951–52.

Langford, C. H. "A Proof That Synthetic A Priori Propositions Exist", *Journal of Philosophy,* 1949.

――――, and C. I. Lewis. *Symbolic Logic,* 1932.

Lazerowitz, M. (1) "Necessary and Contingent Truths", *Philosophical Review,* 1936.

――――. (2) *The Structure of Metaphysics,* 1955.

Lee, O. H., ed. *Essays for A. N. Whitehead,* 1936.

Leibniz, G. (1) *New Essays on the Human Understanding,* 1704.

――――. (2) *The Monadology,* 1714.

Leonard, H. G. "Synonymy and Systematic Definitions", *Monist,* 1967.

Levison, A. B. "Wittgenstein and Logical Laws", *Philosophical Quarterly,* 1964.

Lewis, C. I. (1) "A Pragmatic Conception of the A Priori", *Journal of Philosophy*, 1923; reprinted in Feigl and Sellars and in Nagel and Brandt.

————. (2) *Mind and the World Order*, 1929.

————. (3) "The Modes of Meaning", *Philosophy and Phenomenological Research*, 1943–44; reprinted in Linsky.

————. (4) *An Analysis of Knowledge and Valuation*, 1946.

————, and C. H. Langford. *Symbolic Logic*, 1932.

Lewis, H. D., ed. *Clarity Is Not Enough*, 1963.

Lewy, C. (1) "Logical Necessity", *Philosophical Review*, 1940.

————. (2) "Entailment and Empirical Propositions", *Mind*, 1946.

————. (3) "Why Are the Calculuses of Logic and Arithmetic Applicable to Reality?", *Proceedings of the Aristotelian Society, Supplementary Volume*, 1946.

————. (4) "Entailment and Necessary Propositions", in Black, ed. (1).

Linsky, L., ed. *Semantics and the Philosophy of Language*, 1952.

Liu, Shih-Chao. "On the Analytic and the Synthetic", *Philosophical Review*, 1956.

Locke, D. "Mathematical Statements", *Australasian Journal of Philosophy*, 1963.

Locke, J. *An Essay Concerning Human Understanding*, 1690.

Macdonald, M. "Necessary Propositions", *Analysis*, 1940.

Macdonald, M., ed., *Philosophy and Analysis*, 1954.

MacKinnon, D. M. "Are There A Priori Concepts?", *Proceedings of the Aristotelian Society, Supplementary Volume*, 1939.

Makinson, D. "How Meaningful Are Modal Operators?", *Australasian Journal of Philosophy*, 1966.

Malcolm, N. (1) "Are Necessary Propositions Really Verbal?", *Mind*, 1940.

————. (2) "The Nature of Entailment", *Mind*, 1940.

Marcus, R. B. (1) "Modalities and Intensional Languages", *Synthese*, 1962; reprinted in Copi and Gould.

————. (2) "Essentialism in Modal Logic", *Nous*, 1967.

Marc-Wogau, K. "Kant's Lehre vom analytischen Urteil", *Theoria*, 1951.

Martin, R. M. (1) "On 'Analytic'", *Philosophical Studies*, 1952.

————. (2) *The Notion of Analytic Truth*, 1959.

Mates, B. (1) "Synonymity", *University of California Publications in Philosophy*, 1950; reprinted in Linsky.

————. (2) "Analytic Sentences", *Philosophical Review*, 1951.

Maxwell, G. "The Necessary and the Contingent", in Feigl and Maxwell.

Maxwell, G., and H. Feigl, eds. *Minnesota Studies in the Philosophy of Science*, Volume III, 1962.

McCall, S. "Connexive Implication and the Syllogism", *Mind*, 1967.

McGee, C. D. "Pre-Ceremonial Relations", *Philosophical Quarterly*, 1963.

Meckler, L. (1) "On Goodman's Refutation of Synonymy", *Analysis*, 1953–54.

———. (2) "Are 'Indubitable' Statements Necessary?", *Mind*, 1955.

Menger, K. "The New Logic", *Philosophy of Science*, 1937.

Mill, J. S. (1) *A System of Logic*, 1843; partially reprinted in this collection, in Edwards and Pap, and in Nagel and Brandt.

———. (2) *An Examination of Sir William Hamilton's Philosophy*, 1865.

Moore, G. E. (1) "Necessity", *Mind*, 1900.

———. (2) "External and Internal Relations", *Proceedings of the Aristotelian Society*, 1919–20; reprinted in Moore (3).

———. (3) *Philosophical Studies*, 1922.

Moravcsik, J. M. E. "The Analytic and the Nonempirical", *Journal of Philosophy*, 1965.

Myhill, J. "Some Philosophical Implications of Mathematical Logic. Three Classes of Ideas", *Review of Metaphysics*, 1952–53.

Naess, A. "Synonymity as Revealed by Intuition", *Philosophical Review*, 1957.

Nagel, E. (1) "Logic Without Ontology", in Krikorian; reprinted in Benacerraf and Putnam, in Feigl and Sellars, and in Nagel (2).

———. (2) *Logic Without Metaphysics*, 1957.

———. (3) *The Structure of Science*, 1961.

Nagel, E., and R. Brandt, eds. *Meaning and Knowledge*, 1965.

Nakhnikian, G., and W. P. Alston, eds. *Readings in Twentieth-Century Philosophy*, 1963.

Nell, E. J. "The Hardness of the Logical 'Must' ", *Analysis*, 1961.

Nelson, E. J. "Intensional Relations", *Mind*, 1930.

Nelson, J. O. "Y-Propositions", *Philosophical Studies*, 1961.

O'Connor, D. J. "Incompatible Properties", *Analysis*, 1954–55.

Odegard, D. "The Discovery of Analytic Truth", *Philosophy and Phenomenological Research*, 1965–66.

Olds, M. E. "Synonymity: Extensional Isomorphism", *Mind*, 1956.

Oliver, D. "Logic and Necessity", *Journal of Philosophy*, 1950.

Pap, A. (1) "The Meaning of Necessity", *Journal of Philosophy*, 1943.

———. (2) "The Different Kinds of A Priori", *Philosophical Review*, 1944.

———. (3) *The A Priori in Physical Theory*, 1946.

———. (4) "Logical Nonsense", *Philosophy and Phenomenological Research*, 1948.

———. (5) "Synonymity and Logical Equivalence", *Analysis*, 1948–49.

————. (6) "Are All Necessary Propositions Analytic?", *Philosophical Review*, 1949.

————. (7) *Elements of Analytic Philosophy*, 1949.

————. (8) "Logic and the Concept of Entailment", *Journal of Philosophy*, 1950.

————. (9) "Logic and the Synthetic A Priori", *Philosophy and Phenomenological Research*, 1950.

————. (10) "Belief, Synonymity, and Analysis", *Philosophical Studies*, 1955.

————. (11) "Necessary Propositions and Linguistic Rules", *Semantica*, 1955.

————. (12) "Once More: Colors and the Synthetic A Priori", *Philosophical Review*, 1957; reprinted in this collection.

————. (13) *Semantics and Necessary Truth*, 1958; partially reprinted in this collection.

————. (14) *An Introduction to the Philosophy of Science*, 1962.

Pap, A., and P. Edwards, eds. *A Modern Introduction to Philosophy*, 1957.

Parkinson, G. H. R. "Necessary Propositions and 'A Priori' Knowledge in Kant", *Mind*, 1960.

Parsons, T. "Grades of Essentialism in Quantified Modal Logic", *Nous*, 1967.

Pasch, A. *Experience and the Analytic*, 1958.

Peach, B. "A Nondescriptive Theory of the Analytic", *Philosophical Review*, 1952.

Pears, D. F. (1) "Synthetic Necessary Truth", *Mind*, 1950.

————. (2) "The Incongruity of Counterparts", *Mind*, 1952.

————. (3) "Incompatibilities of Colours", in Flew (2).

Perkins, M., and I. Singer. "Analyticity", *Journal of Philosophy*, 1951.

Pitcher, G., ed. *Wittgenstein*, 1966.

Poincaré, H. *La Science et l'Hypothèse*, 1902; translated *Science and Hypothesis*, 1905.

Pollock, J. L. (1) "Implication and Analyticity", *Journal of Philosophy*, 1965.

————. (2) "Logical Validity in Modal Logic", *Monist*, 1967.

————. (3) "Mathematical Proof", *American Philosophical Quarterly*, 1967.

Popper, K. R. (1) *Logik der Forschung*, 1935; translated *The Logic of Scientific Discovery*, 1958.

————. (2) "Logic Without Assumptions", *Proceedings of the Aristotelian Society*, 1946.

————. (3) "Why Are the Calculuses of Logic and Arithmetic Applicable to Reality?", *Proceedings of the Aristotelian Society, Supplementary Volume*, 1946.

————. (4) "New Foundations for Logic", *Mind*, 1947.

Porteous, A. J. D. "Are There Synthetic A Priori Truths?", *Proceedings of the Aristotelian Society, Supplementary Volume,* 1936.

Prior, A. N. (1) "Determinables, Determinates and Determinants", *Mind,* 1949.

———. (2) *Time and Modality,* 1957.

Putnam, H. (1) "Synonymity and the Analysis of Belief Sentences", *Analysis,* 1954.

———. (2) "Reds, Greens, and Logical Analysis", *Philosophical Review,* 1956; reprinted in this collection.

———. (3) "Red and Green All Over Again: A Rejoinder to Arthur Pap", *Philosophical Review,* 1957; reprinted in this collection.

———. (4) "The Analytic and the Synthetic", in Feigl and Maxwell.

———. (5) "It Ain't Necessarily So", *Journal of Philosophy,* 1962.

Putnam, H., and P. Benacerraf, eds. *Philosophy of Mathematics,* 1964.

Quine, W. V. (1) "Truth by Convention", in Lee; reprinted in Benacerraf and Putnam, in Feigl and Sellars, and in Quine (14).

———. (2) *Mathematical Logic,* 1940.

———. (3) "Notes on Existence and Necessity", *Journal of Philosophy,* 1943; reprinted in Linsky.

———. (4) "The Problem of Interpreting Modal Logic", *Journal of Symbolic Logic,* 1947; reprinted in Copi and Gould.

———. (5) "Two Dogmas of Empiricism", *Philosophical Review,* 1951; reprinted in this collection, in Ammerman, in Benacerraf and Putnam, in H. D. Lewis, and in Quine (7); partially reprinted in Nagel and Brandt.

———. (6) "The Problem of Meaning in Linguistics", in Quine (7).

———. (7) *From a Logical Point of View,* 1953; second edition, 1961.

———. (8) "Three Grades of Modal Involvement", *Proceedings of the XIth International Congress of Philosophy,* 1953; reprinted in Quine (14).

———. (9) "Meaning and Translation", in Brower.

———. (10) "Carnap and Logical Truth", *Synthese,* 1959; reprinted in Schilpp and in Quine (14); partially reprinted in Hook (2).

———. (11) *Word and Object,* 1960.

———. (12) "Reply to Professor Marcus", *Synthese,* 1962; reprinted in Copi and Gould.

———. (13) "Necessary Truth", in Quine (14).

————. (14) *The Ways of Paradox*, 1966.

————. (15) "On a Suggestion of Katz", *Journal of Philosophy*, 1967; reprinted in this collection.

Quinton, A. "The A Priori and the Analytic", *Proceedings of the Aristotelian Society*, 1963–64.

Radford, C. (1) "The Insolubility of the Red-Green Problem", *Analysis*, 1963.

————. (2) "Incompatibilities of Colours", *Philosophical Quarterly*, 1965.

Ramsey, F. P. *The Foundations of Mathematics and Other Logical Essays*, 1931.

Reichenbach, H. (1) "Rationalism and Empiricism: An Inquiry into the Roots of Philosophical Error", *Philosophical Review*, 1948.

————. (2) *The Rise of Scientific Philosophy*, 1951.

Reid, J. R. "Analytic Statements in Semiosis", *Mind*, 1943.

Remnant, P. "Red and Green All Over Again", *Analysis*, 1961.

Rinaldi, F. "Logical Possibility", *Philosophy and Phenomenological Research*, 1967.

Robinson, R. "Necessary Propositions", *Mind*, 1958.

Rozeboom, W. W. "The Logic of Color Words", *Philosophical Review*, 1958.

Rundle, B. "Modality and Quantification", in Butler, ed.

Russell, B. (1) *An Essay on the Foundations of Geometry*, 1897.

————. (2) *A Critical Exposition of the Philosophy of Leibniz*, 1900.

————. (3) *The Problems of Philosophy*, 1912.

————. (4) *Introduction to Mathematical Philosophy*, 1919.

————. (5) *The Analysis of Matter*, 1927.

Ryle, G. (1) "Internal Relations", *Proceedings of the Aristotelian Society, Supplementary Volume*, 1946.

————. (2) "Why Are the Calculuses of Logic and Arithmetic Applicable to Reality?", *Proceedings of the Aristotelian Society, Supplementary Volume*, 1946.

————. (3) " 'If', 'So', and 'Because' ", in Black, ed. (1).

Rynin, D. "The Dogma of Logical Pragmatism," *Mind*, 1956.

Scheffler, I. "On Synonymy and Indirect Discourse", *Philosophy of Science*, 1955.

Schilpp, P. A., ed. *The Philosophy of Rudolf Carnap*, 1964.

Schlick, M. (1) "Gibt es ein materiales Apriori?", *Wissenschaftlicher Jahresbericht der philosophischen Gesellschaft der Universität zu Wien für das Jahr 1930–31*; reprinted in translation, in Feigl and Sellars.

————. (2) "Meaning and Verification", *Philosophical Review*, 1936; reprinted in Alston and Nakhnikian.

Searle, J. R. "On Determinables and Resemblance", *Proceedings of the Aristotelian Society, Supplementary Volume,* 1959.

Sellars, W. (1) "Is There a Synthetic A Priori?", *Philosophy of Science,* 1953; reprinted in Hook (2) and in Sellars (2).

———. (2) *Science, Perception and Reality,* 1963.

Sellars, W., and H. Feigl, eds. *Readings in Philosophical Analysis,* 1949.

Shwayder, D. S. "Mr. Aldrich's Last Word", *Philosophical Studies,* 1955.

Sibajiban. "The Self-Contradictory and the Inconceivable", *Analysis Supplement,* 1964.

Sigwart, C. *Logik,* 1873–8; translated *Logic,* 1895.

Singer, I., and M. Perkins. "Analyticity", *Journal of Philosophy,* 1951.

Skyrms, B., and E. Sosa. "Necessity, the A Priori, and Unexpressible Statements", *Philosophical Studies,* 1965.

Sloman, A. (1) "Color Incompatibilities and Analyticity", *Analysis Supplement,* 1964.

———. (2) " 'Necessary', 'A Priori', and 'Analytic' ", *Analysis,* 1965.

Smart, J. J. C. "Incompatible Colors", *Philosophical Studies,* 1959.

Smullyan, A. F. "Modality and Description", *Journal of Symbolic Logic,* 1948.

Sommers, F. "Meaning Relations and the Analytic", *Journal of Philosophy,* 1963.

Sosa, E., and B. Skyrms. "Necessity, the Priori, and Unexpressible Statements", *Philosophical Studies,* 1965.

Sprigge, T. "Internal and External Properties", *Mind,* 1962.

Srzednicki, J. "Incompatibility Statements", *Australasian Journal of Philosophy,* 1962.

Stebbing, L. S. "The A Priori", *Proceedings of the Aristotelian Society, Supplementary Volume,* 1933.

Stegmuller, W. "Der Begriff des synthetischen Urteils a priori und die moderne Logik", *Zeitschrift fur philosophische Forschung,* 1954.

Stenius, E. "Are True Numerical Statements Analytic or Synthetic?", *Philosophical Review,* 1965.

Strawson, P. F. (1) "Necessary Propositions and Entailment Statements", *Mind,* 1948.

———. (2) *Introduction to Logical Theory,* 1952.

———. (3) "Propositions, Concepts and Logical Truths", *Philosophical Quarterly,* 1957.

Strawson, P. F., and H. P. Grice. "In Defense of a Dogma", *Philosophical Review,* 1956; reprinted in this collection and in Ammerman; partially reprinted in Nagel and Brandt.

Stroud, B. "Wittgenstein and Logical Necessity", *Philosophical Review*, 1965; reprinted in Pitcher.

Suchting, W. A. "Hume and Necessary Truth", *Dialogue*, 1966–67.

Tarski, A. *Logic, Semantics and Metamathematics*, 1956.

Taylor, D. M. "Meaning and the Use of Words", *Philosophical Quarterly*, 1967.

Taylor, R. "Disputes About Synonymy", *Philosophical Review*, 1954.

Terrell, D. B. "On a Supposed Synthetic Entailment", *Philosophical Studies*, 1951.

Thomson, J. F. (1) "Some Remarks on Synonymy", *Analysis*, 1951–52.

————. (2) "What Achilles Should Have Said to the Tortoise", *Ratio*, 1960–61.

Todd, W. "Meaning and Criteria", *Theoria*, 1966.

Toms, E. *Being, Negation and Logic*, 1962.

Toulmin, S. "A Defence of Synthetic Necessary Truth", *Mind*, 1949.

Urmson, J. O. "Are Necessary Truths True by Convention?", *Proceedings of the Aristotelian Society, Supplementary Volume*, 1947.

van der Waerden, B. L. "Synthetische Urteile a priori", *Acta Philosophica Fennica*, 1965.

van Fraassen, B. C. "Meaning Relations Among Predicates", *Nous*, 1967.

von Wright, G. H. *Logical Studies*, 1957.

Waismann, F. (1) *Einführung in das mathematische Denkung*, 1936; translated *Introduction to Mathematical Thinking*, 1951.

————. (2) "Are There Alternative Logics?", *Proceedings of the Aristotelian Society*, 1945–46.

————. (3) "Analytic-Synthetic", *Analysis*, 1949–52; reprinted in Black, ed. (2).

————. (4) "Verifiability", *Proceedings of the Aristotelian Society, Supplementary Volume*, 1945; reprinted in Flew (1).

————. (5) "Language Strata", in Flew (2).

————. (6) *Principles of Linguistic Philosophy*, 1965.

Walsh, W. H. "Analytic-Synthetic", *Proceedings of the Aristotelian Society*, 1953–54.

Wang, H. "Notes on the Analytic-Synthetic Distinction", *Theoria*, 1955.

Watkins, J. W. N. "Between Analytic and Empirical", *Philosophy*, 1957.

Weinberg, J. R., and W. H. Hay. "Concerning Allegedly Necessary Nonanalytic Propositions", *Philosophical Studies*, 1951.

Weitz, M. "Analytic Statements", *Mind*, 1954.

Wheatley, J. "Logical Connection", *American Philosophical Quarterly*, 1967.

White, M. G. (1) "The Analytic and the Synthetic", in Hook (1); reprinted in Linsky.

————. (2) "A Finitistic Approach to Philosophical Theses", *Philosophical Review*, 1951.

————. (3) *Toward Reunion in Philosophy*, 1956.

Whiteley, C. H. "Truth by Convention", *Analysis*, 1936–37.

Whitrow, G. J. "On the Synthetic Aspects of Mathematics", *Philosophy*, 1950.

Wild, J., and J. L. Cobitz. "On the Distinction Between the Analytic and the Synthetic", *Philosophy and Phenomenological Research*, 1947–48.

Williams, D. C. (1) "Analysis, Analytic Propositions, and Real Definitions", *Analysis*, 1935–36; reprinted in Williams (3).

————. (2) "The Nature and Variety of the A Priori", *Analysis*, 1938; reprinted in Williams (3).

————. (3) *The Principles of Empirical Realism*, 1966.

Williamson, C. "Kant and the Synthetic Nature of Geometry", *Dialogue*, 1967–68.

Wilson, F. (1) "Implicit Definition Once Again", *Journal of Philosophy*, 1965.

————. (2) *The Notion of Logical Necessity in the Later Philosophy of Rudolph Carnap*, in Hausman and Wilson.

Wilson, F., and A. Hausman. *Carnap and Goodman: Two Formalists*, 1967.

Wilson, J. C. *Statement and Inference*, 1926.

Wilson, N. L. "Linguistical Butter and Philosophical Parsnips", *Journal of Philosophy*, 1967.

Winch, P. G. "Necessary and Contingent Truths", *Analysis*, 1952–53.

Wittgenstein, L. (1) *Tractatus Logico-Philosophicus*, 1921.

————. (2) *Remarks on the Foundations of Mathematics*, 1956; selections reprinted in Benacerraf and Putnam.

Wood, O. P. "On Being Forced to a Conclusion", *Proceedings of the Aristotelian Society, Supplementary Volume*, 1961.

Woods, J. (1) "The Contradiction Exterminator", *Analysis*, 1965.

————. (2) "Was Achilles' 'Achilles' Heel' Achilles' Heel?", *Analysis*, 1965.

————. (3) "On Species and Determinates", *Nous*, 1967.

————. (4) "The Opacity of Tridence", *Analysis*, 1967.

Yourgrau, W., ed. *Logic, Physical Reality, History*, 1968.

Ziff, P. "On H. P. Grice's Account of Meaning", *Analysis*, 1967.

# INDEX OF NAMES